Whitman Possessed

Whitman
Possessed

POETRY, SEXUALITY,

AND POPULAR AUTHORITY

Mark Maslan

The Johns Hopkins University Press

BALTIMORE AND LONDON

© 2001 The Johns Hopkins University Press
All rights reserved. Published 2001
Printed in the United States of America on acid-free paper

9 8 7 6 5 4 3 2 1

The Johns Hopkins University Press
2715 North Charles Street
Baltimore, Maryland 21218-4363
www.press.jhu.edu

Library of Congress Cataloging-in-Publication Data
Maslan, Mark
Whitman possessed : poetry, sexuality, and popular authority /
Mark Maslan.
p. cm.
Includes bibliographical references and index.
ISBN 0-8018-6701-0 (hardcover : alk. paper)
1. Whitman, Walt, 1819–1892 — Views on sex.   2. Homosexuality
and literature — United States — History — 19th century.
3. Whitman, Walt, 1819–1892 — Political and social views.   4. Power
(Social sciences) in literature.   5. Homosexuality, Male, in literature.
6. Possessiveness in literature.   7. Masculinity in literature.
8. Authority in literature.   9. Gay men in literature.   10. Self in
literature.   11. Sex in literature.   12. Poetics.   I. Title.
PS3242.S47 M37   2001
811'.3 — dc21
00-011756

A catalog record for this book is available from the British Library.

For Ann and Daniel

Whitman is not an artist, but a reflex, the first

honest reflex in an age of papier-mâché letters.

—Ezra Pound, *Patria Mia*

Contents

Acknowledgments xi

Introduction 1

Chapter 1: Sexual Hygiene: The Natural Gates and Alleys of the Body 18

Chapter 2: Sexuality and Poetic Agency 46

Chapter 3: Masses and Muses 93

Chapter 4: Lines of Penetration 142

Abbreviations 171

Notes 173

Index 215

Acknowledgments

I am grateful to Michael Fried for advice given when my work on Whitman was just beginning and for encouragement since. I am also grateful to the English departments of the University of California, Berkeley, and the University of Iowa, as well as the Humanities department of the California Institute of Technology, for the opportunity to deliver portions of the manuscript as lectures and thus receive much useful feedback. At one time or another Maurizia Boscagli, Elliott Butler-Evans, Enda Duffy, Patricia Fumerton, Giles Gunn, Richard Helgerson, and Alan Liu read portions of the manuscript and offered their expertise and support; I am very thankful for their friendship. Michael and Lisa O'Connell have gone beyond the call of duty, providing space to live and work in for two years and, afterward, supplying books, readings, and not a few sumptuous dinners. Kerry Larson and Samuel Otter read the entire manuscript and provided detailed and insightful comments from which I have greatly benefited. Oliver Arnold and Dorothy Hale have read innumerable drafts and versions as well as the final revision; their thoughts and suggestions have helped to shape this book over many years.

Some material in this book has appeared, in quite different form, in journal articles. I wish to thank the publishers for permission to use the material here: "Whitman, Sexuality, and Poetic Authority," *Raritan* 17:4 (Spring 1998): 98–119; "Foucault and Pragmatism," *Raritan* 7:3 (Winter 1988): 94–114; and "Whitman's 'Strange Hand': Body as Text in *Drum-Taps*," ELH 58 (Winter 1991): 935–55.

A number of my central themes evolved out of my conversations with Jeffrey Knapp; he has been a source of wonderful insights as well as an indefatigable reader and critic. Susan Maslan has also been a crucial resource, generously sharing her ideas about democratic culture, reading my work with great care, and offering me endless encouragement. Walter Michaels has been a continuous source of advice and inspiration for well over a decade; I cannot imagine having written this book without his help and example. My greatest debt is to Ann Cumming, who, in addition to sharing with me her expertise as a classicist, has lived through the writing process—sometimes word by word—from start to finish.

Whitman Possessed

Introduction

We are waiting until some tyrannous idea emerging out of
heaven shall seize us and bereave us of this liberty with which
we are falling abroad.
—Emerson, "Inspiration"

In at the conquer'd doors they crowd! I am possess'd!
—Whitman, "Song of Myself"

This book is about possession—primarily the kind that "seizes a tender, virgin soul and stimulates it to rapt passionate expression, especially in poetry," as Socrates puts it in the *Phaedrus*.[1] My core assertion is that Whitman's poetry claims literary and political authority by identifying itself as the product not of a sovereign individual but rather of a possessed one. While possession may sound like a strange route to political authority, it is of course a familiar prerequisite for poetic power.[2] The theory of poetic inspiration has long held that poetry "is not subject to the controul of the active powers of the mind" (*SPP*, 508), as Shelley writes, because it is the result of external forces acting through the poet. Familiar though it is, this theory's relevance to Whitman has received no systematic examination. In part, this is so because the idea that poetry comes from outside the self complicates scholars' longstanding vision of Whitman as an embodiment of American individualism. In this view, the poet's self is primary, and his poetry is its expression and fulfillment. From the mid-twentieth century through the 1980s, Whitman criticism thus tended to focus on the poet's psychology, his peculiarly American egotism, or his negotiation of the egotistical sublime.[3] In the last decade, however, such approaches have largely been replaced by countervailing ones, which assert Whitman's opposition to individualism in its aesthetic, sexual, and political manifestations. For these critics, Whitman's poetry is an experiment in the disintegration of individuality, not the exercise of an imperial self. For instance, Allen Grossman has argued that Whitman's free verse form is not an organic expression of unshackled individuality, as has often been supposed, but a threat to the idea of poetic personality. "It is opposition to the meaning-intending will by the resistance of abstract form that produces, in the English poetic line, the sentiment of the person as a singular individual; and this Whitman could not restore"[4] once he abandoned meter. While Grossman laments this sacrifice of the personal, his view of Whitman's free verse is nevertheless consistent with recent readings that celebrate the poetry's homoeroticism as a means of opposing individualism. According to this interpretation, which has been stated most fully by Michael Moon, the poet's ambiguous treatment of male homosexuality subverts "the chief discourses of (male) embodiment of his time" by rendering "relations between male persons/bodies . . . totally fluid." As Moon sees it, the utopian goal of this project is a mode of human relationship that is free of the inequities of gender and sexual orientation generated by our culture's "strenuous individualism" and "anxiety about the loss of boundaries."[5] In other words, the poetry's homoeroticism enacts thematically the same sort of assault on the sanctity of individuality that its verse form exemplifies structurally.

These readings of Whitman's form and sexuality also correlate with current interpretations of the public, or political, dimension of Whitman's poetry. Indeed, Michael Warner has argued that "Whitman wants to make sex public" through poetry in order to replace the call for self-control that governed individual participation in the public sphere for most antebellum Americans (in causes such as the temperance movement) with the antithetical call for "self-abandonment" that characterizes Whitmanic sexuality.[6] What Moon terms sexual "fluidity" is for Warner the foundation of Whitman's political as well as sexual theory. The idea that Whitman seeks to subvert individuality is evident even among those critics who focus more exclusively on his politics than Warner does. In an influential essay Philip Fisher offers "Crossing Brooklyn Ferry" as prime evidence for his assertion

that "American aesthetics is intrinsically an aesthetics of . . . the subtraction of differences." For Whitman, individual "difference is an aberration,
like the many interesting, diseased conditions of the body from which we
always willingly return to the boredom of health."[7] Wai Chee Dimock's reading of Whitman reinforces this view. In seeking to establish a language of
equal justice, Dimock explains, Whitman's "democratic poetics" dedicates
itself exclusively to "formal universals." It is therefore "silent about those
objects that, for us, are not categoric, not interchangeable or substitutable."
What's missing, she argues, is a vision of individual difference, which "can
materialize only through a particularizing language."[8]

Despite the diversity of their themes and the marked difference in their
views on the ultimate value of individuality, these critics are united in reading Whitman as rejecting the ideal of the sovereign self in favor of a poetic
voice characterized by self-erasure. My own reading of Whitman partici-
pates, to some degree, in this critical reevaluation of what used to be known
as his individualism. It differs from previous revisionist studies, however,
in one crucial respect: whereas others equate Whitman's subversion of the
poetic self with the subversion of authority — whether in the form of literary tradition, masculinist heterosexism, or political and class hierarchies —
I argue that he presents the subversion of the self, by possession, as what
constitutes his authority, and that in doing so he draws heavily upon poetic
precedents. It is therefore significant, in my view, that revisionist work on
Whitman has largely avoided reexamining his ideas about poetic invention
in light of their literary-historical context, instead looking almost exclusively to the social and political history of the period, and to current theories
of sexuality, to situate the subjectivity of his poems. In this, of course, recent
Whitman criticism follows the general trend in literary studies today, away
from literary history and toward social and theoretical explanations.[9] It is
not my intention here to challenge these widespread developments; rather,
I hope to demonstrate that for Whitman the decentering of the subject is
dictated by a specifically literary logic — that of poetic inspiration — whose
purpose is not to subvert authority but to establish it, and that by overlooking the significance of this logic, revisionist studies of the poet fundamentally misread not only his poetics but also his sexuality, his politics, and his
significance for current theories of sexual identity.

The theory of inspiration has always been an attempt not only to explain poetic utterance but also to validate or invalidate it on the grounds of its apparent alterity, that is, its capacity to embody meanings that do not originate in its speaker. To be inspired is to be authorized to speak by and for another, whether that other be natural or supernatural. Poetic authority therefore derives not from the poet's self but from its temporary annulment. Shelley argues that even when poets have no personal claim to moral authority, their words carry authority because they are not personal: "The persons in whom this power resides, may often, as far as regards many portions of their nature, have little correspondence with that spirit of good of which they are the ministers. But even whilst they deny and abjure, they are yet compelled to serve, the Power which is seated upon the throne of their own soul" (*SPP*, 508). The self is understood here as an impediment to authoritative utterance that poetry overcomes.

What makes Whitmanic inspiration distinctive is, above all, the way it fuses the invasive, automatic nature of the poetic impulse thus conceived with the involuntary nature of the sexual drive. But this fusion of the poetic and the sexual is not entirely without precedent. Love poetry has always presented desire as its source (most often in the form of a personified male assailant), and devotional verse has also made occasional use of the sexual impulse to lend substance to the portrayal of religious and poetic rapture. Moreover, both genres traditionally perform an effacement of the poetic subject before its object, whether lover or God. While these precedents undoubtedly influenced Whitman, however, they also imposed generic restrictions—entirely absent from his work—on the use of sexual metaphors and motivations for verse composition. If sexual desire could legitimately inspire love poetry, it was nevertheless incompatible with non-amatory forms and themes in poetry written prior to Romanticism. When Cupid points his arrow at Ovid in the opening poem of the *Amores,* for example, he aims to inflict a specifically elegiac task on the poet, thereby unfitting him for the epic he claims to have intended to write:

> With Muse upreard I meant to sing of Armes,
> Choosing a subject fit for fierce alarmes.
>
> . . . .
>
> When in this workes first verse I trode aloft,
> Love slackt my Muse, and made my numbers soft.[10]

Likewise, John Donne's plea in "Batter My Heart, Three-Personed God" for God to rape him, however astonishing, is licensed by its devotional context, in which the very violation of worldly sexual norms helps transport the poem into the realm of the sacred.

These restrictions began to lift with the advent of Romanticism, when natural forces supplanted supernatural ones as sources of the poetic impulse. In his classic essay "The Correspondent Breeze: A Romantic Metaphor," M. H. Abrams documents the association of creative power with the wind in Wordsworth, Coleridge, and later Romantics, persuasively suggesting that whereas "earlier poets had launched their epics by invoking for inspiration a muse, Apollo, or the Holy Spirit," Wordsworth begins *The Prelude* with lines of "an identical function" on the "gentle breeze" that greets him upon his escape from London. According to Abrams, this inspiring wind that pervades Romantic poetry is not a supernatural but a natural force; it links humanity not to heavenly beings but to "the environment from which, Wordsworth and Coleridge felt, [it] had been divorced by post-Cartesian dualism and mechanism." "For not only are nature's breezes the analogue for human respiration," Abrams observes, but "they are themselves inhaled into the body and assimilated to its substance . . . and so fuse materially, as well as metaphorically, the 'soul' of man with the 'spirit' of nature."[11] An immediate and well-known effect of this shift from the supernatural to the natural was the spread of organic metaphors for poetic invention beyond the bounds of pastoral verse and into every genre of poetry. What has gone unnoticed, however, is that a similar dissemination of sexual metaphors for the creative process began—or at least became logically possible for the first time—during the same period. Once inspiration was understood as an experience arising from the poet's interactions with nature, it followed that the poet's most intimate experience of nature—the familiar urges of his or her own body, its sensations and processes—should likewise bear witness to inspiration's work. Whitman's transformation of sex from generic to general first cause—a defining event in the development of modern literature—was also an outgrowth of Romantic poetics.

Among the various physical urges and functions that contribute to the experience of embodiment, sex fulfilled the requirements for identification with inspiration especially well—even better, in some ways, than breathing. Like inspiration, the sexual urge is involuntary and could therefore be ascribed to an invasive, external force, which it regularly was. For whereas the sexual drive, at least since Freud, has been assigned an internal origin (as has the poetic one), its relative health or morbidity — if not its very existence — was largely attributed to the influence of the external environment in Whitman's era. The reconciliation of self and environment, which the Romantics sought to accomplish by naturalizing inspiration, was thus also implied by inspiration's sexualization, although this is less evident now than it was at the time. Furthermore, the spontaneity and euphoria of orgasm make it easily comparable to the ecstasy of poetic afflatus. Even the cries of orgasm could — and did — take on poetic significance. And, of course, the amatory and devotional traditions supplied a wealth of ready-made metaphors.

Those traditions also help explain why the sexualization of poetic inspiration might take a male homosexual form. Inspiration had always involved the literal or figurative penetration of the poet's body. In amatory verse this was usually the office of Cupid's arrows. Inflicted by a male god upon a male speaker, such penetration could appear homoerotic. (This possibility is not lost on Ovid or his Renaissance translator, Christopher Marlowe, in the passage quoted earlier, which characterizes the role of lover imposed upon the speaker as "soft," or effeminate.) But it need not have appeared primarily or obtrusively so since the desire instilled in the speaker by Cupid was usually heterosexual and since, moreover, Cupid himself was not an actual man but merely a personification of the sexual impulse. However, at the same time that Romanticism began to suggest that inspiration arose out of the poet's impressions of nature instead of descending upon him or her from above, it also assailed conventional uses of personification. In his 1802 preface to *Lyrical Ballads,* for example, Wordsworth warns his readers that "personifications of abstract ideas rarely occur in these volumes" because "I have proposed to myself to imitate and, as far as possible, to adopt the very language of men; and assuredly such personifications do not make any natural or regular part of that language." [12] And Wordsworth's wish to "keep [his] reader in the company of flesh and blood" is endorsed by Whitman in his 1855 preface to *Leaves of Grass* when he calls art "which distorts honest shapes or which creates unearthly beings . . . a nuisance and a revolt" (*LG,* 725). [13]

The naturalization of poetics thus combined with the effort to achieve greater naturalism in poetic diction to rule out conventional personifications of the sexual and poetic drives, such as Cupid. It would no longer be possible to assign the task of invading the poet to mythical figures; figures drawn from nature or those of "flesh and blood" would have to take their place. Poets thus discarded a conventional alibi for the homoerotic implications of inspiration at the same time that inspiration in general was becoming increasingly susceptible to the sexual analogy. Male poets could partly suppress these implications by adopting a feminine role in relation to their inspiration. This is Coleridge's solution in "The Eolian Harp," where he first compares the harp's acquiescence to the wind to "some coy maid half-yielding to her lover" and then to his "indolent and passive brain" abandoning itself to the fantasies that "traverse" it.[14] The heterosexual norm is preserved in this poem through the feminization of the male poet, while homely figures of flesh and blood replace learned personifications. Whitman repeats this maneuver in "The Sleepers" when he assumes the persona of a woman invoking her lover. But for him, as we shall see, this is part of the process of realizing the homoerotic potential of Romantic poetics rather than a way of forestalling that realization.

To say that Whitman seeks to realize the homoerotic potential of Romantic poetics, however, is to underscore the limitations of recent revisionary scholarship on Whitman's sexual politics. When recent critics claim that Whitman stands in opposition to his culture's structures of authority, they effectively discount his involvement in the *literature* that is an integral part of that culture. This involvement cannot be described as one of opposition, nor can Whitman's homosexual poetics be called a renunciation of English Romanticism's presumed heterosexuality. Indeed, the literary history I have sketched makes any radical distinction between heterosexual and homosexual poetics impossible. Whitman's achievement is more audacious than the critical rhetoric of opposition and subversion suggests: rather than affirming male homosexuality as a form of resistance to established modes of authority, he affirms it as a token of poetic authority. By assimilating the sexual penetration of the male poet's body to the theory of poetic inspiration, he turns his homosexuality into a source of legitimation.

Whitman's poetic affiliations also illuminate his response to the sexual reform literature of the period. The so-called sexual scientists of Whitman's time generally claimed that the desires of a healthy male were periodic and infrequent; the idea of an innate, persistent drive (later posited by Freud) was alien to them. Persistent sexual desire was considered a symptom of disease and was attributed to external influences such as unhealthy food, molestation, and the sexual diseases of parents. Sexual reformers thus linked poetic metaphors for desire's penetration of the body to a purportedly physiological foundation: frequent sexual desires really were evidence of possession by external influences. Here was support in the effort to replace outworn personifications of desire with a more naturalistic rhetoric of penetration. For the reformers, however, possession was a pathological state; their goal was to inculcate personal habits that would fortify the body against desire's offensives. It was the theory of poetic inspiration that enabled Whitman to invert the values of sexual hygiene literature by turning sexual possession into a basis for authoritative utterance. Both his affinity for the sexual hygiene movement and his opposition to it were dictated by a logic that was literary in origin. Whitman's opposition to the proponents of sexual discipline should be understood not as a utopian break with the sexual ethos of his culture but rather as part of a struggle over sexuality between connected but conflicting elements of his culture.[15] The point of connection was the vision of desire as a form of possession; the conflict concerned the social and cultural meanings of sexual possession as well as the cultural jurisdiction under which sexuality fell. In this struggle, sexuality was not just something Whitman sought to defend against authority's encroachments. It was an important source of legitimation both for him and his pseudoscientific rivals. A literary history of Whitmanic sexuality thus has the effect of locating him more completely within his cultural milieu than have previous revisionist readings, which tend to characterize Whitman's dissent as isolated even while emphasizing the societal influences on his work. This is not to say that Whitman's dissent from sexual reform orthodoxy was not potent or real. On the contrary, understanding the literary resources out of which that dissent was shaped allows us to appreciate how Whitman changed poetic and reformist discourses alike in order to fulfill his literary and social ambitions. Furthermore, it helps us understand the important role that literary concepts played in the definition and cultural elevation of sex during Whitman's century.

Thus far I have focused on the relationship between sexuality and *poetic* authority, arguing that Whitman identifies sexual penetration with the ingress of poetic voice. But how does this sexualized poetic voice find its way into the political sphere? After all, it has often been claimed that Whitman's poetry of homosexual love conflicts with his ambition to speak for the nation as a whole. While some critics argue that his sexuality threatens to minoritize his poetic voice and therefore requires sublimation,[16] others see his nationalism as a betrayal of the sexual minority to which he owes allegiance.[17] It has also been observed that whereas "Children of Adam," the programmatically heterosexual section of *Leaves of Grass,* appears to eschew interest in the private self in favor of the group, "Calamus," the section devoted to "manly attachment," seems to do the opposite, in some poems even going so far as to renounce the role of national poet in favor of lover.[18] In short, the relationship between Whitman's homosexuality and his politics remains vexed for many critics. Some have argued that he uses his homosexuality to challenge structures of political authority. Even these readers, however, maintain the opposition between homosexuality and established modes of political legitimation. Thomas Yingling describes Whitmanic homosexuality as "the institution which ends institutions . . . the displacement of all cultural centers."[19] Michael Warner suggests that Whitman's published celebration of sex challenges the distinction between public and private upon which representative institutions depend: "Whitman wants to make sex public, and doing so involves jarring conventions of representation."[20] These readings thus converge with descriptions of Whitman's poetry as a critique of representative government. Peter Bellis writes of the poems that they "do not just 'contain' or 'express' political ideas; they work to demonstrate and *enact* them. Their fluid and unstructured form *is* the democratic practice their words proclaim."[21] By abolishing the distinction between form and content, Bellis claims, Whitman makes the challenge to representative institutions his central aesthetic principle.

There is no question that Whitman criticizes American political institutions repeatedly — and sometimes vituperatively — in his antebellum writings. As we shall see, however, the evidence offered as proof of Whitman's hostility to representative government often proves something closer to the opposite. The "Calamus" poems are a case in point. "When I Heard at the Close of the Day" is often cited to demonstrate the cluster's disavowal of the political sphere:[22]

When I heard at the close of the day how my name had been receiv'd with
  plaudits in the capitol, still it was not a happy night for me that follow'd,
And else when I carous'd, or when my plans were accomplish'd, still I was
  not happy,
But the day when I rose from the bed of perfect health, refresh'd, singing,
  inhaling the ripe breath of autumn,
When I saw the full moon in the west grow pale and disappear in the
  morning light,
When I wander'd alone over the beach, and undressing bathed, laughing
  with the cool waters, and saw the sun rise,
And when I thought how my dear friend my lover was on his way coming,
  O then I was happy,
O then each breath tasted sweeter, and all that day my food nourish'd me
  more, and the beautiful day pass'd well,
And the next came with equal joy, and with the next at evening came my
  friend,
And that night while all was still I heard the waters roll slowly continually
  up the shores,
I heard the hissing rustle of the liquid and sands as directed to me
  whispering to congratulate me,
For the one I love most lay sleeping by me under the same cover in the cool
  night,
In the stillness in the autumn moonbeams his face was inclined toward
  me,
And his arm lay lightly around my breast—and that night I was happy.

This poem contrasts success in the Congress with success in homosexual
love. Like the beginning of *The Prelude*, however, it also contrasts a unsat-
isfying urban existence with an inspiring rural one. Indeed, Wordsworth's
inspiring "gentle breeze" turns up here as "the ripe breath of autumn" inhaled by the speaker upon waking at his seaside retreat. And the "plaudits
in the capitol" are contrasted not with the endearments of the lover but
with the voice of nature, in the form of the sea, "whispering to congratulate" the speaker on the lover's arrival. The Wordsworthian elements also
help to underscore the poem's Emersonian agenda, for the poet's renunciation of the Capitol derives only secondarily from Whitman's attitudes at the
time toward Washington and Congress (though he certainly had reason to
mistrust both). Its main source is Emerson's essay "The Poet," which in its

final paragraph dictates this renunciation to the poet: "Thou shalt leave the world, and know the muse only. . . . Thou shalt lie close hid with nature, and canst not be afforded to the Capitol or the Exchange" (*EL*, 467). Yet there is no mention of Emerson's muse in "When I Heard." Instead, Whitman gives us his lover. In fact, the inspiring influence of nature merges so thoroughly with the speaker's elated anticipation of his lover's appearance that the two become indistinguishable. The poem can therefore be said to naturalize the homosexual relationship it celebrates. But it also suggests that the lover is a substitute for the traditional personifications of poetic power. To this end, Whitman introduces the lover in the company of the vocative "O" even though he is not being addressed: "And when I thought how my dear friend my lover was coming, O then I was happy, / O then each breath tasted sweeter." Through its association with apostrophe and invocation, the vocative "O" conjures up the presence of the muse otherwise missing from the poem. "When I Heard" thus exemplifies the replacement of personifications with "flesh and blood" prescribed by Wordsworth, with the result that the scene of inspiration becomes explicitly homoerotic.

In Emerson, however, the poet's renunciation of the Capitol in favor of nature and the muse does not bar him or her from playing a public role. On the contrary, it enables the poet to draw on what Emerson calls "a great public power" (*EL*, 459). By abandoning the world for the muse, the poet also abandons those customs and prejudices that constitute particular social identities: "Thou shalt not know any longer the times, customs, graces, politics, or opinions of men, but shalt take all from the muse" (467). Without a social identity, the poet does not speak for himself or for any particular segment of society. According to Emerson, he therefore "apprises us not of his wealth, but of the commonwealth" (448). The renunciation of the Capitol, which coincides with a renunciation of the self, leads not to a critique of the idea of popular representation but to the legitimation of poetry as a model of representative authority.

Elsewhere in "Calamus" Whitman makes the political consequences of the poet's withdrawal explicit in a way they are not in "When I Heard." The cluster's introductory poem, "In Paths Untrodden," also features a speaker who turns "away from the clank of the world"—this time retiring to "the growth by the margins of pond-waters," where he is "talk'd to . . . by tongues aromatic" of the calamus plant. (The calamus is the section's symbol for "manly attachment." Unmistakably phallic, it is in equal parts a metonymy for nature and for the male lover of "When I Heard" and other poems in the group.) Renouncing "all the standards hitherto publish'd," the speaker nevertheless does not abandon altogether the business of pronouncing upon public matters. Instead, nature dictates "standards not yet publish'd" to him, which he proceeds to publish—that is, to make public—in the poems here introduced. As with Emerson, withdrawal from the world enables the poet to play a public role unavailable to those who continue to participate in worldly affairs. The homoeroticism that Whitman brings to this scenario does not undermine its representational logic. Rather, by humanizing that logic Whitman's homosexuality both completes the Romantic transformation of inspiration initiated by Wordsworth and turns inspiration into a paradigm for popular authority intended to rival that of the Capitol.

As I have presented it thus far, my argument locates itself where the concerns of literary history intersect with those of cultural studies and the new historicism. But it also raises theoretical questions that exceed the bounds of an interpretation of Whitman. It takes particular aim at the assertion that the subversion of personal identity in his writings entails a critique of the way cultural authority was constituted in his time—if not in our own. This assertion, in turn, rests on the belief that the operation and preservation of cultural hierarchies in general demand the existence of stable identities or, conversely, that the demand for stable identities is the root cause of cultural hierarchies. The poststructuralist critique of the subject is clearly the source of this view. To cite a prominent example, one need only think of Foucault's remark that "the soul is the effect and instrument of a political anatomy."[23] Partly because of Foucault's *History of Sexuality,* the poststructuralist critique of the subject has been especially influential in studies of sexuality, where it informs studies of homosexuality by such divergent theorists as Leo Bersani and Judith Butler. By claiming that Whitman's subversion of the autonomous male self actually makes the operation of cultural authority possible in his writings, I am therefore challenging not only several important developments in Whitman scholarship but also the theories of homosexuality—and, more generally, of subjectivity—upon which they rely.

As we shall see in chapter 4, these theories often bear a striking resemblance to the theory of poetic inspiration. Like the inspired poet, the poststructuralist subject is an instrument of forces external to itself. These forces are often specifically described as penetrating the subject and controlling its speech in much the same way inspiration does. And the recent theoretical focus on homosexuality as a paradigmatic example of the trials of subjectification seems to recapitulate Whitman's earlier discovery of how his own sexuality might be shown to bear witness to inspiration's work. In short, it seems reasonable to hypothesize that the poststructuralist critique of the subject has historical roots in the theory of poetic possession and therefore that recent theories of sexuality are in part a distant echo of the nineteenth-century convergence of poetics and sexuality to which Whitman contributed.

According to Romantic poetics, however, if possession undermines the autonomy of the poet's self, it does so in the service of a transcendent and disinterested spirit of which the poet is otherwise an alienated part. As Emerson writes in "Instinct and Inspiration," "the poet must be sacrificed" because "we have a higher than personal interest, which, in the ruin of the personal, is secured."[24] Indeed, personal interest, or what Shelley calls "the principle of self" (*SPP*, 503), is often defined by the Romantic theory of inspiration as exclusion from a larger whole. It is the "sole self" to which Keats is tolled back at the end of "Ode to a Nightingale"[25] and the "impediment" that prevents "the great majority of men" from "report[ing] the conversation they have had with nature" in Emerson's "The Poet" (*EL*, 448) — and poetry is its antidote.[26] Despite its subversion of the poet's self, then, the Romantic theory of inspiration does not actually break with the principle of the constitutive subject as defined by poststructuralism. Instead, as Derrida says of Rousseau's purpose in writing, it undertakes "the greatest sacrifice aiming at the greatest symbolic reappropriation of presence" (*OG*, 143).

For poststructuralism, on the other hand, the idea of a transcendent and disinterested spirit is merely a fiction that masks the presence of hierarchy and the work of domination. The poetic problem of exclusion from a larger whole has thus been recast as the problem of subordination, and as such it now defines not only the subject but also those forces external it, such as Nature, which formerly promised transcendence of exclusion. Selfhood continues to be seen as restrictive, but the transcendence of self has for the most part been replaced by the seemingly more modest project of revealing the latent processes of domination of which the self is supposedly an effect and an instrument. Recently, homosexuality has emerged as a major theme in this poststructuralist project of denaturalizing the subject. Because it is neither reproductive nor open to choice, homosexual desire seems to exemplify the poststructuralist theory of the subject as both construct and constraint.

By making the self a product of external forces, however, poststructuralist theory does not so much eliminate the transcendental subject as reinvent it in the form of those forces by which the self is supposed to be constituted and instrumentalized. These forces—writing for Derrida; power for Foucault; performativity for Butler—now exhibit the will, interests, capacities, and even the desires that used to characterize the subject. Unlike the nature of the Romantics, however, the forces that constitute the subject in poststructuralist theory cannot support the attribution of subjectivity except upon pain of contradiction.[27] After all, poststructuralism adopts as a principal aim the *critique* of transcendental subjects of the kind that Romanticism seeks to affirm. As Foucault himself says of power relations, while social and discursive systems may be "imbued through and through with calculation," they are nevertheless plainly "nonsubjective" (*HS*, 94–95), that is, not people. To state that writers are "governed by the [textual] system" (Derrida, *OG*, 158), that power "penetrates and controls everyday pleasure" (Foucault, *HS*, 11), or that the "strategic aim of maintaining gender within its binary frame . . . cannot be attributed to a subject" because it "found[s] . . . the subject" (Butler, *GT*, 140) is really to return to the type of personifications that Wordsworth and Whitman sought to replace with flesh and blood.[28]

Whitman Possessed consists of two chapters on the poet, preceded by a chapter of contextual analysis and followed by a theoretical conclusion. In chapter 1 I examine the sexual reform literature that contributed to Whitman's vision of male homosexual desire. After briefly introducing the topic of sexual possession in Whitman's poetry, I undertake a detailed analysis of the work of such popular antebellum sexual hygiene authors as Sylvester Graham, William Alcott, Samuel Woodward, and Orson Fowler. Social historians and cultural critics have generally interpreted this literature as an effort to assert control over a newly urbanized young male population that threatened to destabilize the existing social order. However, an analysis of the causes and effects ascribed by these writers to excessive sexual behavior suggests that for them it was the social order that threatened the young men. The prime concern of the discourse of sexual hygiene was the male body's vulnerability to external influences; its model of desire was that of an independent agent that invaded men's bodies and subjugated their wills. By placing men in a role metaphorically equivalent to that of a female rape victim, sexual desire therefore threatened the very idea of male heterosexual identity. An entire logic of homophobia was thus latent within this popular discourse about how sexual desire affected the male body.

In chapter 2 I demonstrate how Whitman adapts this view of sexual desire to his own purposes, first by portraying male homosexual desire as the embodiment of masculine desire per se and, second, by identifying it with the invasive, automating force of poetic inspiration. My examples span Whitman's career as a poet and prose writer, from the early temperance potboiler *Franklin Evans* (1842) to major poems such as "Song of Myself" and "The Sleepers" (1855), the poetry and prose of his Civil War hospital work (1862–65), and the correspondence and conversations of the 1880s and early '90s. Whereas the first chapter was devoted to cultural analysis, here I read Whitman's portrayal of sexual desire in the context of its poetic as well as sexological antecedents. Exploring key poetic precedents, from Ovid to Petrarch to the Romantics, I show how Whitman makes use of the amatory and devotional traditions to extend the Romantic naturalization of inspiration by sexualizing it.

In chapter 3 I connect Whitman's erotics and poetics of possession to his views on poetic and political representation. This chapter provides a counterbalance to the literary history of the preceding chapter, which is international and diachronic, by placing Whitman in the context of the literary and political discussions of slavery and government that occurred in the United States during the 1840s and '50s. Here I focus on the poetry of Whitman's major phase (1855–65) as well as prose works such as "The Eighteenth Presidency!" (1856) and the extraordinary Civil War essays and letters. For Whitman, as for other Northerners of the period such as Douglass and Thoreau, slavery and the federal government were alike in their dependence on dubious theories of delegation: both sought to convince the American public that one person (the slave, the legislator) could be made into the vehicle of another's will. In fact, the realities of slavery demonstrated the impossibility of replacing the slave's will with the master's, while those of the government demonstrated the impossibility of replacing the legislator's will with that of the people. Whereas some writers respond to these failures by urging us to abandon the notion of popular representation altogether, Whitman seeks to redeem the principle of representation and claim it for poetry by assimilating it to poetic possession.

In the final chapter I consider the theoretical implications of Whitman's poetics of possession by means of a critical analysis of four poststructuralist theorists of sexuality: Jacques Derrida, Michel Foucault, Judith Butler, and Leo Bersani. I argue in favor of a relational analysis of the subject, derived in part from Foucault's late essay "The Subject and Power," as a remedy to the contradictions inherent in any theory that, while rejecting the ideal of transcendence, nevertheless attempts to envision a species of agency that is selfless.

As this outline indicates, this study does not conform to the typical format of a single-author monograph. Instead of attempting to provide an exhaustive chronological survey of the poet's career (or some portion thereof), I have tried to present a unified, linear argument concerning the major issues in Whitman's writings — the nature of poetic voice, the poetics and politics of sexuality, the relationship between poetic and political representation — and their significance for recent critical and theoretical approaches to these issues. At times this effort has necessitated that I depart from my discussion of Whitman's works for fairly lengthy stretches in order to fulfill the contextual and theoretical demands of my argument. When I do so, however, it is always in order to support my reading of Whitman and his significance either for his period or for current literary and cultural studies. Given my relatively selective approach to Whitman's oeuvre, some readers may also find my choice of examples surprising. Whereas several major long poems are given extensive treatment — "Song of Myself" in particular — others do not feature in this study at all. In their place, I provide detailed readings of many shorter lyric and narrative poems that usually play a less central role in studies of this poet. Moreover, I have also undertaken to place Whitman's fascinating essays, notebooks, and correspondence on equal footing with his poetry. As does another study by Robert Leigh Davis,[29] I place great emphasis on the still underrated Civil War poetry and prose, which provides the best opportunity we possess for contextualizing Whitman's work not only within his life but also within the sexual and political worlds of nineteenth-century America. It is my hope that in the Civil War sections of the second and third chapters Whitman's life as poet, lover, and popular spokesman emerges — in a way it has not before — as a cultural achievement in its own right. In any event, these writings have a power of their own, and I have tried to make my treatment of them justify the prominence I have given them and compensate for the absence of more thoroughly canvassed works. Ultimately, I have assumed that the value of a critical study lies more in its attempt to transform our sense of a literary project than in its satisfaction of all the formal expectations of its genre.

Sexual Hygiene

The Natural Gates and Alleys of the Body

I

"Lew is so good, so affectionate," Whitman writes about a wounded Union soldier he was tending in Washington's Armory Square hospital in 1863. "When I came away, he reached up his face, I put my arm around him, and we gave each other a long kiss, half a minute long" (*C*, 1:91).[1] Whitman may have hoped that the letter in which this passage occurs would encourage a similar affection in its recipient, Sergeant Thomas Sawyer. While Sawyer proved to be a disappointment,[2] many of the soldiers Whitman nursed on his daily visits to Washington's army hospitals during the Civil War were as affectionate as Lew. "I never was so beloved," Whitman writes to his friend James Redpath in a letter about his hospital work (164). And in another letter on the same topic he reports that "lots of [the soldiers] have grown to expect as I leave at night that we should kiss each other, sometimes quite a number, I have to go round" (162).

These encounters find their way, I would like to suggest, into Whitman's 1865 invocation to the departing spirit of war, "Spirit Whose Work Is Done":[3]

Spirit whose work is done — spirit of dreadful hours!

. . . .

Spirit of hours I knew, all hectic red one day, but pale as death next day,
Touch my mouth ere you depart, press my lips close,

> Leave me your pulses of rage—bequeath them to me—fill me with
>   currents convulsive,
> Let them scorch and blister out of my chants when you are gone,
> Let them identify you to the future in these songs.
>   (ll. 1–18)

These lines carry an erotic charge that at first seems incongruous in a poem addressed to the spirit of war. Read in the context of Whitman's hospital work, however, the poem's eroticism has a familiar ring. The word "hectic," which of course means feverish, invites being read here as an allusion to the soldiers, many of whom suffered from fevers.[4] Not surprisingly, Whitman often describes these sick and wounded men as variously feverish, red, and pale. In a letter to some friends in New York, for example, he writes of the "thousands of American young men" in the hospitals who lie "pallid . . . languishing, dying with fever" (81). And in a letter to his mother written a few months later, he uses language that anticipates that of the poem when he describes a "new lot of wounded" as "pale as ashes & all bloody" (165). Such parallels extend to passages that involve kissing as well. Of his friend-ship with a wounded "young Mississippi captain [with] eyes as bright as a hawk, but face pale," Whitman writes: "Our affection is quite an affair, quite romantic—sometimes when I lean over to say I am going, he puts his arms around my neck, draws my face down, &c." (81). Another letter is more ex-plicit: "Sometimes when I would come in, he woke up, & I would lean down & kiss him" (128), he writes to the parents of a soldier killed by fever.

In "Spirit Whose Work Is Done," however, Whitman is neither seeking nor offering affection. Instead, the speaker in "Spirit" is asking for what Henry James thought this and other poems in *Drum-Taps* (1865) lacked: inspiration. In a scathing review published in *The Nation*, the young James charged that Whitman was simply too self-centered to succeed as a poet. "To sing aright our battles and our glories," James admonishes Whitman, "it is not enough to have served in a hospital (however praiseworthy the task in itself), to be aggressively careless and inelegant, and to be constantly pre-occupied with yourself." The poet's "personal qualities" and experiences are "impertinent," James argues, because "art requires, above all things, a sup-pression of one's self." Poetry comes not from oneself, James tells Whitman, but from the surrender of oneself in the moment of inspiration: "You must be *possessed*, and you must strive to possess your possession. If in your striving you break into divine eloquence, then you are a poet. If the idea which possesses you is the idea of your country's greatness, then you are a national poet."[5] In James's account, being a poet and expressing oneself are mutually exclusive endeavors—assuming, that is, that being a poet is an *endeavor* at all. For the goal toward which the poet strives here is not so much the successful completion of an act as it is the suspension of his or her own agency. To be a poet is to be "possessed," the vehicle of an "eloquence" not one's own but "divine."

This view of poetic agency is not, of course, original to James. As M. H. Abrams has noted, "inspiration . . . is the oldest, most widespread, and most persistent account of poetic invention."[6] Nor is the idea foreign to Whitman, for whom "the great thing is to be inspired as one divinely possessed" (*NUPM*, 4:1404). Indeed, we have already seen that "Spirit Whose Work Is Done" employs this notion of poetic possession in as orthodox a fashion as does any invocation. But we have also begun to see that the poem does a good deal more: it associates Whitman's desire for inspiration with his desire for the soldiers in such a way as to suggest that male homosexual desire might be central to his conception of poetic agency. Why should this be the case? What, in Whitman's view, might his poetic aspirations and his amorous ones have in common? One can begin to answer these questions by examining his portrayal of male-male desire in another poem from *Drum-Taps*, one that also combines the martial and the erotic, though to somewhat different effect than does "Spirit":[7]

> Not my enemies ever invade me—no harm to my pride from them I fear;
> But the lovers I recklessly love—lo! how they master me!
> Lo! me, ever open and helpless, bereft of my strength!
> Utterly abject, grovelling on the ground before them.

Whitman excluded "Not My Enemies Ever Invade Me" from his printed works after 1867, and it is easy to see why.[8] The description of the lovers as invaders and the speaker as "ever open" to their intrusions clearly suggests sexual penetration, which, given the fact that the speaker is male, in turn suggests either oral or anal intercourse. Even the posture of the speaker in the last line—"grovelling on the ground" before his lovers—can be taken to suggest a sexual position in this context, while his sense of abjection (apparent even in the repeated interjection "lo!") shows him to be so mortified by the massively proscribed love he avows that the poem's eventual deletion seems like a logical consequence of the affect of the poem itself.

More important for my purposes than Whitman's mortification, however, is his description of the love that causes it. The physical invasion of the speaker by his lovers—their penetration of his body—illustrates his subjection not just to them but to his desire for them as well. After all, only love renders him "open and helpless"; his enemies achieve no such conquest. Thus, the statement "I recklessly love," which seems to posit the speaker as agent, actually denies self-control: the speaker loves "recklessly," or without the ability to govern his own actions. He is the "helpless" instrument of a power that has "invade[d]" and occupied his body. Indeed, sexual violation is merely the poem's metaphor for the overwhelming power of love, however much the metaphor's vehicle may overshadow its tenor. In short, love here is a state of possession, *like poetry*. The poem's abundant "o" sounds—"no . . . / . . . love . . . lo! . . . / Lo! . . . open . . . / . . . grovelling . . . ground"— give aural testimony to the speaker's sexual permeability, but they also hint equally at the involuntary sounds of sexual pleasure and the apostrophic "O" of traditional poetic invocation.[9]

If love is for Whitman a form of possession, poetic inspiration is, conversely, a form of sexual intercourse. In fact, Whitman's description of the union he desires with the "spirit" in "Spirit Whose Work Is Done" is as erotic as anything in "Not My Enemies": "Leave me your pulses of rage —bequeath them to me—fill me with currents convulsive." In this line, the poet's body, "fill[ed]" by the "pulses" of the spirit's "rage," is imagined to undergo something virtually indistinguishable from sexual penetration. Entering the poet's mouth and filling him, the "spirit" performs an invasion strikingly similar to that perpetrated by the "lovers" on the "ever open" speaker of "Not My Enemies." Further, the word "convulsive" likens the automatism of the inspired poet to orgasm, which Whitman describes in a notebook passage as "spasms more delicious than all before" (*NUPM*, 1:77). By portraying the spirit's entry into his body in sexual terms, Whitman places himself as a poet—and, by implication, the male poet generally—in an unmistakably homosexual role. In doing so, however, he does not mean to suggest that his poetry is an expression of his sexual *identity* but rather that poetry and sexual desire alike *violate* his identity in order to express themselves through him.

In the next chapter I explain how, and to what effect, Whitman identifies these two different kinds of possession. Before we can fully grasp the poetic, sexual, and political significance of this equation, however, we must first understand its components. To begin, what did it mean, in Whitman's time, to portray love as a form of violation?

II

In portraying desire as the subjection of the body to an invasive force, Whitman echoes the sexual hygiene literature of his day, with which he was fully conversant.[10] From the 1830s onward, a growing number of American doctors and reformers warned the public of the potentially devastating effects of sexual desire on its health,[11] describing it as an agent that infiltrates the body from outside in order to enslave it. By the 1850s, when Whitman entered his poetic prime, the views of the sexual hygiene advocates were well on their way to achieving orthodox status both within the medical community and with the public.[12] Whitman was personally acquainted with several prominent figures in the sexual hygiene movement, including Dr. Edward H. Dixon, author of *A Treatise on Diseases of the Sexual Organs* (1845) and *Woman and Her Diseases* (1847); Dr. Russell Thacher Trall, founder of Trall's New York Hydropathic and Physiological School and author of *Sexual Physiology* (1866); and the phrenologists Lorenzo and Orson Fowler, authors of *The Principles of Phrenology and Physiology Applied to Man's Social Relations* (1842) and *Amativeness* (1846), respectively, publishers of periodicals and books on health reform, and distributors of the first two editions of *Leaves of Grass* in 1855 and '56.[13] Whitman reviewed the works of such health reformers as a journalist in the 1840s and '50s, sold their books during his short stint as a shopkeeper from 1851 to 1852, wrote for one of the Fowlers' periodicals, and appended the results of Lorenzo's examination of his head to his anonymous reviews of *Leaves of Grass*. He even appears to have planned a series of lectures on physical culture in the 1840s or '50s.[14] There is thus good reason to believe that the sexual hygiene movement influenced — even if it did not determine — Whitman's poetic treatment of sexuality.

This movement is best remembered today as part of the public campaign against masturbation that took hold in the United States and Europe during the eighteenth century and lasted into the twentieth. Some historians have argued that masturbation was so strenuously combated during this period because, as an asocial substitute for the fundamentally social act of intercourse, it symbolized the breakdown of social ties brought about by the rise of the market economy. "The emphasis in the solitary vice should perhaps be less on 'vice,' understood as the fulfillment of illegitimate desire, than on 'solitary,' the channeling of healthy desire back into itself," writes Thomas Laqueur. "The real problem with masturbation in these dire warnings is . . . that it violates Aristotle's dictum, given new life during the industrial revolution by fears that it might not be true, that man is a social animal."[15]

Others have suggested, by contrast, that the concern about masturbation was fueled at least in part by its *homo*social character. Boys who taught one another to masturbate were perceived as engaging in incipient if not full-fledged homosexual behavior; masturbation "phobia" was partly a species of homophobia.[16] Carroll Smith-Rosenberg argues that "male moral reformers might well have used masturbation as a code for homosexuality. The effeminate masturbator possessed all the stereotypic qualities of the male homosexual. Further, women appeared to repulse him. . . . Moral reformers made the connection even more directly. Masturbation led frequently to overt homosexuality. Young men who taught each other to masturbate, especially in boarding schools, frequently became lovers. Violating nature's constitution in one area, they were led to even more depraved acts."[17] This argument has recently been invoked to demonstrate that male homoeroticism was "the single most increasingly threatened and stigmatized mode of bodiliness" in Whitman's culture.[18]

Neither of these explanations is entirely adequate. While the argument that masturbation was viewed as an individualistic threat to social cohesion may hold true for the eighteenth century, it inverts the pronouncements of the most prominent sexual hygiene advocates of antebellum America. These authors portrayed masturbation as an affliction visited upon individuals by what Sylvester Graham, a founder of the movement, called "the hot-bed influence of civic life" (*LYM*, 64).[19] They did not claim that individual autonomy threatened society; on the contrary, they thought that the depravity of the social whole threatened the autonomy of its members. On the other hand, the claim that masturbation was a code for homosexuality overlooks not only the fact that reformers were quite capable of condemning sexual intimacies between men *without* resorting to a "code" when they wished to but also the fact that the very manner in which masturbation and homosexuality were usually linked — as gradations of sexual corruption — also effected a distinction between them. When Graham, citing the testimony of certain public school students that "almost every boy in the school practiced the filthy vice" of masturbation, added that "many of them went on to the still more loathsome and criminal extent of an unnatural commerce with each other" (43), he simultaneously portrayed masturbation as a potential cause of homosexuality and distinguished it *from* homosexuality as the lesser vice. In other words, the very fact that reformers thought "masturbation led frequently to overt homosexuality" shows that they did not equate the two.[20]

In addition to the pitfalls peculiar to each, these two explanations of the anti-masturbation campaign share a common problem. Sexual hygiene authors denounced masturbation *regardless* of whether it was practiced alone or in a group; therefore, they cannot have denounced it *because* it was practiced in one way or another.[21] But if masturbation was condemned neither because it was asocial nor because it was homosexual, perhaps it was condemned for what it does share in common with homosexuality: both circumvent reproduction. After all, it has been a commonplace for decades that the Victorians opposed all sexual activity whose purpose was not reproductive. Some scholars clearly see the anti-masturbation campaign in this light. Ed Cohen, for example, argues that eighteenth- and nineteenth-century medical authors viewed masturbation as "an act that defies the (re)productive potential of male sexuality."[22] Michael Moon similarly describes antebellum sexual hygiene literature as part of a "proliferating mass of discourse which proscribed non-reproductive sexual activity as well as other kinds of non-'productive' behavior."[23]

Whereas eighteenth-century writers condemned masturbation as a diversion of sexual feelings from their proper conjugal channel, however, the sexual hygiene advocates of nineteenth-century America broadened the definition of harmful sexual behavior to include everything from "lascivious daydreams" to "sexual excesses between husband and wife." The latter, not surprisingly, could include acts of procreation. If these authors merely wanted to promote a reproductive norm, this was an odd way of doing so. Indeed, couples were cautioned against excessive behavior *during the act of conception* on the grounds that it would debilitate them and taint their offspring. The question of what counted as excessive here is, of course, thorny, particularly since the male orgasm, upon which reproduction depended, was regarded by sexual hygiene authors as intrinsically injurious to the male body. While Graham reminded his readers that "propagation" was "the *final cause* of [the] organs of reproduction," he also labeled male orgasms "excesses" capable of "the most terrible effects," adding pointedly that "health does not absolutely require that there should ever be an emission of semen, from puberty, to death, though the individual live an hundred years" (*LYM*, 25, 35, 37, 20, 38). Like Graham, William Alcott seems to have viewed reproductive sex as a necessary evil for the male body: "The life and health of an individual considered without reference to his duties or relations to others, would be quite as well sustained without any indulgence of the sexual propensity, as *with* that indulgence, even though it were in the greatest moderation. It is not, indeed, certain that such restricted indulgence as is barely necessary for the continuance of the species, does not subtract, in some degree, from the sum total of the vital forces, which God, in our constitution has meted out to us."[24] If orgasm was intrinsically debilitating to men, then adherence to a reproductive standard of behavior was no safeguard against debility.

This expansion of the category of "excessive" acts to include marital and reproductive activities undercut earlier arguments against masturbation.[25] Authors could no longer attack "self-pollution" as a diversion of desire from its proper marital expression once marriage was seen as a potential locus of excessive behavior. Graham and others tried to solve this problem by arguing that masturbation involved "forcing a vital stimulation of the parts" in the absence of any natural cause of excitation. The "violence . . . to the system," above and beyond that intrinsic to all sexual stimulation, was in proportion to the "consentaneous effort" required to achieve the "forced effect" (40), Graham reasoned. If masturbation was not uniquely debilitating, it was nevertheless more debilitating than other forms of "venereal indulgence" — not because it circumvented reproduction but rather because of the artificial stimulation it demanded. But this argument could hardly serve to distinguish "self-pollution" from other sexual acts, given Graham's fundamental belief that *most* sexual desire was the result of unnatural stimulation. How was the "mental action" by which the male masturbator stimulated his genitals any different from those "various other stimulants, with which civic life is universally cursed"—stimulants as common as meat and coffee—since these, too, forced unnatural excitation on the genitals? Didn't marital excess also afflict the sexual organs with "demands which exceed the wants of nature?" (25–26, 36).

Graham's attempt to make a special case of masturbation was ultimately belied by his larger critique of the sexual impulse as such. For him and for the movement he helped to inaugurate, masturbation was only one instance of a sexual drive that was unnaturally imposed on the body: "Venery, in Graham's vision . . . *is* itself a form of disease. It is as unnatural in its origins as any other illness, induced by identical causes and practices . . . and symptomatically analogous to a bevy of pathological phenomena." Other sexual reformers shared Graham's view: They "defin[ed] any but the most infrequent sexual act as disruptive and depraved."[26] Indeed, Graham insisted that sexual desire, "long continued," could itself cause "permanent disease, and even premature death, without the actual exercise of the genital organs!" (25). Not only were all behavioral manifestations of sexual desire suspect; the mere presence of desire in the body suggested disease, whether or not it manifested itself in behavior.

Thus, antebellum reformers extolled marriage not as the proper haven for natural desires but as a potential haven *from* desire. Through promiscuity "the genital organs are kept under a habitual excitement, which is . . . diffused over the whole nervous system and disturbs, and disorders all the functions of the body," Graham wrote; but "where there is a proper degree of chastity," husband and wife "become accustomed to each other's body, and their parts no longer excite an impure imagination." For such a couple, "intercourse is the result of the natural and instinctive excitements of the organs themselves [instead of artificial stimulation];—and when the dietetic, and other habits are as they should be, this intercourse is very seldom." Of course, excessive desire could always be introduced into even the most chaste marriage should the "dietetic, and other habits" of either spouse veer from proper standards. But this possibility did not change the fact that marriage *itself* was a valuable tool for inhibiting desire and hence "an institution founded in the constitutional nature of things, and inseparably connected with the highest welfare of man" (33–34).

Graham thus conceived of the "natural and instinctive excitements of the organs themselves" as intermittent; in a state of nature, he insisted, human beings would, like the animals, be "instinctively periodical in their desires." When a person was healthy, the intervals between intercourse were entirely free of sexual urges: "By adopting a proper system of diet and regimen," even married men "troubled with habitual concupiscence" should "be able to abstain from sexual commerce, and preserve entire chastity of body, for several months in succession, without the least inconvenience, and without any separation from their companions." For healthy people, desire was not a component of everyday existence but an infrequent event essentially co-extensive with the rare act of intercourse itself. Anything in excess of this — any sexual feeling outside the immediate scene of periodic marital intercourse — was a form of disease. In short, Graham granted sexual desire no persistent psychological or physiological existence except as a pathological phenomenon. Where desire was "continual," it was also "exceedingly depraved, and unnatural . . . and terribly pernicious in its effects" (13, 35–36, 32). Only excessive sexual feeling constituted a diseased state, but virtually *all* sexual feeling was defined as excessive.

Attempting to account for this vision of sexual desire as intrinsically menacing, Smith-Rosenberg identifies the threat with the group whose sexuality was under most scrutiny. "The purity advocates' protagonist was the male youth," she observes; "his moral education and physical well-being were their espoused goals." The threat of sex symbolized the threat of independent young men in an industrializing society that "had few institutions through which to direct and discipline them": "Male purity writers in the 1830s and 1840s saw young men as a potentially despotic power, cutting through civil and moral law [and] ultimately engulfing and destroying social order." Recent studies echo this view. The notion of masturbatory illness allowed writers to dismiss "counterhegemonic behavior by middle-class male youths" as a symptom of "somatic dysfunction," according to Cohen. The "actual target" of the sexual hygiene movement was "a whole range of emergent forms of male autonomy," which together created a "crisis in the social control of young men,"[27] states Moon.

The young men that populated antebellum purity tracts were more threatened than threatening, however, and it was precisely the social order that authors blamed for their peril. If young men posed a threat to society, it was because society—through its child-rearing practices, dietary customs, clothing styles, schools, literature, and, of course, sexual habits—had imposed "an irresistible power" on them. It was the new habits, goods, and institutions of Jacksonian society, Graham claimed, that kindled "young concupiscence . . . into a passion of despotic power . . . compel[ling] the unwary youth . . . to break through the restraints of moral and civil law" (26, 25).[28] What recent studies call exertions of "male autonomy" and "counterhegemonic behavior" were evidence of constraint to him. Young men were *victims* of despotic power, not authors of it. Through the inculcation of proper habits, the sexual hygiene movement proposed to *liberate* them. The price of that liberty was eternal vigilance over oneself.

The concerns emphasized by analysts of the anti-masturbation crusade—the breakdown of social ties, homosexuality, the circumvention of reproduction, the threat of young men—were at most secondary problems for American sexual hygiene authors. They were less concerned about sexual and social relations than they were about men's relation to desire itself. Masturbation was the representative vice for them because, by dispensing with the sexual partner, it demonstrated desire's potential for becoming a force unto itself, independent of any particular object. *The drive alone* compelled the act of masturbation, and if it compelled masturbation, it could compel other acts as well. It was this vision of a sexual drive as unrestricted as it was involuntary that moved Graham and his colleagues to portray desire in general—and masturbation in particular—as tyrannical.

In the remainder of this chapter I will show how the role of the sexual partner was usurped, in sexual hygiene theory, by an image of desire itself assaulting and subjugating the male body. I will argue that in this vision of sexuality, desire threatened the body from without, the major causes being improper diet, inherited propensities, and the seduction of children by previously infected schoolmates and servants. The male victim of desire experienced increasingly severe symptoms whose automatic character testified to desire's dominion over functions previously subject to his will. The controlling metaphor for this process of automation, grounded in contemporary medical views of the female body as constitutionally vulnerable to external influences, was one of feminization: the more a man came under the sway of desire, the more he resembled a woman.

The reformers' view of desire as an invasive force was evident in their rhetoric. Thus, masturbation was routinely personified as an independent agent forcing itself on the bodies of its young "victims." One physician, inspired to verse by the menace, published these lines in January 1855 — six months before *Leaves of Grass* first appeared:

> In vain we scan the springs of human woe,
> To find a deadlier or more cruel foe
> To erring man, than this sad self-pollution,
> This damning wrecker of his constitution.
>
> In its foul march it tramples vigor down,
> Darkens the soul, usurps the mental throne,
> Preys upon the vitals of its filthy slave,
> And drags him early to a hopeless grave.[29]

If this author's choice of the verse medium was unusual, his personification of masturbation as a kind of monster "prey[ing] upon the vitals" of its victims was not. "Behold lads and lasses by the teeming myriads, half unsexed before puberty by the secret vice," Orson Fowler wrote in 1870; "*Is* it not *high* time some *strong* hand *seized by his horns* this juvenile-slaughtering monster, all reeking with the gore of perishing myriads, to stay his ravages?"[30] Similarly, Dr. Samuel Gridley Howe claimed, in his influential report to the Massachusetts state senate, that "self-abuse . . . vampire-like, sucks the very life-blood from its victims."[31] Graham portrayed the habitual onanist as forced by a personified lust to yield to *its* sexual demands: "The moral sensibilities of his soul may sometimes be aroused, and remonstrate with horror at this terrible defilement . . . but the tyrant lust subjugates everything, and forces the mental and voluntary powers into subserviency to its imperious desires!" (59).

Sexual desires were thus dissociated from the victim and ascribed (redundantly) to "the tyrant lust," which enacted them through coercion of its victim. As this passage also illustrates, the figurative violation of the victim extended to his or her mind as well. "It *takes possession* of his mind," warned the anonymous *Onania* (1724), an early anti-masturbation tract often quoted by

later reformers; "he is prey to the most lascivious ideas which never leave
him."[32] "He cannot rid his imagination of the erotic fantasies which have
so long *possessed* it," wrote Dr. Roberts Bartholow. "During sleep lascivious dreams *beset* him. . . . During the day erotic ideas constantly *invade*
his mind."[33] The so-called solitary vice looks anything but solitary in these
descriptions — *not* because it was frequently practiced in groups but rather
because the "vice" itself was figured as a perpetrator of sexual coercion on
its supposedly solitary practitioners.

A tendency to personify characterizes reformers' accounts not just of masturbation but of sexual desire in general. Graham consistently portrayed desire as a usurping dictator — "tyrant lust" or "despotic lust" — through whom
"our rational powers are brought into vassalage" (59, 62, 32). Phrenology's
compartmentalization of the brain into different faculties, each responsible
for a particular mental function, especially lent itself to this sort of personification. Provide the brain's sexual faculty, or "amativeness," just "a couple
of glasses of wine or ale," wrote Dr. John Cowan, and it "promptly proclaims
'I am excited, and must be exercised ere I am appeased. . . .'"[34] James Jackson personified amativeness as a marauder enlisting its fellow propensities
to waylay unwary victims: "God never yet made a human being to whom
great mental powers were given, and in whom great moral sensibilities were
wrapped up, who could preserve these . . . when the animal passions were
in excess; and of these . . . inordinate amativeness stands the leader. Give to
this unbridled license, and there is not a propensity in human nature that
will not rally at its call like a band of common highwaymen at the whistle
of their captain."[35]

These personifications clearly owed something to the evangelical roots
that the sexual hygiene movement shared with other antebellum reform
efforts.[36] Thus, the Christian spiritualist Andrew Jackson Davis likened the
body to a "wilderness full of animals, passions [and] demons" and the sexual
reformers to exorcists: "The Bible speaks of 'unclean spirits.' Jesus cast them
out. . . . Dr. Trall, of this city, also does something in the line of exorcism."[37]
But the rhetoric of sexual hygiene was also informed by theories of human
physiology and pathology. While antebellum physicians did not view diseases as distinct invasive entities (as we do viruses and pathogenic micro-
organisms), they did see them, according to Charles Rosenberg, as "the sum

of one's transactions with the environment."[38] Certain transactions were necessary either for the maintenance of individual life (eating, drinking, breathing) or for the production of new life. But they all posed a potential danger as well: any of them might introduce debilitating substances into the body or drain vital energy from it. This danger was considered acute by Graham, whose systematic exposition of the relations between sex, diet, and disease served as the theoretical foundation for sexual reform in this period. For Graham, Stephen Nissenbaum writes, "the human body [was] an exceedingly fragile and vulnerable organism exposed to constant assaults from the outside world."[39] The personification of desire as a sexual assailant was merely the rhetorical expression of what to him, and other reformers, was a physiological fact: persistent sexual desire signaled the intrusion of deleterious substances or influences from the outside world into the body.

The body's vulnerability lay in its dependence on its environment for survival: "By continually ingesting a portion of its environment in order to insure even temporary survival, it was forced literally to open its gates to the enemy."[40] This innate vulnerability dictated strict regulation of the body's intake. Dietary reform was thus central to the sexual hygiene agenda. Foods considered "stimulating"—meat, tea, coffee, alcohol, seasonings of all kinds—were proscribed, by Graham, on the grounds that they "increase the concupiscent excitability and sensibility of the genital organs, and augment their influence on the functions of organic life, and on the intellectual and moral faculties" (19).[41] Persistent sexual sensibility resulted from the consumption of external irritants, and health demanded its minimization. "If an unmarried man finds himself troubled with concupiscence, let him be more abstemious, and less stimulating and heating in his diet," Graham wrote. "And if a married man finds himself inclined to an excess of sexual indulgence, let him adopt the same regimen, and he will soon find that he has no reason to complain of what he calls his natural propensity" (39). On the other hand, Graham argued, "If we will train our offspring into the early and free use of flesh-meat, and accustom them to high-seasoned food, and richly prepared dishes, and learn them to drink tea, and coffee, and wine . . . we shall be more indebted to their want of *opportunity to sin*, than any other cause, for the preservation of their bodily chastity,—if, indeed, we escape the heart-rending anguish, of seeing them the early victim of passions, which we have been instrumental in developing to an irresistible power!" (25–26). Other sexual hygiene advocates followed Graham's lead. Whereas the mechanics of heterosexual intercourse might have suggested a view of masculine sexuality as penetrative volition, the digestive system illustrated something like the opposite: sexual desire literally entered men's bodies from outside in the concrete form of food. Lust was a mark of the body's permeability, not its virility.

While individuals could, with some effort, reduce the perils of their diet, they could not avoid inheriting a predisposition to sexual excess from their parents. According to Cowan, the "first great cause [of the] abnormal growth and exercise" of amativeness — greater even than diet — was its transmission "from parents to offspring."[42] Assuming that "acquired characteristics, even patterns of behavior, could be inherited," reformers reasoned that parents' sexual behavior and ailments — the two were nearly synonymous in their minds — would predispose their offspring to the same sexual destiny.[43] The act of conception itself could be particularly disastrous for the child, even if the parents were married, should it involve immoderate sensual delight.[44] "The Psalmist David uttered simply a physiological truth," James Jackson argued, "when . . . he declared that he 'was shapen in iniquity, and in sin did his mother conceive him.' . . . There is no evidence that David was not begotten in wedlock," Jackson acknowledged, "but when . . . he found his sexual passion running away with him, and . . . submerging all considerations . . . in its overbearing impulse, he was compelled . . . to ascribe it to a constitutional tendency . . . and he plumply 'owns up'. . . that his mother conceived him in a way . . . which, though it were within the boundaries of wifely obligation, was nevertheless sinful."[45]

While an inherited predisposition might be kept dormant through sexual and dietary temperance, any deviation from strict regimen could activate it. Should this occur, Jackson argued, the "victim . . . must have his responsibility largely qualified; and the sin which will attach to him . . . may be so lightened in degree . . . as to make his parents carry its heaviest share."[46] "Excessive" behavior reflected parental victimization. Desire was thus attributed less to the individual whose actions exhibited it than to an anterior cause implanted in his or her body. Such people could hardly be held responsible for urges not their own. In search of the best metaphor to dramatize heredity's operation, Edward Dixon finally settled on poisoning as illustrated by the Ghost's speech in *Hamlet:*

> We have attempted to show how the very sources of [the child's] earliest exis-
> tence in its mother's womb, are impressed by the vices of its parents; and to
> trace the web of error that is wound round the nervous system of the little
> infant, even from the pure fountain of maternal love, till having entered the
> "dark labyrinth of sin," he presents himself to the surgeon, a fellow-being of
> ungoverned passion . . . ; he has imbibed
>
> > "The leperous distilment, whose effect
> > Holds such an enmity with blood of man
> > That, swift as quicksilver, it courses through
> > The natural gates and alleys of the body —
> > Curdling like eager droppings into milk,
> > The thin and wholesome blood." [47]

On the face of it, the quotation from Shakespeare seems unsuited to the topic of hereditary illness; after all, here a father narrates his *brother's* poisoning of *him*, not *his* contamination of his son. Nevertheless, Dixon's application of old Hamlet's speech powerfully depicts hereditary sexual propensities as enemy invaders of the vulnerable "gates and alleys" of children's bodies. Like diet, heredity was a means by which sexual desire was regarded as infiltrating the individual body from without.

Young men spared infection through heredity or diet were at risk of acquiring sexual impulses directly from other people. In fact, the threat of transmission through sexual coercion was already fairly explicit in warnings about hereditary predisposition and diet. By indulging in sensuality before or during conception (or even during gestation or lactation, in the mother's case), by feeding them stimulating foods during childhood, parents effectively violated their children — a point the penetrative metaphors for these processes made clear. The agents of direct sexual transmission, on the other hand, were usually servants and schoolmates, not parents. Masturbation was seen as a disease communicated from one victim to the next: "The child finds, on his first arrival [at school], a focus of contagion, which soon spreads itself around him; the vice is established endemically, and is transmitted from the old pupils to those newly arriving." [48] Cajoled or coerced by others into masturbating, boys would soon find the habit itself assuming the role of oppressor: "One of the most melancholy and remediless cases I ever knew commenced in very early childhood, under the care, and by the immediate instruction of a nurse; and before the boy was old enough to know the dangers of the practice, the habit had become so powerful, that he was wholly unable to resist it; and when he had reached the age of twenty, with a broken down constitution, — with a body full of disease, and with a mind in ruins, the loathsome habit still tyrannized over him, with the inexorable imperiousness of a fiend of darkness!" (42).

The unspoken assumption of passages like this one is that were it not for some more or less forceful "instruction," masturbation would never occur. The notion of desire as something that could be sexually transmitted is thus a further example of how the hygienic etiology of desire assigned it an external cause. If it could not gain entry through heredity or food, desire needed a personal envoy to make its way into the body. Since such agents were themselves seen as victims of "contagion," their responsibility, like that of the hereditary sensualist, had to be "largely qualified": they did not so much impose *their* lust on others as become vehicles by which "the tyrant lust" imposed *its*. Embodiments of desire, they personified its exteriority to the naturally chaste body it menaced. Their sometimes coercive initiation of children too young "to know the dangers of the practice," and therefore too young to qualify as consenting, simply dramatized the manner in which desire assaulted the body and subjugated the will. Sex was always something done *to* people but never entirely done *by* them.

The direct or indirect duress of parents, schoolmates, or servants only marked the beginning of desire's dominion. Desire's subjugation of the will was also evident in the compulsive masturbation that ensued in its victims. Masturbation was not only a disease or a cause of disease but also a symptom of foreign occupation. Once installed in the body, sexual desire became a "despotic power," "controlling the decision of the understanding; and, at times, even forcing the will, against the remonstrance of the moral sense" (26–27). As one victim of masturbation ingenuously wrote to a medical advisor, "This habit produces most singular results, in spite of one's self." [49] Explaining that masturbation's dominance of the moral faculties made moral appeals to the victim useless, James Jackson commented that he "do[es] not . . . approach the masturbator so much in the light of a voluntary and outrageous sinner, as in that of a victim and sufferer."[50] Not only did masturbation commence under duress; it was itself a kind of duress.

In addition to displaying desire's capacity to control its victim's behavior, compulsive sexual activity also served to tighten that control and to expand its domain throughout the interior of the body. The more frequent the indulgence, the more insatiable the desire and the more enslaved its victim.[51] Thus established, sexual excess soon led to an even greater erosion of physical self-control. In men, the first sign of this erosion was most often "spermatorrhoea," or involuntary seminal emissions. Philadelphia surgeon George R. Calhoun defined spermatorrhoea as "the involuntary loss of . . . the Seminal fluid, either by the spasmodic action of the genital organs after lascivious dreams during sleep, or by constant daily discharges, before or after passing urine, or at stool, during the waking hours."[52] Doctors believed these emissions constituted a diseased state, of which "self-abuse" and "venereal excess" were the chief causes.[53] According to François Lallemand, the French physician who pioneered the study of spermatorrhoea, such excessive sexual behavior eventually induced "a constant disposition in the seminal vesicles to contract spasmodically and expel their contents."[54] Dr. Marris Wilson described how sexual excesses were thought to have this effect, reporting that "repeated exercise" of the sexual function establishes an "unhealthy state of excitement in the organs," which, "assuming by continuance a chronic character, takes on an action independent of its cause, progresses gradually, and occasions a constant secretion of seminal fluid."[55] The task of creating "excitement" was assumed by the genitals themselves, which began to convulse spontaneously, or without the aid of the victim's participation. The "convulsive paroxysms" of orgasm, themselves pathologized by Graham as "excesses [causing] the most powerful agitation to the whole system, that it is ever subject to" (20), produced through repetition an ingrained genital automatism. Even should he succeed in giving up all forms of sexual "excess," the victim thus faced the likelihood that his body would persevere, as it were, without him — indeed, against his wishes. The direct or indirect coercion initially inflicted on him by others was now inflicted by the "unhealthy" genitals themselves, as the testimony of one young man illustrates:

> When I was *thirteen* and *fourteen* years of age . . . I was enduced by a young man with whom I slept, to follow the practice of masturbation, though not

without some threats on his part, and indeed was forced to by him. After a while I needed neither forcing nor threatening, but did it voluntarily from three to twelve times a week, till I was between seventeen and eighteen, when I became convinced it was sinful, and abandoned it; and never, to my knowledge, have practiced it since, no, not even once, as I made it a matter of conscience; but I have had the spontaneous or involuntary emissions, and the nocturnal pollution more or less ever since, especially in lascivious dreams; and sometimes in female company, the involuntary emissions have troubled me greatly.[56]

Like the drama of the compulsive masturbator struggling to resist "incontrollable propensities," only to be overpowered "in spite of himself," the involuntary emissions engendered by such habitual sexual activity illustrated, above all, the autonomy of the sexual urge from its victim, who not only did not *want* to indulge it but, in this case, maintained he succeeded in not consciously doing so.[57]

As a "reflex act," orgasm itself suggested the presence of an agent inside the body but distinct from the will.[58] While the same might be said of the body's myriad other automatic functions, sexual hygiene writers reserved their apprehension for orgasm. In part this was because the healthy body's other automatic functions did not make themselves felt. Indeed, as Graham liked to point out, "The nerves appertaining to organic life, which preside over the general function of nutrition, are, in their natural and healthy state, entirely destitute of sensibility; and the perfect healthfulness and integrity of this general function, require such a state of these nerves" (17). When healthy, the functions of "organic life," though automatic, were therefore not available to be *felt* as in conflict with the will. Orgasm, by contrast, not only made itself felt but extensively and violently so. "The brain, stomach, heart, lungs, liver, skin . . . feel it sweeping over them, with the tremendous violence of a tornado. . . . [T]his violent paroxysm is generally succeeded by great exhaustion, relaxation, lassitude, and even prostration" (20). The combination of automatism and violent feeling was essential to the hygienic construal of orgasm as a *felt violation* of the body and the will. While it is true, as Smith-Rosenberg vividly remarks, that for sexual hygiene writers "it was not the emission of sperm or the penetration of a woman's body that threatened, but the orgasmic thrust itself, wild and unstructured,"[59] what made orgasm threatening was not any outwardly directed male violence it might be supposed to betoken but rather its negation of masculine volition. Male orgasm signaled male disempowerment, not male power.

The pursuit of orgasm thus appeared to sexual hygiene authors simultaneously as a misguided invitation to violation and as a sign that violation had already occurred. And if the spasms of orgasm were "excesses," as Graham termed them, by reason of their sensible yet automatic character, their unsought, or involuntary, occurrence suggested an expansion of automatic activity into somatic terrain previously controlled by the will. For while orgasm as such was "automatic or uncontrollable," the sexual act of which it was a part was supposed to require a man's willful exertion.[60] The production and ejection of semen are automatic functions, explained Graham, "but the power to *exercise* the organs of generation . . . depends on the nerves of animal life" or "voluntary motion" (16, 15; my emphasis). As the culmination of an act initiated voluntarily — at least by men — under even the best of circumstances orgasm suggested a supersession of the voluntary by the involuntary. Thus, John Humphrey Noyes proposed that the male orgasm simply be eliminated from the sexual act except in those infrequent cases where reproduction was the goal — a proposal he put into practice in 1848 at the Oneida community. Noyes suggested this not merely as a means of avoiding unwanted pregnancies but, more important, because he wished to introduce "moral culture" into the sexual act itself. While he admitted that "some cannot 'contain'" — "men of certain temperaments and conditions are afflicted with involuntary emissions of every trivial excitement in their sleep," he conceded — he viewed these as "exceptional morbid cases that should be disciplined and improved," insisting that "in the normal condition, men are entirely competent to choose in sexual intercourse whether they will stop at any point in the voluntary stages of it, and so make it simply an act of communion, or go through to the involuntary stage, and make it an act of propagation." While Noyes' proposal would never have satisfied someone like Graham, for whom sexual excitement itself was physically perilous, it actually differed from hygienic views on continence only in that it introduced self-discipline, as Noyes himself wrote, "at another stage of the proceedings." His innovation was to extend the pursuit of self-control to the sexual act, making the latter a means toward the former: "It is the glory of man to control himself, and the Kingdom of Heaven summons him to control himself in ALL THINGS."[61] With proper discipline, Noyes argued, the sexual act itself could be purged of automatism.

If automatism superseded the will during orgasm, the avid and repeated enactment of that supersession implied a wish for self-surrender so perverse that writers could explain it only by reference to some prior experience of coercion. The appearance of involuntary emissions, or "spermatorrhoea," in turn marked a further transition from the momentary automatism of orgasm, repeatedly induced, to a progressive deterioration of the body's voluntary powers. Sleep, during which these spontaneous emissions typically took hold, was understandably viewed as the body's most vulnerable state since it was when the will resigned control of the body wholly to its automatic functions — "when the powers of the body are prostrate," as one author put it.[62] Masturbation itself could occur automatically during sleep, once commenced, despite the victim's abstention from it while conscious.[63] (Thus, the young man who wrote that he had "never, *to [his] knowledge* . . . practiced it" since the age of eighteen was making a significant qualification.) But the symptoms occasioned by sexual excesses soon manifested themselves during waking hours as well. "Nocturnal pollutions" were joined or succeeded by "diurnal" ones. The entire body began to exhibit an array of convulsive symptoms that both mimicked and generalized the spasms of orgasm.

As a "violent paroxysm," orgasm itself was generically identified with various convulsive ailments, especially epilepsy: "It approximates in many of its phenomena to epilepsy, and is accompanied in some persons with epilepti-form seizure."[64] Further, it was not a local but an all-encompassing corporeal event, "all the body participating at this moment in a strange convulsion, as though nature at the instant forgot every other function."[65] A violent spasm affecting the whole body, it could, when too often repeated, so debilitate the nervous system as to engender related forms of chronic spasm outside the genital area. One author warned that "patients are apt to experience occasional jerks or contractions of the muscle of the eye."[66] Graham claimed that as a consequence of habitual masturbation "the food will often cause great distress in the stomach, and frequently be thrown off with violent eructations"; "spasmodic disorders" will "reduce the intestines to a deplorable state" (48–49). Samuel Woodward quoted the testimony of a former masturbator who remained an "unwilling captive" not only of spontaneous emissions but of what he described as "constant little twitchings or spasms in various parts of my body, and frequently in my face. Sometimes . . . they are so violent as to affect the whole limb with a sudden convulsion." William Alcott predicted the same symptoms when he cautioned that "St. Vitus [*sic*] dance . . . is another disease which is often brought on some of our most promising young men, as a consequence of masturbation. . . . It is not by any means pleasant to the sufferer to find his arms or legs twitching about, when he would gladly control them." Extending its sway from the genitals outward, sexual desire quickly annexed other parts of the body, wresting control of them away from the will and remaking them in the image of the perpetually convulsed sexual organs. Sometimes the entire body assumed — whole for part — a phallic likeness. In his treatise on onanism, the eighteenth-century Swiss physician Samuel Tissot described the case of a watchmaker whose masturbation provoked a recurrent "convulsive action of the extensor muscles of the head, which drew it strongly backward, while the neck was very much swelled" and the mouth "foamed"; he also cited the "perhaps unique case of a man who, in the middle of the act [of intercourse], was seized with a spasm which rendered his whole body stiff" for twelve years.[67]

Like involuntary emissions — indeed, like the sexual activity that supposedly occasioned them — these convulsive symptoms were evidence of "a lack of power to bring the body . . . under the action of the will."[68] This lack of power on the part of the victim of sexual excesses in turn testified to the power exerted over him by desire. While the symptoms through which desire demonstrated its reign sometimes worked to identify the male body exclusively with its genitals, this exaggerated masculinity actually betrayed the victim's sexual subjection. As if to emphasize this subjection even further, in their survey of automatic symptoms sexual hygiene writers focused special attention on the loss of control over orifices. In part this emphasis reflected concern about the male body's need to "keep in [its] contents" — above all its semen — in order to retain its health and masculinity.[69] But to keep in its contents the body had to be able to prevent intrusions, and it was the loss of this ability, more than anything else, that the loss of control over orifices indicated. The natural gates and alleys of the victim's body — his throat, anus, seminal ducts — became increasingly spasmodic or open as his "disease" progressed. According to Graham, the masturbator's famously dilated pupils made his eyes "weak and excessively sensible; so that wind, light, &c., irritate and distress them." The body became a helplessly permeable entity, its very skin pores "exceedingly susceptible to the injurious effects of cold, heat, moisture, malaria, and other noxious agents" (55, 53). After breaching the body's defenses, desire thus set about "opening the gates to other diseases."[70] By focusing on paths into the body, sexual hygiene authors could identify the physical effects of desire, like its causes, almost explicitly with sexual penetration: "Patients are seized with . . . morbid contractions of the throat, with sudden stoppage of breath, as if a foreign body had lodged in this region."[71]

As the ultimate involuntary state, insanity was the logical culmination of desire's erosion of the will. "No cause is more influential in producing Insanity . . . than Masturbation," Woodward typically asserted.[72] In fact, masturbation was itself sometimes viewed as an insane, because unwilling, act. Noting that "loss of the power of will is one of the sad effects of this diseased habit," one Grahamite reformer argued that victims recalcitrant to treatment "should be treated as already insane, and put under any necessary degree of constraint."[73] Conversely, insanity caused by masturbation was considered nearly incurable precisely because it destroyed whatever vestige of resistance the sufferer might previously have retained, thereby resulting in increased masturbation and further mental deterioration: "Thus the cause is perpetuated; and in spite of every effort, the disease increases, the powers of body and mind fail together, and are lost in the most deplorable, hopeless, disgusting fatuity!"[74] In madness desire reigned without hindrance. The onanist became a sexual automaton, incapable of turning his thoughts or actions to other objects. At a time when the criminal responsibility of the insane was beginning to be systematically questioned on the grounds that they lacked "liberty of will and action," the notion of masturbatory insanity took the hygienic equation of sexual activity with the abridgment of liberty to its logical extreme. In his groundbreaking treatise on insanity (1838), Isaac Ray reinforced this connection when he argued that the "medico-legal importance" of "morbid activity of the sexual propensity . . . has never been so strongly felt as it deserves." "Filling the mind with a crowd of voluptuous images, and ever hurrying its victim to the grossest licentiousness," Ray insisted, "erotic mania" nullified the "free choice of the intellectual faculties" essential to an enlightened conception of legal responsibility. While Ray himself did not state that masturbation or venereal excess necessarily led to insanity, he clearly believed that sexual desire could constitute such a state: "If insanity — or . . . morbid activity of the brain inducing a deprivation of moral liberty — ever exists, it does in what is called erotic mania."[75] Beginning by penetrating the body, desire completed its conquest by dominating the mind.

The encompassing metaphor for this process of deterioration was one of feminization: the more a man came under the sway of desire, the more he resembled a woman. William Acton attributed what he called Jean-Jacques Rousseau's "pettish feminine temper and conceit," as evidenced in his *Confessions,* to his enslavement to the "vile habit." Various authors complained of "the unmanliness of the act" and warned that "the masculine traits are gradually weakened" by it. Onanism, they cautioned, would cause the male voice to become "effeminate and shrill," "almost like that of a woman." According to Fowler, the "pitiable victims" of "excessive" intercourse also "lost their distinctive sexual characteristics," becoming "practically neuter genders." Graham held that even "amorous reveries" could cause "effeminacy," not to mention disease and death, "without the actual exercise of the genital organs" (25).[76]

This vision of the feminizing effects of male sexual desire reflected contemporary medical views of female sexuality. If desire was dangerous to men in part because it threatened to subject the entire bodily economy to domination by the reproductive organs, such domination was often thought to be normal for women. One doctor claimed that "woman's reproductive organs are pre-eminent. . . . They exercise a controlling influence upon her entire system."[77] Since these organs, unlike their counterparts in the male body, functioned with complete independence from the will, it followed that women were by nature less volitional, more automatic beings than men even when healthy. Further, by defining women in terms of those parts of their bodies penetrated by men and inhabited by the fetus, Victorian doctors made the permeability that threatened men with the loss of self-rule central to female identity. Women's genital permeability thus came to define aspects of their physiology seemingly unrelated to reproduction. For example, medical discourse described the female nervous system as, in the words of one physician, "sooner affected by all stimuli . . . than that of the male."[78] Another doctor claimed that "the nerves themselves are smaller, and of a more delicate structure. They are endowed with greater sensibility, and . . . are liable to more frequent impressions from external agents."[79] In short, women's nervous systems showed them to be more pervious and therefore less individuated than men. This relative lack of individuality explained their distinctive virtues — sympathy, altruism, selflessness, and spirituality — but it it also explained their potential instability: "The female sex is far more sensitive and susceptible than the male, and extremely liable to those distressing affections which . . . have been denominated nervous."[80]

For women, in other words, the preeminence of the reproductive organs entailed a specifically feminine vulnerability to external influences and, along with that, to disease. This view of women also informed medical opinions about their susceptibility to sexual desire. These opinions are notoriously contradictory, so much so that one historian sees them as constituting "one of the central analytical dilemmas in the understanding of nineteenth-century social history."[81] But whether women were believed to be "not very much troubled by sexual feeling of any kind," as Acton declared, or, on the contrary, "much under its dominion," they were consistently viewed as subject to sexual possession. For example, when Orson Fowler wrote that "woman is made to crave everything with resistless intensity, so that her maternal cravings may overcome all prudential considerations," he pointed to women's desires as evidence for his belief that their sexuality compelled them to sacrifice their physical self-control. On the other hand, the belief that women were *devoid* of sexual desire affirmed even more strongly the notion of their subservience to their reproductive function. Incapable of wanting sex themselves, women could — and did — want it only for the sake of others: "A modest woman seldom desires any sexual gratification for herself. She submits to her husband's embraces, but principally to gratify him; and were it not for the desire for maternity, would far rather be relieved of his attentions." By construing women as passionless, doctors like Acton thus presented female sexual activity as a form of altruistic surrender. But women's selflessness in intercourse, as in other respects, was less a matter of choice than of biology. Their sexual acquiescence was dictated by their sex, which, by furnishing them with only the slightest of barriers between self and other, persuaded them to adopt the sexual promptings of their husbands as their own. Whereas Fowler's passionate woman evinced her possession by sacrificing personal safety to maternal cravings, Acton's passionless one evinced hers, if anything, more dramatically by obeying cravings *she* didn't even feel. In other words, Acton's theory of female sexuality only *emphasized* women's subjection to sexual desire by locating desire *outside* the female body. Thus, while Acton thought women had "a natural repugnance of cohabitation," he saw an unwillingness to overcome this repugnance as a symptom of disease. Aversion to intercourse was normal, but expression of that aversion to one's husband indicated a "selfish indifference to please" incompatible with the body's normal functioning. Acton suggested that such women were most likely victims of masturbation, which was thought to produce in women an atypical egotism curiously at odds with the erosion of will it brought about in men.[82]

When these writers argued that sexual desire and its indulgence made men like women, they thus relied on a notion of women as permeable, nonvolitional, underindividuated beings. In other words, desire feminized men both by penetrating their bodies and by defining them as permeable in the process. Since this notion of femininity was articulated, in large part, through an account of the inherent vulnerabilities of the female nervous system, it should not be surprising that sexually overactive men were believed to suffer from the same sort of nervous disorders that were thought to plague women. Bartholow argued, for example, that "those [men] in whom the nervous apparatus predominates in activity over the muscular and digestive" were particularly liable to masturbation, and that the "spermatorrhoea" which usually attended such cases was itself a form of neurosis.[83] Other writers described the onanist's sensitivity to external stimuli in terms nearly identical to those used to characterize the "greater sensibility" of the female nervous system. "The whole body becomes . . . sensible to the slightest impression," one author claimed. "Their bodies becom[e] as keenly delicate to external and atmospheric agencies as the most perfect barometer," wrote another.[84] This equation of male masturbatory disease with female nervous ailments was often more explicit. According to R. J. Culverwell, the habitual onanist "sighs and weeps like a hysterical woman"; sinking "into the effeminate timidity of womanhood, [h]e becomes truly hysterical," stated Hayes.[85]

This feminization of the male nervous system was often said to be accompanied by an even more dramatic transformation of the male reproductive system itself. Sexual hygiene writers argued that frequent or improper sexual activity would lead not only to impotence but to the shrinking, if not the disappearance, of the male sexual organ. Whereas popular opinion may have held that "through want of exercise, the male organ will decrease in size," Cowan insisted that "when any such decrease in size does occur, it will be found to be caused by exactly the reverse — namely, excessive exercise by self-abuse."[86] Graham made an even more sensational assertion: "A general withering, and impotence and decay of the parts, commences and continues on, with the continuing vice, till almost every vestige of the *insignia*, and all the power of virility are gone" (60). More was at stake here than simple emasculation: sexual hygiene authors imagined not only that masturbation could make the male genitals disappear but that it could transform them into something like their female equivalents. Thus, writers such as Graham claimed that habitual masturbation would produce "bloody semen" or bleeding from the urethra — possible analogues for menstruation (61). And the disappearance of the male organ was sometimes described as occurring *via* absorption into the abdominal cavity: "Cases have been known" in which the male onanist's genitals, once "faded and entirely decayed . . . have disappeared into the abdomen."[87]

What *replaces* the penis here matters as much as its disappearance. According to Thomas Laqueur, medical science prior to and, in some cases, during the nineteenth century held that the female reproductive system was merely an inverted and less perfect version of the male. As the sixteenth-century surgeon Ambroise Paré put it, "women have as much hidden within the body as men have exposed outside; leaving aside, only, that women don't have so much heat, nor the ability to push out what by the coldness of their temperament is held bound to the interior."[88] Laqueur explains that Paré and others credited tales of women turning into men on the grounds that increased bodily warmth — resulting from puberty, intense physical activity, or even intercourse — could "break the interior-exterior barrier and produce on a 'woman' the marks of a 'man.'" They dismissed the notion that men could become women, however, insisting, in the words of one writer, that "Nature tends always toward what is most perfect and not, on the contrary, to perform in such a way that what is perfect should become imperfect."[89] But if nature, in the view of Renaissance physicians, tended always toward perfection, violations of nature like masturbation or "venereal excess" could drive human anatomy in the opposite direction, according to nineteenth-century sexual hygiene advocates. The disappearance of the male onanist's genitals turned external organs into ones that were internal, like women's —

a metamorphosis that presumed the creation of a vagina-like opening into which the organs supposedly vanished. The *metaphor* of sexual penetration, so often used to describe desire's infiltration and subjection of the male body, materialized as an anatomical stigma: the male organ of penetration was replaced by the orifice into which it disappeared. By invading and subjugating men, desire cast them as "feminine" victims of its own "masculine" assault. The ensuing physical transformation made the male body illustrate that subjugation by making it look female.

Earlier in this chapter I argued that, contrary to what some scholars have suggested, sexual hygiene writers did not use masturbation as a "code for homosexuality." What I have tried to demonstrate instead is that they propounded a theory of sexuality that condemned male sexual desire *in general* as a feminizing invasion of the male body. The coercive nature of sexual desire, revealed in masturbation, was both figured and theorized in terms that to us suggest male homosexual rape. In other words, the homophobic legacy of the sexual hygiene movement is to be found not in any confused or euphemistic use of terminology, nor even in its virulent yet sporadic condemnations of sodomy, so much as in *its vision of how sexual desire as such acted upon the male body.*[90] Yet the analogy between desire's violation of the male body and violent homosexual intercourse, whether oral or anal, went unremarked in the discourse; none of the passages on sodomy exploited it. As the next chapter will demonstrate, it was Whitman who activated this analogy—laden though it was with homophobic implications—as a means of endowing male-male desire with the paradigmatic status previously assigned to masturbation. But it required a further equation between homosexual love and poetic invention—an equation Whitman forged using tools provided by a long poetic tradition in startling new ways—to make male homosexuality represent more than the despotism of desire that masturbation already exemplified. In Whitman's hands that despotism would turn its victim into a vehicle not of vice but of virtue.

℘ℕ CHAPTER 2

Sexuality and Poetic Agency

> I think Swedenborg was right when he said there was a close
> connection — a very close connection — between the state we call
> religious ecstacy and the desire to copulate. I find Swedenborg
> confirmed in all my experience. It is a peculiar discovery.
> —Horace Traubel, *With Walt Whitman at Camden*, 5:376

I

Sexual hygiene authors defined desire as a form of possession: lust entered the body from outside, disabled the will, and set about operating the machinery of the body for its own ends. Whitman often employs this definition of desire quite straightforwardly. While his interest in autoeroticism has been read as solipsistic,[1] he actually tends to portray the compulsion to masturbate as though it were externally imposed. In "Spontaneous Me," for example, a young man's struggle to resist nocturnal urges is likened to an attempt to fight off an assailant:

> The young man that wakes deep at night, the hot hand seeking to repress
>   what would master him,
> The mystic amorous night, the strange half-welcome pangs, visions, sweats,
> The pulse pounding through palms and trembling encircling fingers, the
>   young man all color'd, ashamed, angry . . .
>   (ll. 32–34)

Even in poems more conspicuously concerned with heterosexual dynamics, female love objects tend to be upstaged, as they are in sexual hygiene rhetoric, by the presence of desire itself. Readers have rightly noted the marginality of particular women in Whitman's poems of procreation, "Children of Adam," ever since their initial appearance in the third edition of *Leaves of Grass*. "Walt Whitman assumes to regard women only as an instrument for the gratification of his desires, and the propagation of the species. To him all women are the same," a contemporary reviewer writes. "An ordinary man aches with love for Belinda, or his Native Land, or the Ocean, or the Stars." Whitman's women, by contrast, are mere "muscles and wombs. They needn't have had faces at all," D. H. Lawrence observes. A more recent critic concurs: "The madness of the speaker's desire rings untrue . . . because the object of his desire is insufficient. His lover is a nobody. . . ."[2] What these readers neglect to note, however, is that the marginality of Whitman's women results from the centrality he grants to the desire for them. If these poems are not about being possessed by a *beloved,* they are nevertheless very much about being possessed by *love.* Whitman's longest and most delirious paean to heterosexual passion, "From Pent-up Aching Rivers," manages to focus on the actual object of desire for no more than a few phrases, but it provides an extensive report on desire's sway over the speaker:

The female form approaching, I pensive, love-flesh tremulous aching,
The divine list for myself or you or for anyone making,
The face, the limbs, the index from head to foot, and what it arouses,
The mystic deliria, the madness amorous, the utter abandonment,
(Hark close and still what I whisper to you,
I love you, O you entirely possess me. . . .)
The furious storm through me careering, I passionately trembling,
The oath of the inseparableness of two together, of the woman that loves me
    and whom I love more than my life, that oath swearing,
(O I willingly stake all for you,
O let me be lost if it must be so!
O you and I! what is it to us what the rest do and think?
What is all else to us? only that we enjoy each other and exhaust each other
    if it must be so;)
From the master, the pilot I yield the vessel to,

The general commanding me, commanding all, from him permission
taking.
(ll. 23–39)

Master, pilot, general: the multiple incarnations of desire in this poem contrast sharply with the abstract anonymity of "the female form." The poem
focuses less on lover or beloved than on the drive animating and subordi-
nating both. The poet's body is a mere vessel under desire's command. Even
his defiance of social conventions — "what is it to us what the rest do and
think?" — is not an act of self-assertion but rather an act of compliance with
a will more potent than society's or his own: "From the master . . . / . . .
permission taking." Male heterosexuality is defined here not by a will to
command or to penetrate but by a willingness to *yield.*

It is no wonder, then, that some recent scholars have likened Whitman's
views on sexuality to those set forth by the sexual hygiene movement. "Whitman does not celebrate masturbation," writes Betsy Erkkila. "On the contrary, his attitude is closer to the antimasturbation tracts published by Fowler
and Wells."[3] His celebration of procreative sex can be viewed in a similar
light: after all, from its very beginnings the hygienic supervision of sexuality was animated by a professed reverence for the human reproductive
system in many respects comparable to Whitman's.[4] More to the point, like
the sexual hygiene writers, Whitman takes the personification of desire to
such an extreme that the sexual urge itself is often presented as seducing or
molesting the poems' male figures.

Detached from the hygiene movement's rigid taxonomy of sexual acts,
however, Whitman's scenes of solitary sex — even his scenes of consensual
heterosexual sex — can become genuinely difficult to distinguish from scenes
of one man being ravished by one or several others. The "mystic amorous
night" of "Spontaneous Me" and the interloping "master" of "Pent-up Aching Rivers" suggest the potential for such confusion. In fact, the phrase
"amorous night" alludes to two earlier passages in *Leaves of Grass* where the
night is explicitly invoked as a lover.[5] The first is from "Song of Myself":

Press close bare-bosom'd night — press close magnetic nourishing night!
Night of south winds — night of the large few stars!
Still nodding night — mad naked summer night.
(ll. 435–37)

This stanza fully elaborates the portrayal of night as lover implied in "Spontaneous Me." Whitman's allusion to this passage thus reinforces the impression that the "amorous night" in "Spontaneous Me" serves, however fleetingly, to personify as a lover the urge that would "master" the young man. The second passage, from "The Sleepers," gives that lover a sex:

> I am she who adorn'd herself and folded her hair expectantly,
> My truant lover has come, and it is dark.
>
> Double yourself and receive me darkness,
> Receive me and my lover too, he will not let me go without him.
>
> I roll myself upon you as upon a bed, I resign myself to the dusk.
>
> He whom I call answers me and takes the place of my lover,
> He rises with me silently from the bed.
>
> Darkness, you are gentler than my lover, his flesh was sweaty and panting,
> I feel the hot moisture yet that he left me.
>
> My hands are spread forth, I pass them in all directions,
> I would sound up the shadowy shore to which you are journeying.
>
> Be careful darkness! already what was it touch'd me?
> I thought my lover had gone, else darkness and he are one,
> I feel the heart-beat, I follow, I fade away.
>   (ll. 47–59)

All of the examples we have examined thus far substitute a personification for a beloved. This passage is *about* that displacement. Darkness "takes the place" of the speaker's lover, first caressing her gently — "Darkness, you are gentler than my lover" — but then, it seems, entering her impetuously if not forcibly: "Be careful darkness!" In other words, the male darkness imposes itself sexually on the female speaker in the same way that the personifications of desire we have already discussed impose themselves figuratively on the male will. By temporarily turning the usually male speaker of *Leaves of Grass* into a woman, "The Sleepers" thus makes sexual penetration a metaphor for desire's suppression of the will — a suppression evident in the final phrase of the passage: "I fade away." Being possessed by desire — here darkness — is like being possessed by a man. And in "The Sleepers" being possessed by a man is like being a woman.

"Spontaneous Me" distills this tale of nocturnal possession into a single animistic phrase: "The mystic amorous night." By now the latent homoeroticism of this phrase should be evident: amorous male night ravishes sleeping young man. "From Pent-up Aching Rivers," on the other hand, connotes its homoeroticism somewhat differently by infusing it into the poem's more heavily advertised heterosexual program. For example, it is easy to forget that the parenthetical apostrophes of "Pent-up Aching Rivers" address "the female form" rather than the personified male sexual drive, especially since the poem regularly introduces parts of the woman's body by using the definite article — "*the* face, *the* limbs" — instead of the more intimate possessive pronoun "your." Whitman thus quietly disjoins *the* generic woman that is the speaker's ostensible love object from the familiar *you* of the parentheses. This disjunction, accentuated by effects of contiguity, invites the reader to mistake desire itself for the object of address:

> The face, the limbs, the index from head to foot, and what it arouses,
> The mystic deliria, the madness amorous, the utter abandonment,
> (Hark close and still what I now whisper to you,
> I love you, O you entirely possess me. . . .)

Given that the poem personifies desire as male — as master, pilot, general — the suggestion that desire itself might be the object of the apostrophes is partly a homoerotic one. And this suggestion is only reinforced by the phrase "O you entirely possess me," which, though presumably addressed to the woman, nevertheless describes the male speaker as subject to possession in a way that seems anything but heterosexual — indeed, in a way that anticipates the surrender of his body to his male "master." As in "Not My Enemies Ever Invade Me," moreover, the apostrophic "O" reinforces the reader's impression of the speaker's sexual permeability.

Neither "Pent-up Aching Rivers" nor "Spontaneous Me" is primarily homoerotic in design, yet both briefly suggest that *surrendering to desire is like surrendering to a man*. Elsewhere this suggestion is less fleeting. In "Song of Myself," for example, the poet is ravished by a group of "prurient provokers" who seem alternately to be actual assailants and personifications of his own sexual yearnings. Betrayed by his sense of touch as well as his other senses — personified as "sentries" who have been "bribed" to desert their posts — the speaker finds himself powerless to resist the ambiguous onslaught:

> Is this then touch? quivering me to a new identity,
> Flames and ether making a rush for my veins,
> Treacherous tip of me reaching and crowding to help them,
> My flesh and blood playing out lightning, to strike what is hardly different
>   from myself,
> On all sides prurient provokers stiffening my limbs,
> Straining the udder of my heart for its withheld drip,
> Behaving licentious toward me, taking no denial,
> Depriving me of my best as for a purpose,
> Unbuttoning my clothes, holding me by the bare waist,
> Deluding my confusion with the calm of the sunlight and pasture-fields,
> Immodestly sliding the fellow-senses away,
> They bribed to swap off with touch and go and graze at the edges of me,
> No consideration, no regard for my draining strength or my anger,
> Fetching the rest of the herd around to enjoy them a while,
> Then all uniting to stand on a headland and worry me.
>
> The sentries desert every other part of me,
> They have left me helpless to a red marauder,
> They all come to the headland to witness and assist against me.
>
> I am given up by traitors,
> I talk wildly, I have lost my wits, I and nobody else am the greatest traitor,
> I went myself first to the headland, my own hands carried me there.
>
> You villain touch! what are you doing? my breath is tight in its throat,
> Unclench your floodgates, you are too much for me.
> . . . .
> Blind loving wrestling touch, sheath'd hooded sharp-tooth'd touch!
> Did it make you ache so, leaving me?
>   (ll. 619–43)

This mock captivity narrative has been read alternately as autoerotic and as homoerotic — and understandably so. Statements like "I myself first went to the headland, my own hands carried me there" seem clearly enough to suggest masturbation. And the "red marauder" seems like a malignant member of that large family of metaphors for sexual desire in *Leaves of Grass* that includes the more benevolently despotic general of "Pent-up Aching Rivers"—a resemblance that strengthens the reading of the episode as auto-erotic, given the absence of any female object for that desire. The passage thus appears to take the displacement of the *object of* desire by a *figure for* desire one step further than does "Pent-up Aching Rivers," with the consequence—familiar from the discussion of sexual hygiene literature in the first chapter—that desire, no longer restricted to an object, assumes a malevolent role.

Yet here the "prurient provokers," engaged in "unbuttoning [the poet's] clothes" and "holding [him] by the bare waist," are much too tangibly human not to be viewed primarily as *people*. Even the object of the poet's apostrophe seems to fluctuate undecidably between personification and person: the "touch" could be that of another man—"Did it make you ache so, leaving me?" suggests postcoital withdrawal—instead of the speaker's own hand.[6] In fact, if the "red marauder" seems to resemble some of Whitman's more transparent, though nonetheless ambiguous, figures for sexual desire, "touch" calls to mind the more nebulous figure of darkness in "The Sleepers," a poem written concurrently with "Song of Myself." Compare, for example, "You villain touch! what are you doing?" to "Be careful darkness! already what was it touch'd me?" Although darkness in "The Sleepers" *is* a personification, it so thoroughly assumes the role of the male lover that it necessarily assumes some of the lover's physical reality in the process. The same is true of "touch" in "Song of Myself." Indeed, the suggestion of penetration in both passages can be read as Whitman's way of affirming each figure's substance: the reader will inevitably ascribe an independent body to any figure described as penetrating the speaker's body. Even the "red marauder," though in some respects analogous to the general of "Pent-up Aching Rivers," is most obviously a metaphor for the engorged penis, and as such could just as easily represent somebody else's as it could Whitman's. Ultimately the attribution seems irrelevant: the "red marauder" plays the same irruptive role here that the poet's male lovers play in less ambiguously homosexual poems like "Not My Enemies Ever Invade Me" *regardless* of to whom it belongs. Whitman here implies that when men's masturbatory and heterosexual urges are defined as forms of surrender to an invading force, *all* male desire begins to look homoerotic.

No doubt this fusion of sexual acts results, in part, from Whitman's effort to cloak his homosexuality in the sexual hygiene movement's language for autoeroticism. While the encounter with touch is clearly comparable to hygienic descriptions of desire, however, the comparison does not entirely clarify our understanding of the sexual act or acts Whitman describes. Instead, it suggests that he is as audacious in molding the language of sexual hygiene to fit the contours of his own sexual agenda as he is cautious in disguising that agenda in hygienic rhetoric. For example, Whitman's "herd" of "prurient provokers," led by a "red marauder," strikingly resembles James Jackson's portrayal, in *The Sexual Organism,* of the "animal passions" as a "band of common highwaymen" with amativeness as their "captain." Yet the comparison is as striking for the differences it reveals as for the similarities. Jackson offers his portrayal as a reifying simile: "Give to [amativeness] unbridled license," he writes, "and there is not a propensity in human nature that will not rally at its call like a band of common highwaymen at the whistle of their captain." He wants to endow the abstract concept of amativeness with some visceral immediacy in order to lend urgency to his message. By contrast, the ambiguity of Whitman's personifications results from the fact that he does not tell us what abstract concepts, if any, they embody. His "prurient provokers" do not explicitly or exclusively allegorize the animal propensities and his "red marauder" does not directly represent amativeness. Instead, like the sexual urge itself in both Whitman and Jackson, these figures take on a life of their own.

The effect of this autonomy is to endow what would otherwise be mere personifications with the more solid particularity of *characters.* If they generate a sense of immediacy, therefore, it is not on behalf of an abstract concept so much as in their own right. And the less like metaphors and the more like characters they seem, the more like actual assailants or lovers they seem — which is to say the more homoerotic the whole episode seems. The passage does assimilate the allegorical figures of sexual hygiene literature, then, but this doesn't mean it is simply about masturbation, nor that it merely seeks to disguise its homoeroticism. Rather, by detaching the allegorical figures of sexual hygiene literature from their framing allegory, Whitman fashions his own form of male homosexual melodrama.

The same confusion of ravisher and ravished occurs during another defining sexual encounter in "Song of Myself" — the poet's conjunction with his soul:

> I believe in you my soul, the other I am must not abase itself to you,
> And you must not be abased to the other.
>
> Loafe with me on the grass, loose the stop from your throat,
> Not words, not music or rhyme I want, not custom or lecture, not even the
>   best,
> Only the lull I like, the hum of your valvèd voice.
>
> I mind how once we lay such a transparent summer morning,
> How you settled your head athwart my hips and gently turn'd over
>   upon me,
> And parted the shirt from my bosom-bone, and plunged your tongue to my
>   bare-stript heart,
> And reach'd till you felt my beard, and reach'd till you held my feet.
>   (ll. 82–90)

Here, too, Whitman personifies what might ordinarily be considered part of himself—his soul—as an independent agent that takes violent, if amorous, possession of his body. In fact, Whitman's soul is not only independent of him but, as the erotic ferocity of the encounter makes plain, independently *embodied* as well. This soul has a head, throat, and tongue; it can loaf on the grass, nestle, or pierce the poet's breastbone. Its capacity to inflict bodily injury—to puncture not just flesh but solid bone—demands that we attribute physical autonomy to it. However paradoxical it may seem, we have no choice but to view Whitman's soul as effectively its own person. As in the encounter with touch, the more independent his soul appears, the more it seems like an actual lover—a male lover, presumably, given its graphic penetration of the poet's body. For while Robert K. Martin tentatively identifies the act that occurs here as "apparently a part of fellatio"[7]—and the phrase "you settled your head athwart my hips and gently turn'd over upon me" does suggest this—Whitman quickly discards this option, perhaps because it fails to capture the sense of possession he intends to convey. Instead, he moves the point of contact from his hips to his chest and replaces gentle touching—as he does in "The Sleepers"—with sudden and violent entry. Were it not for this choice, the passage might seem essentially autoerotic; after all, the poet's lover here *is* his own soul. If choosing penetration makes the soul a more physically compelling figure, however, that compelling male presence conversely marks this scene as homosexual.

Of course, the homoeroticism of Whitman's poetry is not in dispute, and it is not my purpose here merely to document its pervasiveness. Instead, my goal thus far has been to show how the sexual hygiene movement's view of desire as something that penetrates men's bodies allows Whitman to portray male homosexual intercourse as *the objective correlative of male sexual desire per se.* Once it is assumed that all masculine desire constitutes a violation of the male body, it becomes possible to suggest that actual *sexual* penetration of that body is not an anomaly but an enactment—an incarnation—of the essential logic of *all* sexual desire. Sometimes, as in "Spontaneous Me" and "Pent-up Aching Rivers," Whitman suggests this quite subtly; at other times, as in "Song of Myself" and "The Sleepers," he is more audacious. Whether subtle or audacious, however, Whitman's inclusion of homoeroticism in ostensibly autoerotic or heterosexual scenes (or scenes that mix the two) indicates more than his very real need both to voice and to conceal his passion for men. More fundamentally, it demonstrates that he views homosexuality as the template for male sexuality in general. Male homoeroticism so pervades *Leaves of Grass,* in other words, partly because its author views all other forms of masculine desire as variations on an archetypically homosexual theme.

Being possessed by desire is like being possessed by a man; for Whitman, being possessed by desire is therefore like being a woman. Sexual hygiene tracts made the latter claim incessantly, warning their young male readers of the mental and physical effeminacy—even the metamorphosis of sex characteristics—that would befall them if they yielded to their urges. Whitman links the two claims, seeing in male homosexuality something like the natural expression of the invasive work of desire and in feminine sexuality perhaps the ultimate model for the self-surrender to which he believes masculine desire also inevitably leads. Thus, he speaks as a woman in "The Sleepers" not simply in order to present himself as an object of sexual penetration—something he obviously could not do as explicitly in the persona of a man—but also to identify the possession of his body by desire, and the surrender of his body in intercourse, with feminine sexuality. For the same reason, in "Song of Myself" he represents his love of men through the yearnings of a female character:

> Twenty-eight young men bathe by the shore,
> Twenty-eight young men and all so friendly;
> Twenty-eight years of womanly life and all so lonesome.

She owns the fine house by the rise of the bank,
She hides handsome and richly drest aft the blinds of the window.

Which of the young men does she like the best?
Ah the homeliest of them is beautiful to her.

Where are you off to, lady? for I see you,
You splash in the water there, yet stay stock still in your room.

Dancing and laughing along the beach came the twenty-ninth bather,
The rest did not see her, but she saw them and loved them.

The beards of the young men glisten'd with wet, it ran from their long hair,
Little streams pass'd all over their bodies.

An unseen hand also pass'd over their bodies,
It descended tremblingly from their temples and ribs.

The young men float on their backs, their white bellies bulge to the sun,
    they do not ask who seizes fast to them,
They do not know who puffs and declines with pendant and bending arch,
They do not think whom they souse with spray.
    (ll. 199–216)

Whitman links the twenty-ninth bather to his own persona through a number of allusions to passages about himself in "Song of Myself" and elsewhere.[8] For example, the "richly drest" woman's fantasy of undressing and entering the water with the men recalls the speaker's startling announcement near the opening of the poem—"I will go to the bank by the wood and become undisguised and naked" (l. 19)—as well as the stripping of the poet by his soul prior to ravishing him: "you ... / ... parted the shirt from my bosom-bone, and plunged your tongue to my bare-stript heart." It also anticipates his voluptuous invocation to the sea later in the poem:

You sea! I resign myself to you also—I guess what you mean,
I behold from the beach your crooked inviting fingers,
I believe you refuse to go back without feeling of me,
We must have a turn together, I undress, hurry me out of sight of the land,
Cushion me soft, rock me in billowy drowse,
Dash me with amorous wet, I can repay you.
    (ll. 448–53)

The reciprocal wetting of this passage likewise echoes the splashing with water and sousing with spray in the group bathing scene. (Whitman merges elements of both scenes in a single line of "Spontaneous Me": "The souse upon me of my lover the sea, as I lie willing and naked" [l. 35].) In addition, the woman's imagined emergence from "aft the blinds of the window" resembles a number of crucial passages closely related to the scenes of disrobing, in which Whitman presents himself as emerging into view from behind some form of cover. This group of passages includes the Wizard of Oz–like proclamation in the 1860 poem "So Long!": "My songs cease, I abandon them, / From behind the screen where I hid I advance personally solely to you" (ll. 51–52). The prototype, however, is a passage on style in the 1855 preface to *Leaves of Grass:* "I will not have in my writing any elegance or effect or originality to hang in the way between me and the rest *like curtains.* I will have nothing hang in the way, not the *richest* curtains" (719, emphasis added). The "richly drest" woman who emerges from "aft the blinds" thus appears to be a surrogate for Whitman *specifically in his role as poet.*

This may help to explain some other curious parallels. The unseen hand of the woman evokes the night-shrouded hands of the female speaker in "The Sleepers," for example, another figure closely associated with Whitman himself: "My hands are spread forth, I pass them in all directions, / I would sound up the shadowy shore to which you are journeying." Reaching blindly in all directions, this persona gestures, in turn, toward the undiscriminating eros of the twenty-ninth bather. Moreover, the bather's tremulous exploration of the men's bodies — "An unseen hand also pass'd over their bodies, / It descended tremblingly from their temples and ribs" — brings to mind several other sexually charged passages in which Whitman emphasizes *his own* trembling, from the shudder elicited from him by touch in another section of the same poem ("Is this then touch? *quivering me* to a new identity") to his sense of "passionately trembling" in "Pent-up Aching Rivers." Granted it is hardly surprising that erotic scenes should feature quivering and quaking of this kind, whether by the speaker or by others, but these instances of automatism have special connotations when ascribed to the poet or his surrogate. In the first chapter, it will be recalled, such shivers were interpreted as symptoms of disease by sexual hygiene writers, who associated them with involuntary phenomena as varied as orgasm and epileptic seizures. For them tremors of erotic excitement signaled an assault on one's sovereignty over one's own body. As was also noted, however, shudders of sexual arousal and delight can be invested with quite another significance. They can be tokens of *poetic* arousal, as in "Spirit Whose Work Is Done":

> Touch my mouth ere you depart, press my lips close,
> Leave me your pulses of rage—bequeath them to me—fill me with
>   currents convulsive.

The convulsions of orgasm are here no less a threat to self-control than they are in the discourse of sexual hygiene. The difference is that *the logic of poetic possession renders self-control counterproductive.* In this context, the unseen hand of the twenty-ninth bather takes on new meaning. Its passionate trembling begins to look like that of the *poet's* hand, seized by the spirit and convulsively executing its commands.[9]

But if the trembling woman represents the rapt Whitman, why does he make her a woman? Obviously, self-protection plays a role here, as it does in "The Sleepers"; openly describing a *man's* sexual longings as he watches a group of younger men bathe wasn't a promising idea for a poet of national ambition in 1855. But this doesn't explain why Whitman chooses to emphasize his surrogate's female silhouette so explicitly in the penultimate line of the passage, by which time her sex has already been firmly established: "They do not know who puffs and declines with pendant and bending arch." This line exquisitely describes a woman bending over the horizontal body of a man, her breasts pendant, her breathing hard, as she raises and lowers herself in the act of lovemaking.[10] If Whitman merely intended to use the woman as a cover, he need not have highlighted her female anatomy so strikingly. However, he seems to have given her body some fairly precise thought. It appears, in other words, that he wanted not only to hide his own pleasure in the male body behind a female front but also to present both erotic and poetic rapture as feminine.

It should be clear by now why Whitman sees erotic rapture as feminine. His views of sexual desire and of his own homosexuality are rooted in a notion of possession that derives, in part, from the discourse of sexual hygiene. As Whitman employs it, this notion of possession renders sexual pleasure in general—and male homosexual pleasure specifically—analogous to a woman's penetration by a man during sexual intercourse, whether that penetration involves her passive receptivity, as in Acton, or — what amounts to the same thing in the logic of sexual hygiene — her compulsive action, as in Fowler and here Whitman himself. For Whitman as for the sexual hygiene writers, penetration and automatism are the essential constants defining male sexual desire and joining it to femininity. One of his innovations was to add male homosexuality to the equation.

Penetration and automatism: Whitman links the female bather to himself on the basis of their shared appetite for erotic possession and their shared experience of it. But in the process he also links her sexual rapture to another experience that might otherwise be considered unrelated to sexuality — that of composing poetry. The blinds are like the curtains of poetic rhetoric and convention that Whitman rejects in his 1855 preface, as are the woman's clothes; the "unseen hand" is like the invisible hand of the author; its trembling like the spasms of poetic possession the poet seeks in "Spirit Whose Work Is Done." And, finally, the woman's spontaneous vocalizations — "They do not know who *puffs* and declines" — suggest something on the order of poetic automatism. The resemblances between the woman and Whitman thus imply a larger parallel between sexuality and poetry, a parallel based upon the suspension of the will that Whitman considers integral to both. The narrative of the twenty-eight bathers is bound up with Whitman's writings about himself as a poet not just because the woman it describes embodies his own sexual yearnings but because the story it tells of joyful surrender to an overwhelming urge is a story about poetic creation.

II

In connecting the sexual drive to the poetic, Whitman was preceded, to some extent, by the same sexual hygiene writers from whom he borrowed much of his theory of sexuality. We have already seen that these writers likened sexual desire to demonic possession. While Noyes and other radical reformers associated the "nervous exaltation" of sexual intercourse with an influx of the Holy Spirit, Graham and like-minded writers saw revival meetings and other popular forms of religious exaltation as organized offensives against the chastity of their participants.[11] In each case spiritual possession and sexual excitement were linked.

Vocal automatism was a regular item in the moral reformers' catalogues of bodily movements and functions over which the victims of masturbation and venereal excess gradually lost control. Masturbators displayed "trembling of the voice, hesitation of speech [and] stuttering"; some talked "in a wild and incoherent manner."[12] William Acton quoted from the *Confessions* of avowed onanist Jean-Jacques Rousseau to illustrate his belief that "incoherence of language" was one of "the most characteristic mental phenomena . . . resulting from masturbation in young men": "Instead of knowing how to hold my tongue when I have nothing to say, it is just then that, to pay my debt as quickly as possible, I have a mania for talking. I try in a hurry to stammer, promptly, words without ideas, only too happy if they mean nothing at all. In trying to conquer or hide my inaptitude, I seldom fail to display it." Rousseau's "mania for talking" was for Acton a sexually induced "chronic dementia"; his stammered "words without ideas" expressed only desire's subversion of his capacity for intentional self-expression. To Acton's medically trained ear, these inept words constituted masturbation's announcement of its mastery over their speaker. In fact, he seems almost to have viewed the entire *Confessions* along the same lines — as nothing more than one massive instance of automatic talking: "Displaying as they do at once the terrible ease with which the vile habit can make a human being its slave, and the kind of judicial blindness which comes over its besotted victim, [they] are of no small value."[13] Graham went a step further in his description of the effect of excessive sexual desire on speech. Explaining how mental disorders begat sexual ones, and vice versa, he noted that "insanity . . . is generally attended with excessive sexual desire." In this case a consequence rather than a cause of the disintegration of self-control, sexual desire here manifested itself not in "words without ideas" but in obscenities: "Many people who were perfectly modest while in health, become exceedingly obscene in their conduct and talk, when insane" (*LYM*, 18). Whereas Rousseau's onanism, as analyzed by Acton, merely inhibited his capacity for spoken self-expression, the ungovernable desire of the insane turned them into its mouthpieces.

All this suggests a distrust of spontaneous utterance that would naturally have extended to theories of spontaneous *poetic* utterance as well. It is hardly surprising, then, that François Lallemand viewed a gift for poetry as a symptom of diseased sexuality: "Individuals endowed with the spirit of poetry, whom we call *nervous*, frequently attach the most seductive colors to their recollections, and embellish them with imaginary charms; but their devouring passions are badly supported by their weak and irritable organs. ... [S]uch individuals are very liable to the occurrence of spermatorrhoea."[14] According to Lallemand, the spirit of poetry and the despotism of desire are one.

III

When Whitman links sexuality to poetic automatism, however, he has more than the sexual hygiene movement as a precedent. At least as important is the Western poetic tradition itself.[15] Since antiquity, love has been presented as a source of the poetic impulse. In fact, the classical personification of love, which remained vital in the lyric tradition throughout the seventeenth century and beyond, bears a striking (and perhaps not coincidental) resemblance to the hygienic one described in the first chapter. Although the form of desire portrayed in the lyric tradition is usually heterosexual — especially after the classical era — and the victim of desire is usually male, given the predominance of men among lyric poets, desire is nevertheless personified as male too. Heterosexual desire is thus frequently portrayed as arising out of the relationship between a male god and a male poet. Further, the act that traditionally instigates desire is one of physical coercion and penetration: Cupid wounds the unsuspecting or reluctant poet with an arrow, thereby filling him with desire. In other words, it is *possible* to see the conventions defining Love and his relation to the male poet as suggestive of homoeroticism.[16] And with love comes poetic expression:

> With Muse upreared I meant to sing of arms,
> Choosing a subject fit for fierce alarms.
>
> . . . .
>
> When in this work's first verse I trode aloft,
> Love slacked my Muse, and made my numbers soft.
> "I have no mistress, nor no favorite,
> Being fittest matter for a wanton wit";
> Thus I complained, but love unlocked his quiver,
> Took out the shaft ordained my heart to shiver,
> And bent his sinewy bow upon his knee,
> Saying "Poet here's a work beseeming thee."

Oh woe is me, he never shoots but hits,
I burn, love in my idle bosom sits.

. . . .

Elegian Muse, that warblest amorous lays,
Girt my shine brow with sea-bank myrtle praise.[17]

This first poem of Ovid's *Amores* (in a translation by Christopher Marlowe that Whitman probably read)[18] presents an ironic twist on what was already a conventional scenario: Love injects desire into the poet's body and thus directs — in this case redirects — his poetic endeavors. Ovid's twist on this scenario is to portray himself as filled with desire, and the elegiac ambition that accompanies it, before he has even begun looking for a beloved to serve as their focus: "I burn, love in my idle [*vacuo*] bosom sits."[19] By highlighting the relationship between himself and Cupid at the expense of that between himself and his as yet undetermined beloved, Ovid thus emphasizes the fictive male-male tie underpinning elegiac heterosexuality. Love, not a beloved, provides both the erotic and poetic impetus here. Finally, Ovid suggests that by forcibly diverting him from epic to love elegy, Cupid also forces him out of a masculine role and into an effeminate one: "When in this work's first verse I strode aloft, / Love slacked my Muse, and made my numbers soft." These lines trace a movement from epic tumescence to elegiac detumescence or softness.[20] The shift in genre and meter is also a shift in gender roles. Marlowe accentuates the sexual connotations of this shift in his translation of the poem's first line: "With Muse upreared I meant to sing of arms."[21] The descent from masculine to effeminate coincides with the change in subject matter — from men and arms to women and sex. But the change in subject matter is imposed in a manner that is itself feminizing: Love pierces and occupies the poet's breast. The poem not only attributes the poet's sexual and poetic arousal to the male god instead of a female beloved; it also describes the transmission of the sexual and poetic impulse from god to poet as an infringement on the poet's masculinity.

Many of the same elements can also be found in the Petrarchan tradition.[22] Feminist scholarship on the Petrarchan portrayal of sexuality has tended to focus on its fragmentation of the female body. In this account, Petrarch and his followers respond to the shattering effects of their encounter with the female body — that is, with castration anxiety — by projecting the fragmentation they fear onto the women they praise. In doing so, it is argued, they salvage not only their masculinity but also their poetry, which femininity likewise threatens with disintegration.[23]

Petrarchan praise certainly fragments the female body. But this reading mistakes the character and role of male fragmentation in the Petrarchan tradition. While the object of the poet's love is a woman, the love that wounds and even dismembers him is personified as *male* in both the Petrarchan and Ovidian lyric—a fact entirely omitted, despite its conspicuousness, by recent critics of Petrarchan heterosexuality. Take, for example, the following sonnet from Sidney's *Astrophil and Stella:*

Fly, fly my friends, I have my death wound, fly;
See there that boy, that murth'ring boy I say,
Who like a thief hid in dark bush doth lie,
Till bloody bullet get him wrongful prey.
  So tyrant he no fitter place could spy,
Nor so fair level in so secret stay
As that sweet black which veils the heavn'ly eye;
There himself with his shot he close doth lay.
  Poor passenger, pass now thereby I did,
And stayed, pleased with the prospect of the place,
While that black hue from me the bad guest hid:
But straight I saw motions of lightning grace,
And then descried the glist'ring of his dart:
But ere I could fly thence, it pierced my heart.[24]

Here the figure of Stella, in whose dark eyes Love sets up his ambush, functions primarily as a blind for fictional male-male aggression. The threat of love is figured here as masculine and irruptive, in other words, not as feminine—despite the fact that the object of the speaker's desire is a woman.[25] Further, while Love's assault may indeed be shattering for the poet—Sidney says he has received his "death wound"—it is clearly integral to his *poetry,* which originates in the event that wounds him.[26] The poet's loss is poetry's gain. Thus, in another sonnet Sidney defends himself against Stella's charge of having used her as a pretext for augmenting his own fame by maintaining that his poetry is not the product of his volition but rather of Love's violation of it:

Stella, think not that by verse I seek fame;
  Who seek, who hope, who love, who live, but thee:
  Thine eyes my pride, thy lips my history;
If thou praise not, all other praise is shame.
Nor so ambitious am I, to frame
  A nest for my young fame in laurel tree;
  In truth I swear, I wish not there should be
Graved in mine epitaph a poet's name:
  Ne if I would, could I just title make,
That any laud to me thereof should grow
Without my plumes from other wings I take.
For nothing from my wit or will doth flow,
  Since all my words thy beauty doth indite,
  And love doth hold my hand, and makes me write.[27]

By linking love's shattering effects upon the self to poetic invention, Sidney follows his model, Petrarch, for whom the disintegration of the self by love and the process of poetic utterance are, in fact, virtually coextensive:

  Since it's my fate
To speak, forced by a fiery passion
That's driven me to sigh and sigh—
Love, who've spurred me in this fashion,
Be my guide, show me the gate,
And let my desire fit my rhyme;
  But please, not in too perfect time—
So sweet a song my heart would break:
I dread what aches where none can see.
For speaking burns and stings me;
Nor does my skill—this makes me quake—
As favors some,
The great blaze of my mind abate;
Instead I dissolve in the sound of my tongue,
A man of ice beneath the sun.[28]

Petrarch's speaker here suffers the kind of disintegration against which his fetishistic praise of Laura is supposedly meant to protect him.[29] Yet his disintegration does not stifle his poetry. On the contrary, *he dissolves in his own eloquence.*[30] Or, rather, *Love's* eloquence: the words that speed his dissolution, though spoken by him, are inspired by Love, to whom, in turn, the poet addresses his invocation. The power that dissolves the poet empowers his utterance, which thus quite logically contributes to his further undoing. The poet speaks not in hope of defending or restoring his wholeness but purely out of compulsion:

> But still I must follow the high enterprise,
> Continue my amorous notes,
> So strong is the will that transports me.
>   (ll. 22–24)

One of Petrarch's principal metaphors for this compulsion is the wind — a particularly fitting one for his purposes, since the Italian word *l'aura* is a homonym for the name of his beloved Laura.[31] The use of the wind as a metaphor for the poetic compulsion had a long history by the time he took it up.[32] What's distinctive in Petrarch is the way he puns on this metaphor in order to equate the promptings of the poetic spirit with the force of the sexual drive. Thus, he figures the wind as the ultimate metaphorical weapon Love wields against him through the medium of Laura:

> Love's propped me up like a target for arrows,
> Like snow in the sun, like wax in a furnace,
> Like a cloud in the wind; and with begging for kindness,
> Lady, I'm hoarse, yet still you slight my sorrows.
>
> Not time nor place restore me from the blow,
> The mortal blow that came out of your eyes,
> The sun and fire and wind that cause my cries,
> They spring from you (without a thought, I know).
>
> Thoughts of you are arrows; your face, a sun;
> Desire, a furnace; with this array of arms,
> Love pierces, dazzles, and destroys me;
>
> And your angelic song and conversation,
> With your sweet breath — I can't resist such harm —
> Are all a wind before which my life flees.[33]

Yet the same wind that helps to work Petrarch's personal destruction empowers and immortalizes his poetry:

I recognize it by its murmuring breath:
The soft wind that washes the fog from the hills,
And wakens the flowers in woods dim and still;
Wind on which my pains, my fame, must rest.[34]

Ovid, Petrarch, and Sidney personify love as, among other things, a source of poetic inspiration. Writing in the wake of this tradition, seventeenth-century male devotional poets sometimes do the opposite, investing religious inspiration, from which they also seek to gain poetic impetus, with something of the ravishing physical intensity of the sexual encounter. Since, like Cupid, the god in this case is also male, and since the notion of inspiration — whether poetic, religious, or both — has always entailed some form of penetration, any suggestion of eroticism in a male poet's supplication to God may run the chance of arousing associations with male homosexual intercourse, however unlikely that may seem.[35] But even if one grants this possibility, Donne's bold exploitation of those associations comes as a bombshell:

Batter my heart, three-personed God; for, you
As yet but knock, breathe, shine, and seek to mend;
That I may rise, and stand, o'erthrow me, and bend
Your force, to break, blow, burn and make me new.
I, like a usurped town, to another due,
Labour to admit you, but oh, to no end,
Reason your viceroy in me, me should defend,
But is captived, and proves weak or untrue,
Yet dearly I love you, and would be loved fain,
But am betrothed unto your enemy,
Divorce me, untie, or break that knot again,
Take me to you, imprison me, for I
Except you enthral me, never shall be free,
Nor ever chaste, except you ravish me.[36]

This sonnet performs an almost systematic inversion of Petrarchan topoi. The torments associated by Petrarch with unfulfilled desire — puncture wounds, consuming flames, driving wind — are turned by Donne into metaphors for God's love and desire's consummation, with the consequence that they now appear to be torments very much to be coveted. Petrarch's pleas to Laura for relief become in Donne's sonnet a plea for destruction and redemption: "bend / Your force, to break, blow, burn and make me new." The desire that shatters the speaker of the *Rime Sparse* is replaced in Donne by the desire *to be* shattered. Most important, in a metaphor that makes Petrarchan figures for desire's subjugation of the male will seem almost timid by comparison, Donne transforms the reluctant lover's plangent remonstrations with Cupid for piercing and inspiring him into an invocation to God to rape and thereby redeem him (since, while eager, he is unable to open himself to God voluntarily).[37] Despite these reversals, Donne, like Petrarch, identifies inspiration (the sonnet is an invocation) with the violent—here overtly sexual—penetration of his body by another male figure.

Like the male devotional poets of the seventeenth century, male English Romantic poets seem less interested in desire's potential as a *source* of the poetic impulse than in the idea that poetic rapture itself might somehow be *equivalent* to sexual violation.[38] This analogy rests on a number of basic assumptions about poetry and the poet shared by the major Romantics, assumptions for which Shelley's *A Defense of Poetry* may serve as an index.[39] Most of these views are familiar; nevertheless, their importance for a proper understanding of the relationship between poetry and sexuality in the nineteenth century has yet to be fully grasped. The most fundamental of these assumptions is the belief in inspiration itself: "poetry is the record of the best and happiest moments of the happiest and best minds. We are aware of evanescent visitations of thought and feeling . . . always arising unforeseen and departing unbidden, but elevating and delightful beyond all expression. . . . It is as it were the interpenetration of a diviner nature through our own; but its footsteps are like those of a wind over a sea, which the coming calm erases, and whose traces remain only as on the wrinkled sand which paves it" (*SPP*, 504). As the record of these visitations, Shelley continues, "poetry redeems from decay the visitations of the divinity in man" (505).

Such subtle, fleeting visitations demand an instrument of the utmost sensitivity to register them. This instrument is the poet. "Poets are . . . subject to these experiences as spirits of the most refined organization," Shelley explains; the poet "is more delicately organized than other men" (505, 507).[40] This description of the poet's sensitivity to external stimuli should sound familiar: it is essentially the same as the medical reports of the onanist's nervous sensitivity cited in the first chapter—reports themselves modeled on medical portrayals of the female nervous system.[41] As we have seen, this nervous sensitivity was linked in the medical literature to abnormal forms of automatism on the theory that excessive receptivity to external influences threatened to undermine the capacity for physical and mental self-control. Here, too, the *Defense* runs a course that, while time-honored, is also strikingly parallel to nineteenth-century medical thought. According to Shelley, of course, poetic creation is involuntary; like sexual desire in the hygienic account, it operates apart from reason and the will: "Poetry is not like reasoning, a power to be exerted according to the determination of the will. A man cannot say, 'I will compose poetry.' The greatest poet even cannot say it: for the mind is as a fading coal which some invisible influence, like an inconstant wind, awakens to transitory brightness . . . and the conscious portions of our natures are unprophetic either of its approach or its departure" (503–4).[42] Furthermore, since it operates independently of the will, this influence is also capable of acting in *opposition* to the will: "The persons in whom this power resides, may often, as far as regards many portions of their nature, have little correspondence with that spirit of good of which they are the ministers. But even whilst they deny and abjure, they are yet compelled to serve, the Power which is seated upon the throne of their own soul" (508).

Like sexual desire in the hygienic view, the poetic power in Shelley's description is a despot. It invades the vulnerable poet, usurping control from reason and the will. We can even say of this occupying force, as Graham does of "the tyrant lust," that it "forces the mental and voluntary powers into subserviency to its imperious desires!" (*LYM*, 59). The difference is that, unlike Graham's despot, Shelley's is benevolent, a "spirit of good" that "desires" to cultivate the good in its recipient: "The great secret of morals is Love; or a going out of our own nature, and an identification of ourselves with the beautiful which exists in thought, action, or person, not our own. A man, to be greatly good, must imagine intensely and comprehensively; he must put himself in the place of another and of many others; the pains and pleasures of his species must become his own. The great instrument of moral good is the imagination; and poetry administers to the effect by acting upon the cause. Poetry enlarges the circumference of the imagination . . ." (487–88). In surrendering to inspiration, the poet thus relinquishes his or her individual vices—relinquishes, one might say, the vice *of individuality*—instead of capitulating to them. And to put it this way is to highlight a fundamental conflict between sexual hygiene and Romantic poetics, one that goes beyond the question of whether the *source* of rapture is benevolent or not to the question of whether rapture *itself* is an instrument of good or evil. For Graham and his followers, rapture—even religious rapture—is evil because it overthrows the self; hence the hygienic horror of automatism. For Shelley rapture is good—and *for the very same reason.* Only by suppressing the self, as James puts it, only by going out of our own nature (or admitting another nature into ours), can moral improvement of the kind envisioned by Shelley be accomplished. "Poetry, and the principle of Self," writes Shelley, "are the God and the Mammon of the world" (503).[43]

The analogy between nineteenth-century figurations of sexual and poetic rapture as I have thus far described it is, of course, only that—an analogy. But this analogy is not a critical invention. On the contrary, it is not only at work in the margins of medical thought of the period (witness Lallemand) but also at the heart of the Romantic transformation of English poetry.[44] For example, Coleridge's poem "The Eolian Harp" (1796) is credited with initiating a genre of verse meditation that decisively transformed the poetic landscape of the time.[45] It also initiates the Romantic form of the analogy I have been pursuing:

My pensive Sarah! thy soft cheek reclined
Thus on mine arm, most soothing sweet it is
To sit beside our Cot, our Cot o'ergrown
With white-flower'd Jasmin, and the broad-leav'd Myrtle,
(Meet emblems they of Innocence and Love!)
And watch the clouds, that late were rich with light,
Slow saddening round, and mark the star of eve
Serenely brilliant (such should Wisdom be)
Shine opposite!

. . . .

           And that simplest Lute,
Placed length-ways in the clasping casement, hark!
How by the desultory breeze caress'd,
Like some coy maid half yielding to her lover,
It pours such sweet upbraiding, as must needs
Tempt to repeat the wrong! And now, its strings
Boldlier swept, the long sequacious notes

Over delicious surges sink and rise,
Such a soft floating witchery of sound.

. . . .

   And thus, my Love! as on the midway slope
Of yonder hill I stretch my limbs at noon,
While through my half-clos'd eye-lids I behold
The sunbeams dance, like diamonds, on the main,
And tranquil muse upon tranquillity;
Full many a thought uncall'd and undetain'd,
And many idle flitting phantasies,
Traverse my indolent and passive brain,
As wild and various as the random gales
That swell and flutter on this subject Lute! [46]

Here Coleridge introduces what would quickly become the prime Romantic topos for poetic inspiration: the wind harp.[47] In recent years, this metaphor has received a good deal of criticism, especially deconstructive. As a figure for the poet's voice and, therefore, his presence, the Eolian harp has been condemned as a mystification of the representational nature of poetic language.[48] Like its practical counterpart in Romantic verse, the invocation, the Eolian model of poetic expression, it is argued, personifies the source of poetry only as a way of asserting the speaking presence of the poet.[49] As in the feminist critique of Petrarch, the poet's entreaties and celebrations are seen as concealed efforts to defend and project an ultimately factitious image of undivided masculine poetic presence.

Yet "The Eolian Harp" itself has been viewed as an attempt to appropriate the generative power of feminine sexuality, not to dispel its disintegrative threat. In this reading, Coleridge's comparison of the Eolian harp first to "some coy maid half yielding to her lover" and then to himself suggests that he sees inspiration as a form of spiritual impregnation—like sexual reproduction, but presumably transcending it. In other words, Coleridge is thought to see poetry as a way of contending with feminine creative, not destructive, power.[50]

Different though they are, both these arguments—the general one about Eolian poetics and the specific one about Coleridge's poem—rest on the same confusion: they confound the poet with the poetic power. Eolian poetics is not, as one critic has written, a "fiction of unmediated expression."[51] It is instead a fiction of *mediated* expression, that is, a fiction according to which the poet is a passive medium upon which the poetic power acts and through which it makes itself — or, rather, a version of itself — heard. It is not a mystification of representation but an effort to imagine how representation arises. Nor does it highlight the presence of the poet. Rather, it relegates him or her to an ancillary role. In fact, the individuality of the poet's voice comes to the fore in the Eolian fiction in two ways, both negative: as an expression of *privation* for which the self's submission to inspiration is the desired remedy (as in invocation: "O lift me as a wave, a leaf, a cloud! / I fall upon the thorns of life! I bleed!")[52] and as an *impediment* to the perfect reproduction in language of the inspiring force, for which it therefore becomes an inadequate substitute: "All poetry was written before time was, and whenever we are so finely organized that we can penetrate into that region where the air is music, we hear those primal warblings, and attempt to write them down, but we lose ever and anon a word, or a verse, and substitute something of our own, and thus miswrite the poem" (*EL*, 449).

Similarly, viewing "The Eolian Harp" as an attempt to co-opt female generative power mistakes the source and gender of power in the poem. The figure for creative power in the poem is the wind, not the harp, and Coleridge portrays the wind quite emphatically as *male*: "hark! / How by the desultory breeze caress'd, / Like some coy maid half yielding to her lover, / It [the harp] pours such sweet upbraiding." In comparing himself to the harp, Coleridge identifies himself with feminine *vulnerability*, not power. Lying on a hillside with "half-clos'd eyelids" while "phantasies, / Traverse [his] indolent and passive brain," he likens himself indirectly to a girl "half yielding" to rape. The point of the similes is clear: being inspired is like being a wind harp, which is like being raped and therefore like being a woman.

By describing the poem as an attempt to seize creative power, on the other hand, the feminist reading effectively identifies the poet not with the harp and the maid but with the masculine figures for power, that is, the wind and the rapist.[53] It thus neutralizes Coleridge's suggestion that being inspired might be like being raped. Further, if Coleridge's adoption of femininity is not an appropriation of power but rather of powerlessness, neither is it clear that it constitutes a figurative assumption of women's *procreative* role. In fact, the poem has nothing to say about reproduction per se. The "coy maid" simile dwells exclusively on the sexual act, never mentioning its potential biological consequences. The parallel to inspired utterance is neither impregnation nor parturition but rather the inarticulate cries of female sexual delight to which Coleridge likens the "long sequacious notes" and "delicious surges" of the wind harp. Parenthood is no more an issue here than it is in Whitman's parable of the twenty-ninth bather. Coleridge's interest focuses on the penetration of the maid and her—which is to say *his*—ensuing vocal automatism. (The fact that the maid puts up at least token resistance underscores the involuntary nature of her utterance.) For Coleridge poetry is like a woman's moans of half-welcome sexual pleasure.

Coleridge thus expands the application of the analogy between sexual and poetic rapture beyond its amatory uses in Ovid and Petrarchism as well as its devotional use in Donne. The analogy no longer defines a particular type of inspiration suitable to a particular type of poem; instead, it contributes to Romanticism's general inventory of figures for poetic invention. But Romantic poets could make use of it in amatory contexts as well, as Shelley does in the opening lines of "With a Guitar. To Jane":

> Ariel to Miranda;—Take
> This slave of music for the sake
> Of him who is the slave of thee;
> And teach it all the harmony,
> In which thou can'st, and only thou,
> Make the delighted spirit glow.
>   (*SPP*, 60)

When Shelley is in need of amatory metaphors, he turns not to Ovid or Petrarch but to his Romantic predecessors, whose wind harp he turns into a guitar. "Slave of music . . . slave of thee": the poet, for whom the guitar is a token, remains the passive instrument of an external force, but that force is now the beloved (a change Coleridge's Sara might have appreciated). In this poem Shelley synthesizes the amatory tradition's portrayal of the poet as "forced by a fiery passion" to express his love in verse with the Romantic movement's vision of the poet—and, indeed, humanity—as "an instrument over which a series of external and internal impressions are driven, like the ever-changing wind over an Æolian lyre, which move it by their motion to ever-changing melody" (*SPP*, 480) In doing so he combines the poetic tradition's major topoi for equating poetic rapture with sexual ravishment.

IV

The poetic tradition's various figurations of sexual desire presented Whitman with many specific parallels to the way desire was portrayed in the literature of sexual hygiene. In both cases desire is personified as a man assaulting and entering other men; desire's assault tends to effect a metaphorical feminization of its male victim; the victim trembles and speaks involuntarily; and the male victim's relation to the female object of his desire is mediated, if not entirely displaced, by his relation to desire itself. To some extent, then, these apparently quite different discourses of desire are mutually reinforcing.

While much in their *descriptions* of desire coincides, however, their *evaluations* of it are largely divergent. In the poetic practices I have outlined, desire's rape-like penetration of the male poet's body is equated, in one way or another, with poetic inspiration. The most personally debilitating passions can thus find powerful affirmation in the words they compel the ravaged poet to speak, even when, as in Petrarch, those words seem to provide no great personal consolation to their speaker. For unlike the sexual hygiene movement, the amatory, devotional, and Romantic poetic traditions tend to identify virtue with the violation of the self and not with the preservation of its boundaries. Poets may "have little correspondence with that spirit of good of which they are the ministers. But even whilst they deny and abjure, they are yet compelled to serve." Or, as Emerson, a veteran of the devotional and Romantic traditions, starkly declares, "The poet must be sacrificed," for "we have a higher than personal interest, which, in the ruin of the personal, is secured." [54] Whereas sexual hygiene advocates seek to minimize the body's vulnerability to external sources of excitation, even to the point of aspiring to desensitize the body, the poetic traditions I have charted thus often glorify that vulnerability and even attempt, as Wordsworth recommends, to augment it in the reader: "The human mind is capable of being excited without the application of gross and violent stimulants; and . . . one being is elevated above another, in proportion as he possesses this capability. . . . To endeavour to enlarge this capability is one of the best services in which . . . a writer can be engaged." [55] Whereas sexual hygiene writers browbeat their readers with case after case of dreadful convulsive ailments resulting from sexual indulgence in order to convince them that by having sex they are effectively surrendering their bodies to perpetual coercion, poets from Ovid to Shelley identify poetic invention with sexual desire precisely because both are involuntary.

The poetic and hygienic descriptions of desire each give Whitman ways of presenting male homosexual intercourse as a physical dramatization of the male sexual drive's fundamental structure. What the poetic resources provide Whitman are the means for incorporating the sexual hygiene movement's description of male sexual desire into his verse, which he often does quite faithfully, while at the same time inverting the movement's moral program. By itself, the analogy between desire as depicted in the hygiene tracts and one man's sexual penetration of another is of little value to Whitman, given that the theory enabling the analogy condemns not just homosexuality but sexual desire in general. However, when Whitman brings his poetic precedents to bear on this analogy (as he also does quite faithfully), he creates something entirely new: a portrait of male homosexuality as a mark of poetic vocation. If male homosexual intercourse renders the penetration of the body by desire in objective but abjected form, *the poetic equation of violation with inspiration turns that abjection into an artistic and moral imperative.*

Let us return to "Song of Myself." I have already suggested that when the twenty-ninth bather "puffs and declines with pendant and bending arch" over the bodies of the young men in section 11 of the poem, her gasps not only express her sexual pleasure but also suggest the involuntary character of inspired poetic utterance. Having examined Coleridge's "The Eolian Harp"— in which the harp's wind-made music is first compared to the "sweet upbraiding" of a young woman "half-yielding" to her lover, then to her cries of sexual pleasure, and finally to the thoughts traversing the poet's "indolent and passive brain"—we can see that reading the bather's panting in poetic as well as sexual terms is by no means farfetched. The analogy was already on the books; Whitman merely turns Coleridge's similes into a metaphor.

Yet when it comes to identifying sex with inspiration, other passages in "Song of Myself" are considerably more direct. Section 5, in which the poet is ravished by his soul, is one example. In fact, like the bather's panting in section 11, the setting of the poet's ravishment is strongly reminiscent of Coleridge. Both scenes are set outdoors on a summer's day and both feature indolent speakers reclining on the ground—Coleridge "on the midway slope / Of yonder hill," Whitman loafing "on the grass." Whitman's passage can be read as condensing Coleridge's analogies — wind/harp, lover/maid, thought/poet — into a single rapturous encounter. Moreover, the story of the poet's ravishment is preceded by a slyly informal but nevertheless recognizable *invocation* in which the speaker asks his soul for voice:

> Loafe with me on the grass, loose the stop from your throat,
> Not words, not music or rhyme I want . . .
> Only the lull I like, the hum of your valvèd voice.

This invocation deliberately echoes the equally casual one that is part of the poem's playful variation on the traditional epic opening:

> I loafe and *invite* my soul,
> I lean and loafe at my ease observing a spear of summer grass.
>   (ll. 4–5, my emphasis)

Playful though he may be, Whitman thus takes pains to make sure that we understand the poetic function of the soul in these two passages: this is his epic muse. It naturally follows, then, that his soul's entry into, and filling of, his body constitutes a scene of *poetic* as well as sexual possession. This is why Whitman has his soul enter his body *tongue first:*

> You settled your head athwart my hips and gently turn'd over upon me,
> And parted the shirt from my bosom-bone, and plunged your tongue to my
>   bare-stript heart,
> And reach'd till you felt my beard, and reach'd till you held my feet.[56]

The tongue is an unmistakable metonymy for voice; by plunging it into the speaker's chest, therefore, his soul both ravishes *and* inspires him.

As with "Song of Myself," so too again with "The Sleepers." Before the woman speaker in this poem is ravished by the darkness, she issues her invocation — "Double yourself and receive me darkness" — and receives her visitation: "He whom I *call* answers me and takes the place of my lover" (my emphasis). When darkness then enters her, the poem enters upon its visionary phase. This passage rewrites section 5 of "Song of Myself" as an ostensibly heterosexual nocturne.

Even the speaker's sexual encounter with touch in section 28 of "Song of Myself" serves a plainly inspirational function. For one thing, the "marauder" metaphor reads like an extravagant refashioning of the conventional amatory scene — as we have seen it in Ovid, Petrarch, and Sidney — in which Love ambushes the unwitting poet and shoots him full of love-inspiring but also *verse*-inspiring arrows. Further, when Whitman describes himself as surrounded "on all sides [by] prurient provokers" and, later in the passage, when he exclaims "my breath is tight in its throat, / . . . you are too much for me," he has in mind not only similar scenes from the literature of sexual hygiene but an apparently dissimilar one in Emerson's archetypically Romantic essay "The Poet": "He [the poet] hears a voice, he sees a beckoning. Then he is apprised, with wonder, *what dæmons hem him in.* He can no more rest; he says, with the old painter, 'By God, *it is in me, and must go forth of me'*" (*EL*, 466; my emphasis).[57] In fact, once it is in Whitman, one way it goes forth from him is in the form of spontaneous utterance. "Given up" by his senses and "left . . . helpless" to the "red marauder," the speaker tells us: "I talk wildly, I have lost my wits." As it happens, this announcement faithfully echoes Emerson's essay as well: "The poet . . . speaks adequately . . . only when he speaks somewhat *wildly*," Emerson explains, "not with the intellect, used as an organ, but with the intellect released from all service" (459, my emphasis). This the poet achieves by "unlocking, at all risks, his human doors, and suffering the ethereal tides to roll and circulate through him."[58] In effect, "Song of Myself" rewrites this account of poetic inspiration as one of homosexual rape, with the "floodgates" of the male body replacing Emerson's "human doors" and the "red marauder" his "ethereal tides."[59] The parallel with Emerson's essay is even closer in Whitman's notebook draft, which has "the torrent of touch" in place of the "red marauder" (*NUPM*, 1:76). But Whitman does not simply replace inspiration with rape. Instead he combines the two in a single scenario of possession, according to which sexual incursion and poetic afflatus are one and the same. Betrayed from within and overwhelmed by the invader, the speaker of section 28 "talk[s] wildly," with his "intellect released from all service." A notebook draft of the same passage emphasizes the logic of inspired utterance even more. In two lines that subtly and concisely blend inspiration with seduction, Whitman writes of the touch that has "unhaltered all my senses but feeling": "It talks for me with a tongue of its own / It finds an ear wherever it rests or taps" (76).

In replacing Emerson's "ethereal tides" with the rather more carnal "red marauder," moreover, Whitman again appears to have deliberately evoked Emerson's poetics while at the same time infusing the passage with the rhetoric of sexual hygiene. For Whitman's marauder, redolent though he is of the Fowlers and Wells booklist, also has a literary precedent in another, equally extravagant, rape metaphor in Emerson's early lecture "The Poet and the Times": "We are a little afraid of poetry,—afraid to write and afraid to read it; are we not? . . . *Poetry always descends as a foreign conqueror from an unexpected quarter of the horizon, carries us away with our wives and children, our flocks and herds, into captivity,* to make us, at a later period, adopted children of the new land, and, in the end, to disclose to us, that this is really our native country."[60] Whitman attended this lecture as a young newspaper editor in 1842, and it seems to have made a powerful impression (more so, apparently, than the "Grahamites" he noted in the audience).[61] In "Song of Myself" he combines the old-fashioned sense of rape as abduction, evoked here by Emerson, with the more specific modern meaning of forcible intercourse. In both cases, however, rape serves as a metaphor for *poetic* transport.

In linking such notoriously erotic passages as this one from "Song of Myself" to so traditional a literary theme as inspiration, and such canonical treatments of that theme as those by Coleridge and Emerson, I may appear to be domesticating Whitman's dramatically new poetic approach to sexuality. But comparing Whitman's treatment of desire to previous ones does not, I think, make him seem less audacious; rather, it helps us recognize the precise nature of his audacity—as well as its literary-historical implications. If Whitman looks rather different as a result, so too do the traditions and conventions he seizes upon and quite freely transforms. Further, linking Whitman's portrayals of male homosexuality to inspiration (as he himself does) in no way diminishes the eroticism of the scenes we have examined. What we see in Whitman is not a sublimation of homosexual desire into art but a highly developed vision of male poetic agency as intrinsically homoerotic.

One can see the beginnings of this development as early as 1842. A few months after he attended Emerson's lecture, Whitman published his temperance potboiler *Franklin Evans, or The Inebriate: a Tale of the Times.*[62] As chapter 20 opens, the title character (who is also the narrator) is suffering the psychological aftereffects of one of the several unfortunate and improb-

able female deaths of which his intemperance is indirectly the cause. (The
abandon with which this story dispatches female beloveds is noteworthy.) In
this state, which he describes, not very helpfully, as "a kind of morbid pecu-
liarity" (*EPF*, 219), Evans has a vision of the future in which the population
of a prosperous American empire gathers to celebrate the conversion of the
last drinker of alcohol to temperance:

> Yielding myself to the passage of those about, I wended on, until at last we
> came into a wide field in the middle of which was an uncovered scaffold. Upon
> it was the person whom I had noticed in the procession — the Last Vassal. Far
> around, on every side, countless multitudes of nothing but human heads were
> to be seen, in one compact body.
>
> "Rejoice!" cried a man from the crowd. "Our old enemy is deserted, and we
> triumph!"
>
> . . .
>
> And now, he who stood on the scaffold spoke:
>
> . . .
>
> "This day . . . I throw off my chains, and take upon myself the pleasant bond-
> age of good. It may not be a truth to boast of, That I am the *last* of the serfs of
> Appetite; yet I joy that I occupy my position before you now, as I do!" (222)

Phrases like "the Last Vassal" and "serfs of Appetite" are reminiscent of
the sexual hygiene movement — and for good reason: sexual hygiene was an
outgrowth of the temperance movement, and some of its most prominent
speakers and authors began their public careers as temperance speakers.[63]
Furthermore, the temperance movement's view of alcohol as an invasive
agent that usurped control over the bodies and minds of its users coincides
entirely with the hygienic vision of sexual desire. In other words, temperance not only preceded sexual hygiene; in its demonization of alcohol it also
provided a physical paradigm for what hygiene writers said desire did to
the body. Whitman's rehearsal of that paradigm prepared him — as it did
Graham and others — for addressing the issue of sexuality in similar terms.

Like Evans, however, Whitman seems to find alcohol's suppression of the
self as seductive as it is threatening. For what's striking about Evans' dream
vision is not so much the content in itself (though, to be sure, that is curious
enough)[64] as the glaring discrepancy between its content and its *cause:* "It
was the result, no doubt, partly of my confinement and the sombre reflec-

tions I held—and partly of my former intemperate habits. It was a species of imaginative mania, which led to giving full scope to my fancy—and I frequently remained for two hours at a time in a kind of trance, beholding strange things, and abstracted from all that was going on around me. On one of these occasions, the incident occurred which I shall now relate" (219–20). What's perplexing here, of course, is that Evans attributes his dream vision of temperance triumphant to his *in*temperate habits and their consequences. Without all that alcohol, it turns out, he never would have suffered the "imaginative mania" of which the vision is so edifying an example. Without servitude to Appetite, there is no liberating vision. For while "mania" characterizes Evans' state as an illness, the fact that it leads to "giving full scope to [his] fancy" makes his imaginative state sound more emancipatory than oppressive. In short, it seems as though intemperance can be quite inspiring. Perhaps this is why Evans' description of the immediate circumstances leading up to the vision resemble Coleridge's famous description of the circumstances that led to his composition of "Kubla Khan": "I was sitting in an easy chair at twilight one evening, near the open window," Whitman writes. "Upon my knees lay a newspaper, which I had been reading. It contained some extracts from an eloquent temperance address. The quietness of the scene, and the subdued light, and the peculiar influences that had been surrounding me for a few days past, had their full chance to act at such a time, as may well be imagined" (220). Compare this to Coleridge: "In the summer of 1797, the Author, then in ill health, had retired to a lonely farmhouse. . . . In consequence of a slight indisposition, an anodyne had been prescribed, from the effects of which he fell asleep in his chair at the moment he was reading the following sentence . . . in 'Purchas's Pilgrimage': 'Here the Khan Kubla commanded a palace to be built. . . .' The Author continued for about three hours in a profound sleep, at least of the external senses. . . ."[65]

Like Coleridge, Evans falls into a trance while sitting in a chair reading; and, as in Coleridge, his reading provides the starting point for his vision. Evans is in self-imposed confinement; Coleridge has retired to an isolated farmhouse to restore his health. Evans is "abstracted from all that was going on around" him; Coleridge is in a "profound sleep, at least of the external senses." Evans' "imaginative mania" is caused by alcohol and its attendant evils; Coleridge's poetic inspiration is brought on by an "anodyne," that is, by laudanum. Instead of merely repeating the temperance movement's equation of drinking with servitude, Whitman summons up the Romantic vision of poetic automatism to make prophecy one of servitude's effects. Similarly, instead of just rehearsing the sexual hygiene movement's view of stimulating food and drink as seducers and destroyers of their victims, he identifies the inebriate's surrender to drink with the poet's surrender to poetic possession. The basic structure of sections 5 and 28 of "Song of Myself" is already in place here; all that is needed is the elevation of the male homoerotic theme — which is only hinted at in Whitman's phallic personification of alcohol as the "Snake-Tempter" (221).[66] In fact, the connection between alcohol and inspiration seems to have been one of the few ideas Whitman actually retained from *Franklin Evans.* "Parke Godwin . . . came to see me about writing it," he explained to Traubel in 1888. "Their offer of cash payment was so tempting — I was hard up at the time — that I set to work at once ardently on it (with the help of a bottle of port or what not)" (*WWC*, 1:93). This excuse for the novel echoes Evans' description of the intemperate state that provokes his dream vision. Whitman thus renews his commitment to the analogy between being a "serf to Appetite" and a servant to the muse in the very act of dismissing the novel.[67]

The same paradoxical logic is at work in another, more famous, disavowal. In 1890, after years of beating around the bush, the English critic John Addington Symonds, a pioneer in the study of same-sex desire, wrote Whitman to inquire whether his "conception of Comradeship . . . is calculated to encourage ardent & *physical* intimacies between men" (*C*, 5:72).[68] Although Whitman's response employs the same equation of sexual and poetic possession that he projects in *Franklin Evans* and fully realizes in the poems of his major period, this time he adroitly turns this equation into grounds for denying responsibility for any suggestion of homosexuality in his poetry: "Such a construction as mention'd is terrible — I am fain to hope the pages themselves are not to be even mention'd for such gratuitous and quite at the time entirely undream'd & unreck'd possibility of morbid inferences — wh' are disavow'd by me & seem damnable. Then the one great difference between you and me, temperament & theory, is *restraint* — I know that while I have a horror of ranting & bawling I at certain moments let the spirit impulse (?demon) rage its utmost, its wildest, damnedest — (I feel to do so in my L. of G. & I do so)" (*C*, 5:72–73). Whitman here uses the notion of poetry as inspired utterance to deflect Symonds' attempt to make him divulge his own sexual "inversion." (In this same letter he proceeds to manufacture six children and a grandson in order to lend credence to his denial.) But by claiming that any apparent endorsement of physical intimacy between men in his poems must be attributed to "the spirit impulse (?demon)" instead of himself, Whitman does more than provide himself with cover. He recapitulates his notion of poetry and male homosexuality as congruent forms of possession. Indeed, in admitting his willingness to "let the spirit impulse (?demon) rage its utmost, its wildest," he goes so far as to echo his 1860 announcement of the homoerotic theme in "Starting from Paumonok":

> I will sing the song of companionship,
>
> . . . .
>
> I will therefore let flame from me the burning fires that were threatening
>   to consume me,
> I will lift what has too long kept down these smouldering fires,
> *I will give them complete abandonment.*
>   (ll. 86–91, my emphasis)

At the same time that he disavows Symonds' "morbid inferences," Whitman attributes his love of men to the poetic process itself. The homoeroticism of the poetry is a token of the state of possession that produced it: the former demonstrates the latter. Whitman thus affirms his poetic portrayal of male homosexuality as possession by denying responsibility for it.

Conversely, Whitman's private struggles to curtail his homosexual longings usually also involve a struggle to curb the "spirit impulse." In the summer of 1870 Whitman experienced a crisis in his relationship with Peter Doyle, his lover at the time, a crisis he expressed and attempted to overcome in a small ten-page notebook. The notebook alternates between abstract sketches of "a superb calm character" and written pledges similar to those recommended for drinkers in temperance tracts and for onanists by sexual hygiene writers. Here Whitman renounces "this diseased, feverish, disproportionate adhesiveness" (*NUPM*, 2:889–90).[69] The "Wise Man," he writes, "observes himself with the nicety of an enemy or spy, and looks on his own wishes as betrayers." "His appetites are always moderate" and he "Praises nobody / Blames nobody, / *Nor even speaks of himself*" (886).[70] Whitman goes on to reprimand himself, in language strongly reminiscent of the lines about self-betrayal in "Song of Myself" (section 28), for failing to live up to this ideal: *"Cheating, childish abandonment* of myself, fancying what does not really exist in another, but is all the time in myself alone— utterly deluded & cheated by *myself,* & my own weakness . . ." (887). Then comes the pledge (888–89):

> TO GIVE UP ABSOLUTELY & <u>for good, from the present hour, this</u> FEVERISH, FLUCTUATING, <u>useless</u> UNDIGNIFIED PURSUIT. . . . <u>avoid seeing her, or meeting her, or any talk or explanations</u>—<u>or</u> ANY MEETING WHATEVER, FROM THIS HOUR FORTH, FOR LIFE
>
> July 15 '70

"Her" is Doyle; the erased word "him" remains visible in the manuscript.[71] The renunciation of "any talk" in the pledge applies specifically to Doyle. But elsewhere in the notebook Whitman makes more general pledges to reform his speech habits:

> No more attempts at smart sayings, or scornful criticisms, or harsh comments on persons or actions, or private or public affairs.
>
> . . .
>
> SAY little—make no explanations—<u>give no confidences</u>—never attempt puns, or plays upon words, or utter sarcastic comments, or . . . hold any discussion [or] arguments. (887)

Whitman's effort to "depress the adhesive nature" (889) seems to depend, in his mind, on his ability to control what he says—or, rather, on his ability to say as little as possible. His fear of speaking appears to indicate a fear of self-exposure; the wise man never speaks specifically *"of himself."* The desire to avoid talking thus seems to be part of an ideal of emotional self-sufficiency: don't speak of yourself, don't express your desires, and you will be invulnerable, Whitman tells himself. The "superb calm character['s] . . . emotions &c are complete in himself, irrespective of whether his love, friendship, &c are returned or not. . . . His analogy is as of the earth, complete in itself" (889). On the face of it, the fear of speaking would not appear to apply to *poetic* utterance, which for him transcends mere *self*-expression.

Another way to put this, however, is to say that what Whitman fears from speaking is not just the exposure of his desires—and consequently his vulnerability—to others but rather the *submission* to desire itself that speech would entail. It is as though merely allowing desire expression were some-how tantamount to yielding oneself to its promptings—indeed, as though its main prompting *were* for expression. The real fear behind these stric-tures upon his speech is not one of self-expression but of *dispossession*— the loss of control over one's words, one's feelings, and ultimately one's ac-tions. Speaking, it turns out, is a form of self-surrender, not self-assertion. Like betraying oneself to the "red marauder," it is a *"cheating, childish aban-donment* of [one]self"—an opening of one's gates to the enemy. The agent that threatens betrayal and dispossession through speech here is the same one that denotes poetic possession elsewhere: homosexual desire. Giving up Doyle thus begins to look like giving up not only talking but poetry as well.

Whitman suggests as much in an 1860 "Calamus" poem from which the earth analogy in the Doyle notebook is drawn:

Earth! [My likeness!]
Though you look so impassive, ample and spheric there—
I now suspect that is not all,
I now suspect there is something terrible in you, ready to break forth,
For an athlete loves me,—and I him—
But toward him there is something fierce and terrible in me,
I dare not tell it in words—not even in these songs.[72]

"Earth, My Likeness" dramatizes the personal dilemma posed for Whitman by his equation of homosexual desire and poetic utterance. Were it not for the Doyle notebook, we might assume that Whitman's fear of reporting his passion "in words" is merely a matter of self-censorship—an internalization of the legal formula for sodomy as "the unnameable sin."[73] That notebook suggests, however, that Whitman's primary concern here is not to protect himself against public denunciation (not publishing the poem would have been better protection) but rather to avoid the *self-abandonment* that the surrender to speech—and thereby to desire—entails. Whitman's dilemma here is that his aversion to surrender, if persisted in, can only lead to a re-nunciation of poetry itself, which demands the poet's disavowal of all merely selfish considerations. Thus the poem's last line, while poignant, represents an impasse: the refusal to "tell it in words . . . even in these songs" marks not just the end of the poem but the point at which poetic utterance itself must come to a halt.

Faced with this choice, Whitman consistently chooses poetry, even though it means the "abandonment of [him]self" to that "incessant <u>enormous &</u> <u>abnormal</u> PERTURBATION" that he vows to escape in his notebook (887–88). Yet his fitful attempts to choose otherwise—to "SAY little"—dramatize the fact that what binds authorship and male homosexuality together for Whitman is not a quest for identity or self-expression, as we might assume, but the sacrifice of both. Whitman's homosexuality, like his poetry, originates in a disjunction between himself and his actions, himself and his body. This is why, in the poems we have examined, the union of poet and spirit, poet and lover, is consistently so violent. Whitman's lovers are invaders and marauders; his spirits pierce and convulse his body. The injury inflicted on the poet in these encounters bespeaks the rending of personal identity they entail. The coupling of poet and soul in "Song of Myself," for example, while traditionally seen as a moment of mystical wholeness or unity for the poet, is actually quite the opposite: the soul in effect remains another person—a "you"—throughout the passage, and the speaker's sensation of being physically penetrated and occupied by this person is not one of difference overcome but of difference internalized.[74] Here as elsewhere, authorship and homosexuality are not attributes of Whitman's identity but instances of its disruption. His homosexuality marks his poetic vocation not because his poetry expresses his sexuality but because his sexuality represents the violation of identity that poetry requires.

In "Spirit Whose Work Is Done," as in "Song of Myself," the agent of this disruption is a spirit that enters and fills the poet's body—a spirit modeled (as we saw in chapter 1) on the soldiers Whitman nursed during the war. In fact, when Whitman asks the spirit of war to "fill" him in "Spirit," he is echoing not only "Song of Myself" but also his wartime letters, where he describes himself as internalizing what he sees in the hospitals. Writing to his brother in February 1863, after having spent less than two months in Washington, he describes with alternating wonder and disapproval the splendor of the Capitol's interior, which he has recently seen for the first time. He ends his account by contrasting the scenes depicted in its "costly frescoes" with those he has been witnessing in the hospitals: "Filled as I am from top to toe, of late with scenes and thoughts of *the hospitals* (America seems to me now, though only in her youth . . . brought *already here* feeble, bandaged and bloody *in hospital*) . . . all the poppy-show goddesses and all the pretty blue & gold in which the interior Capitol is got up, seem to me out of place beyond anything I could tell" (*C,* 1:75; Whitman's emphasis).

This letter compares three different interiors: the Capitol's, the hospitals, and Whitman's own. The work of "imported French and Italian artists," the Capitol's interior is dismissed as "un-American and inappropriate" (74). The hospitals, on the other hand, house "America." Finally, Whitman himself is "filled . . . from top to toe . . . with scenes and thoughts of *the hospitals.*" The latter phrase recalls "Song of Myself," where the occupying spirit reaches from the speaker's head to his feet; it also anticipates the invocation in "Spirit Whose Work Is Done," where the speaker asks the spirit to "fill" him. But here Whitman is "filled" neither with his soul nor with a spirit that resembles the wounded soldiers but rather with thoughts of the soldiers themselves. Whereas in "Spirit" he portrays his muse as a wounded soldier, here he portrays the soldiers as muses. The letter is thus concerned with the hospitals not only as literary subject matter but as a source of inspiration (as opposed to the inspiration of European models represented by the frescoes in the Capitol). Writing to his friend James Redpath eight months later, Whitman makes this connection between his writing and his internalization of the hospitals more explicit. Redpath had just published Louisa May Alcott's *Hospital Sketches* (1863) — a fictionalized account of her stint as a nurse in one of Washington's army hospitals — and Whitman writes to him to propose a book of his own, "beyond mere hospital sketches," though with "many hospital incidents." [75] "I have been & am in the midst of these things," he writes of the scenes to be described in the new book. "I feel myself full of them" (171–72).

Elsewhere in his correspondence Whitman describes his inspiration by the wounded in terms of ingestion. Of the soldiers' ability to retain their composure in the face of "all pains and bloody mutilations" he writes: "It is immense, the best thing of all, nourishes me of all men" (82). "Filled" with scenes of the hospitals and "nourishe[d]" by the "immense" fortitude of the wounded, Whitman's body, as viewed through his letters, consequently seems to *expand.* In the same letter in which he describes his hospital visits as nourishing, he assures his friends in New York that as a result of these visits his "health, strength, personal beauty &c. are . . . without diminution, but on the contrary quite the reverse." This sense of increase is made concrete in the next sentence, where, as though it were an effect of his contact with the wounded, he goes on to give his weight: "I weigh full 220 pounds avoirdupois, yet still retain my perfect shape — a regular model" (83). In fact, Whitman reports his size in one letter after another, repeatedly rejoicing that he is "fat" or "large" throughout the period of his most intense involvement in the hospitals. A letter to Redpath is typical: "I am running over with health, fat, red & sunburnt in face &c. I tell thee I am just the one to go to our sick boys" (164).[76] Here the image of expansion through nourishment merges with one of sexual excitement. Enlarged, red, and overflowing, Whitman in this self-portrait is an embodiment of phallic arousal. His desire for the soldiers appears to imprint itself on his entire physique. At the same time, the suggestion of internal superabundance in the phrase "I am running over with health" recalls his earlier remark about being "filled . . . from top to toe . . . with scenes and thoughts of *the hospitals.*" He thus links his embodiment of phallic potency, or what he calls "health," to his possession by the soldiers: he is "running over" because he is "full of them." "I am large, I contain multitudes": as in "Song of Myself," his arousal is indistinguishable from his internalization of others. In the image of the large, red, overflowing Whitman, virility and permeability merge.[77] The possession that defines authorial agency for Whitman defines his love of men in his hospital letters as well.

In the Petrarchan tradition, poetic creation is, at least implicitly, a substitute for procreation: poetry compensates the male poet — though perhaps inadequately — for the fact that his beloved is unattainable. Whitman takes this idea a step further. By portraying inspiration as a form of sexual penetration, and thus placing his own body in the role occupied by the woman in traditional heterosexual intercourse, he presents himself as *incarnating* the substitution of poetic for biological reproduction. The expansion of his body that seems to occur in his letters hints at gestation as well as phallic arousal. Whitman seems to have this idea in mind when he takes up the issue of "Female Nurses for Soldiers" in the Civil War portion of *Specimen Days:*

> Few or no young ladies, under the irresistible conventions of society, answer the practical requirements of nurses for soldiers. . . . [M]others of children are always best. Many of the wounded must be handled. A hundred things which cannot be gainsay'd, must occur and must be done. . . . [T]he expres-

sive features of the mother, the silent soothing of her presence, her words, her knowledge and privileges arrived at only through having had children, are precious and final qualifications. It is a natural faculty that is required. . . . One of the finest nurses I met was a red-faced illiterate old Irish woman; I have seen her take the poor wasted naked boys so tenderly up in her arms. (*PW,* 1:88)

If to nurse the sick and wounded is to mother them, where does this leave Whitman, who devotedly attended the same soldiers during the war? The Irish woman's skill as a nurse is a "natural," which is to say, maternal faculty, a fact Whitman emphasizes by noting that she is "illiterate" and therefore cannot have acquired her skills through any kind of formal schooling. Yet Whitman's portrait of this "red-faced illiterate old Irish woman," who is apparently large enough to hold "the poor wasted naked boys" like infants in her arms, almost seems calculated to resemble his repeated description of *himself* in the letters as large, strong, "red and sunburnt in face." Further, taking the boys "up in her arms," she also evokes his self-portrait in "The Wound-Dresser": "Many a soldier's loving arms about this neck have cross'd and rested" (l. 64). His idealized mother-nurse figure is, among other things, a feminized image of himself.

Unlike an actual mother's care, however, the attention Whitman lavished on the sick and wounded cannot be traced to any "knowledge and privileges arrived at only through having had children," however much of "a great tender mother-man" some of his contemporaries may have thought him to be.[78] Nor was his literacy extraneous to the care he actually provided: Whitman both read to the soldiers regularly and wrote letters for them to send to loved ones (see *PW,* 1:38, 50–51, 56). Further, he took notes and sometimes worked on his own poetry and prose in notebooks he carried with him during his hospital visits (see 1:2n.). If he suggests that his absorption of the hospital scenes and consequent swelling in size are analogous to insemination and gestation, then these writings are the offspring of that process. "I gave myself for them," Whitman says in 1889 of the soldiers. "But for this I would never have had Leaves of Grass — the consummated book" (*WWC,* 3:581–82). Female nurses need the natural faculty that comes with maternity; for Whitman, the male homosexual poet, however, the poetic faculty simultaneously resembles and replaces the maternal one.

But if the poetic faculty triumphs here, it is at the poet's expense. "Fill me with currents convulsive," Whitman pleads to the soldier-spirit of "Spirit Whose Work Is Done." The convulsions Whitman calls down upon himself here are not simply those of orgasm or poetic automatism. Nor do they *merely* represent the political turmoil of a time that he says could "best be described by that very word *convulsiveness*" (*PW*, 1:122)—although Whitman clearly has all of these meanings in mind. Like the convulsive ailments supposedly visited upon those who violate the laws of sexual physiology, and like the actual convulsions of the sick and wounded upon whom Whitman's spirit here is modeled, they are also symptoms of *injury*—a sexual and poetic injury that always separates him from the "superb calm character" whose "emotions &c are complete in himself."[79] "I gave myself for them: myself: I got the boys: then I got Leaves of Grass," Whitman says in old age. "My body? Yes—it had to be given—it had to be sacrificed: who knows better than I do what that means?" (*WWC*, 5:582). By the time Whitman made these remarks, he had been suffering from partial paralysis for sixteen years as a result, he believed, of his arduous hospital service during the war. With this interpretation of his postwar physical decline, he presents himself as an actual embodiment of the principle of self-negation that is central to his theories of sexuality and poetry. Not surprisingly, he describes his devotion to the soldiers as *involuntary*—the result of an unnamed external force having seized control of him and taken his body as sacrifice: "Every man has a religion: something . . . which he will give up everything else for—something which absorbs him, possesses itself of him, makes him over into its image: something: it may be something regarded by others as being very paltry, inadequate, useless: yet it is his dream, his lodestar, it is his master. That . . . seized upon me, made me its servant, slave. . . . I had to give up my health for it—my body—the vitality of my physical self . . ." (581–82).

In this chapter I have argued that the unnamed—and perhaps unnameable—religion that seizes upon Whitman time and again in his poetry, prose, and daily life is one in which poetic vocation and same-sex desire are inseparable and often indistinguishable. As I have tried to demonstrate, this view of the relation between sexuality and poetry is not entirely Whitman's own creation: much of it derives from the poetry and reform movements that preceded him. His originality is twofold. First, he employs the hygienic vision of desire as something that penetrates and feminizes men's bodies in order to portray homosexuality as the template for *all* male sexual desire. And, second, by adapting aspects of amatory, devotional, and Romantic poetry, he reverses the hygienic evaluation of desire by identifying it with another invasive, automating force: inspiration.

V

Some critics view Whitman's homosexuality as an obstacle to his achievement of poetic authority on the grounds that it threatens to confine him and his message to "a marginal . . . order of loving men." In this account, homosexuality is a "perturbance" for Whitman, above all because of its "potential dissonance" with his broader democratic message. According to Betsy Erkkila, "It is only by transforming his homoerotic feelings into bonds of democratic comradeship that Whitman is able to present these feelings as safe, normal, and nameable in the public sphere."[80] Other readers, less patient with Whitman's apparent efforts to sublimate his sexuality into a form of mainstream masculine nationalism, have nevertheless come to similar conclusions about the dissonance between his sexuality and his national poetic ambitions: "Every creation of an identity, every claim of a space from which to speak, is purchased at the price of participation in some larger whole," advises Robert K. Martin. "But for those for whom that right to speak has been at best illusory, the price may seem well worth paying."[81]

As we have seen, however, identity and sexuality are antithetical concepts for Whitman, as are identity and poetic speech. For him, as for the Romantics, the creation of a place from which to speak demands the suppression of one's identity. By equating male homosexual desire with inspiration, Whitman makes it a token for that suppression. For him, therefore, the structure of male homosexual desire and the structure of poetic authority are not incompatible. As assaults on identity, they're analogous. Whitman's homosexuality thus serves as a mark of his inspiration, and inspiration, as Emerson makes clear, is the foundation of poetic authority in the period: "Let the poet, of all men, stop with his inspiration. The inexorable rule in the muses' court [is] *either inspiration or silence*."[82] In Whitman's view, his "marginal" sexuality actually indicates that he is the vehicle of an authority greater than himself.

Critics have also tried to connect Whitman's vision of sexuality to his poetics by suggesting a "link between the persona's phallicism and his vocalism."[83] At times this connection is presented as again occurring through sublimation: sexually aroused, the poet expresses his excitement through language instead of through orgasm, thus transforming what might have been a debilitating sexual event into a transcendent work of art.[84] In this view, as in the one discussed previously, Whitman must suppress his sexuality in order to achieve poetic expression. At other times, though, it is argued that ejaculation and poetic utterance are congruent for Whitman. Even this view, however, restricts the connection between sexuality and poetry to the issue of the poet's powers of *expenditure* — sexual, poetic, or both. Since ejaculation, unlike the sexual penetration of the male body, is potentially common to *all* forms of male sexual activity, Whitman's homosexuality need not — and, in fact, *does not* — arise as an issue in this reading. Yet, as we have seen, Whitman's metaphors for tumescence and orgasm are generally preceded by ones for invasion and possession. When he is large, red, and running over it is because he is "filled . . . from top to toe . . . with scenes and thoughts of the *hospitals*"; and when "pulses of rage . . . / . . . blister out of [his] chants," it is because he has been "fill[ed] with currents convulsive." By overlooking the poet's subjection to penetration, this reading misconstrues the basis upon which poetry and sexuality — specifically male homosexuality — are identified in Whitman's writings.

A third group of critics, by contrast, has recently championed Whitman's portrayals of same-sex desire as the foundation of his poetics. Wishing also to portray that desire as fundamentally egalitarian in structure, however, these critics have sought to dissociate Whitman from what some, at least, recognize as the violent, rending characteristics of Whitmanic sex. In this they participate in the dominant trend in recent theoretical work on sexuality, which seeks in same-sex desire a model for equality with which to counteract what is perceived to be a hierarchical social system grounded in heterosexual gender inequality.[85] The goal of these critics is to enlist Whitman's work in this cause. To that end they argue that Whitman's association of same-sex desire with violence and violation must be understood either as a sign of his inability to reimagine fully the oppressive cultural system to which his poetry is nevertheless opposed or as evidence of his effort to deconstruct that system along with the artificial boundaries between persons it dictates. Whitman sometimes "fail[s] to critique" his "oedipal culture" and "to imagine an alternative system of desire," writes Michael Moon, who attributes this failure to "the extreme difficulty . . . of resisting and subverting" sociosexual norms. Yet this resistance demands that the poetry exert what he calls its "de-compositional powers of rewriting and revising its culture's boundaries around bodies."[86] In the first view, the sexual violence of the poetry represents the violence done to Whitman himself by his culture — a violence he attempts but is not always able entirely to erase. In the second view, the violence merely signals Whitman's effort to achieve that erasure. In neither case is the rending character of Whitmanic sex considered integral to his sexual vision. Either it intrudes on the poetry from the culture "without" or it is a means to an end that is itself egalitarian and nonviolent.[87]

However well-intended, these arguments miss Whitman's point. Sexual violence is not marginal but central to his poetics. Only by portraying sex as an assault on his body and a disruption of his identity can Whitman equate it with poetic possession. Further, it is difficult to see how this equation of sexual ravishment and poetic rapture could represent an effort to disrupt his culture's definitions of bodily identity, given that his ideal of self-surrender is not only hierarchical — as ravishment generally is — but also deeply rooted in his culture's amatory, devotional, and Romantic literatures. As I have argued, Whitman's poetics of possession *does* constitute an incisive and ingenious reversal of the sexual hygiene movement's moral and physiological program.[88] But Graham and Fowler no more define the culture of Whitman's period than do Coleridge and Shelley — arguably far less so — and the conceptual tools Whitman brings to his critique of the sexual hygiene movement largely derive from these and other poetic predecessors. The conflict, in other words, is between different discourses that help make up the culture and not between Whitman and his culture as such. He brings that conflict between discourses into the open.

But the main reason Whitman's poetics of ravishment and rapture cannot be said to undermine authority is that *it is itself a fiction of authorization.* When Whitman invokes his soul or the spirit of war — when he surrenders his body to the "red marauder" or to the hospitals full of wounded soldiers — he is seeking external authority for his language, not subverting the language of external authority. Critics have sought to portray his treatment of sexuality as a critique of the ideal of inviolate identity that sexual and political norms are presently thought to entail. We are now in a position to see the fallacy of this view. Whitman's violability is, in his eyes, the *basis* for his authority. His significance for contemporary discussions of sexuality lies in his synthesis of what are today mistakenly assumed to be antithetical phenomena: the renunciation of an ostensibly masculinist and heterosexist model of identity, on the one hand, and the legitimation of power, on the other. And Whitman's model of authority is not restricted, in his view, to the literary and sexual arenas. As we shall see in the next chapter, he views possession as providing a paradigm for *popular* authority as well.

CHAPTER 3

Masses and Muses

I   The morality of the act I dispose of as follows: I am myself;
     you are yourself; we are two distinct persons, equal persons.
     What you are, I am. You are a man, and so am I. God created both,
     and made us separate beings. I am not by nature bond to you, or
     you to me. Nature does not make your existence depend upon me,
     or mine to depend upon yours. I cannot walk upon your legs,
     or you upon mine.
     —Frederick Douglass, "Letter to His Old Master," 1848

Critical efforts to connect Whitman's treatment of male homosexuality to
the politics of his period have been contradictory: by arguing that his sexuality threatens to undermine the wider political force of his poetry or, conversely, that his treatment of sexuality stands opposed the social and political
structures of mid-nineteenth-century America, recent work on these issues
in Whitman has actually dichotomized the sexual and the political in the
name of bringing them together. Indeed, those readers most convinced of
Whitman's sexual radicalism often echo the most traditional arguments for
the autonomy of the work of art in their efforts to protect the antithetical purity of his sexual vision from worldly contamination. Thus, *Leaves of
Grass* becomes, in Michael Moon's words, an "*ideal medium* for the inter-
mingling of (male) bodies"—one that incorporates "the chief discourses of
(male) embodiment of his time" only to make "the referents of those discourses indeterminate." In other words, the text achieves its autonomy as a
medium for male homoeroticism—what this critic elsewhere calls its "uto-

pian potential"—by isolating itself linguistically from the sexual politics of the period.[1] This is not political criticism but its opposite.

Readings of Whitman's politics, on the other hand, have tended to present the poetry as profoundly antiliterary, by which I mean opposed not only to the conventions of poetic representation of his period but to the very idea of poetry *as representation*. The assumption here seems to be that if Whitman's homoeroticism requires an "ideal medium" in which to flourish, his engagement in democratic politics demands that he renounce the very of idea of representational mediation. Betsy Erkkila, seeking "to repair the split between the private and the public, the personal and the political, the poet and history, that has governed the . . . evaluation of Whitman's work in the past," describes the poet as "refusing to stay put on the literary page" and "dissolv[ing] the boundaries between . . . art and life."[2] If the utopian reading of Whitmanic sexuality proposes that his work be viewed as a "creative medium that will not remain a slave to the world of referents,"[3] this approach to reading Whitman politically attacks the idea that his text should be viewed as a *medium* at all. We are thus presented with a critical situation in which the analysis of Whitman's sexuality and that of his politics are implicitly treated as separate and incompatible.

In presenting Whitman's poetry as opposed to literary representation, critics receive ample encouragement from the poet himself. Whitman *does* present his poetry as though it were equivalent to his personal presence; furthermore, he often does so by explicitly renouncing linguistic mediation. One of his notorious unsigned reviews of his own book, for example, describes the 1855 *Leaves of Grass* as the "attempt . . . of a naive, masculine, affectionate, contemplative, sensual, imperious person, to cast into literature not only his own grit and arrogance, but his own flesh and form."[4] And even the slight acknowledgment of the difference between body and language underpinning Whitman's metaphor here of "cast[ing]" his "flesh" "into literature" disappears in the poem "So Long!" (1860) when he announces to the reader: "Camerado, this is no book, / Who touches this touches a man" (ll. 53–54). Whitman thus seems determined to reduce the literary representation of his body to the presence of the body itself. In "A Song for Occupations" his preference for personal presence over artificial substitutes extends to the presence of others as well:

When the psalm sings instead of the singer,
When the script preaches instead of the preacher,
When the pulpit descends and goes instead of the carver that carved the
supporting desk,
When the sacred vessels or the bits of the eucharist, or the lath and plast,
procreate as effectually as the young silversmiths or bakers, or the
masons in their overalls,
When a university course convinces like a slumbering woman and child
convince,
When the minted gold in the vault smiles like the nightwatchman's
daughter,
When warrantee deeds loafe in chairs opposite and are my friendly
companions,
I intend to reach them my hand and make as much of them as I do of men
and women.
    (*LG* 1855, ll. 171–78)[5]

This is Whitman at his most iconoclastic, identifying his language with the living presence of people instead of the representational artifacts they create. Even the Eucharist, as closely connected to physical presence as any symbol in Western culture, is rejected in favor of the (highly fertile) people who bake it.[6] As he baldly states at another point in the poem, "[I] send no agent or medium. . . . and offer no representative of value—but offer the value itself" (ll. 46–47). Yet his language itself is a medium, as are the psalm, script, and Eucharist he repudiates. Whitman attempts to neutralize this problem at the beginning of the poem by calling attention to the material presence of the printed page and then quickly subsuming it into the fiction of his own physical presence:

Come closer to me,
Push close my lovers and take the best I possess,
Yield closer and closer and give me the best you possess.

This is unfinished business with me . . . . how is it with you?
I was chilled with the cold types and cylinder and wet paper between us.

I pass poorly with paper and types . . . . I must pass with the contact of
bodies and souls.
    (ll. 1–6)

The effectiveness of this gambit is debatable (Whitman dropped these lines some years later), but the intention to place his page before the reader as though it were himself seems clear.

The political point seems fairly clear too. When Whitman first published "A Song for Occupations" in the 1855 edition of *Leaves of Grass,* the controversy over the potential expansion of slavery into the western territories was raging anew as a result of the passage of the Kansas-Nebraska Act the previous year. Disaffected Northern members of the Democratic and Whig Parties were defecting to the newly formed Republican Party, which was organized with the purpose of opposing slavery's expansion. Like the more radical abolitionists, most Republicans denied "that there CAN be MORAL RIGHT in the enslaving of one man by another," as Lincoln put it in 1854.[7] Unlike the abolitionists, however, Republicans focused less on the evil of slavery as it existed in the South than on the moral good of free labor and the economic threat posed by competition with a slave-labor economy bent on expanding westward. This approach was calculated to appeal to the economic interests of white Northern voters who may have felt no great urge to oppose slavery on moral grounds but might be persuaded to do so if convinced that their own prosperity was at stake. "We are all personally interested in this question, not indirectly and remotely as in a mere political abstraction—but directly, pecuniarily, selfishly," argued an Indiana Republican. "Free labor languishes and becomes degrading when put in competition with slave labor," warned another from Wisconsin.[8]

As a journalist, Whitman was a keen exponent of free labor ideology from the late 1840s onward. He lost his job as editor of the Democratic Brooklyn *Daily Eagle* in 1848 after writing editorials supporting the Wilmot Proviso against the wishes of his employer; later he briefly edited a free soil newspaper called the Brooklyn *Freeman.*[9] As early as 1847, before the Mexican War was even settled, Whitman sounded the free soil theme in his editorials: "The question whether or no there shall be slavery in the new territories which it seems conceded on all hands we are largely to get through this Mexican War, is a question between *the grand body of white working men, the millions of mechanics, farmers, and operatives of our country,* with their interests on one side—and the interests of a few thousand rich, 'polished,' and aristocratic owners of slaves at the South, on the other side" (*GF,* 1:208).

It is no wonder, then, that Whitman published a poem in praise of free labor in 1855. Nor is it surprising that this poem should eagerly disavow the "agent or medium" in favor of "the value itself." For slavery was in large part, for Whitman as for other advocates of free labor in the period, a problem of mediation—a problem, as Whitman puts it in another editorial, of "men who work only with other men's hands" (*GF*, 1:204). By claiming the fruit of other people's labor instead of working with their own hands, their opponents argued, slaveholders ignored the inviolable unity of the human body. For Lincoln the unity of the body demonstrates that God himself dictated the free labor system:

> Free Labor argues that, as the Author of man makes every individual with one head, and one pair of hands, it was probably intended that head and hands should co-operate as friends, and that that particular head should direct and control that particular pair of hands. And as each man has one mouth to be fed, and one pair of hands to furnish food, it was probably intended that that particular pair of hands should feed that particular mouth—that each head is the natural guardian, director and protector of the hands and mouth inseparably connected with it.[10]

Slavery was a system for the forced and unnatural delegation of labor. It therefore fueled doubts in its opponents' minds about the delegation of labor in general—and did so, as the passage from Lincoln demonstrates, in a intensely visceral way. These doubts also found expression in critiques of the conditions in Northern factories, which were often compared to slave plantations by Northerners and Southerners alike. Thus, in another *Eagle* editorial of 1847 Whitman excoriates "the manufactory lords who own the blood and sinews there" (157–58). And Horace Greeley confesses that he is "less troubled concerning the Slavery present in Charleston or New-Orleans" than he is about "Slavery in New-York."[11] Whitman expresses these concerns poetically in much the same way Lincoln does politically: he instructs us to identify the products of labor with the people who toil to produce them, and not to prize the product at the expense of the person. In aesthetic terms, this leads him to identify his language as closely as possible with his own body and to protest—sometimes too much—against the idea that his poetry is merely an "agent," "medium," or "representative" of himself or of others. The insistence on physical immediacy in "A Song for Occupations" suggests a free labor poetics.

As Whitman's use of the word "representative" implies, slavery raised doubts not only about the delegation of *labor* but also about *political* delegation. "A Song for Occupations" makes a point of reminding its readers that "the President is up there in the White House for you . . . it is not you who are here for him" (*LG* 1855, l. 83). The operations of the American political system were yet another example of the potential dangers of substituting another person's actions for one's own. Further, the two forms of delegation were directly related, not only because of the federal government's manifest aversion to the idea of opposing Southern interests throughout the 1850s but also because of the Constitution, which included slave populations in its method for apportioning Southern seats in the House of Representatives. According to the bizarre and oblique formula of article 1, section 2, "Representatives and direct taxes shall be apportioned among the several States . . . according to their respective Numbers, which shall be determined by adding to the whole Number of free Persons, including those bound to Service for a Term of Years, and excluding Indians not taxed, three fifths of all other Persons." All other persons meant slaves. For apportionment purposes at least, a slave thus constituted three-fifths of a human being. The more slaves Southern states accumulated, the more seats they held in the House. For many Northerners the obvious injustice of the formula struck at the foundation of the House's claim to proportional representation and thereby impugned the federal government's whole claim to representative legitimacy. Lincoln called the method of apportionment "manifestly unfair" and compared the Constitution's tolerance of slavery to that of an "afflicted man [who] hides away a wen or a cancer, which he dares not cut out at once, lest he bleed to death; with the promise, nevertheless, that the cutting may begin at the end of a given time."[12]

While Republicans like Lincoln proposed a gradual cutting and therefore a gradual progress toward just representation, others with more radical views saw the slavery issue as reason to question the idea of delegated authority *as such.* In *The Social Contract* (1762) Rousseau had equated political representation with slavery on the grounds that "a will cannot be represented: it is either the same will or it is different." When the people believe they are *delegating* their will, therefore, they are really *abdicating* their authority to another will altogether: "The English people thinks it is a free people; it is greatly mistaken; it is free only during the election of the members of parliament; as soon as they are elected, it is enslaved."[13] The critique of Southern slavery also employed the idea that a will cannot be represented, but it did so somewhat differently. In the *Narrative of the Life of Frederick Douglass* (1845), for example, it is not the people but their delegates who are compared to slaves:

> Few privileges were esteemed higher, by the slaves of the out-farms, than that of being selected to do errands at the Great House Farm. It was associated in their minds with greatness. A representative could not be prouder of his election to a seat in the American Congress, than a slave on one of the out-farms would be of his election to do errands at the Great House Farm. They regarded it as evidence of great confidence reposed in them by their overseers; and it was on this account, as well as a constant desire to be out of the field from under the driver's lash, that they esteemed it a high privilege, one worth careful living for. He was called the smartest and most trusty fellow, who had this honor conferred on him the most frequently. The competitors for this office sought as diligently to please their overseers, as the office-seekers in the political parties seek to please and deceive the people. The same traits of character might be seen in Colonel Lloyd's slaves, as are seen in the slaves of the political parties.[14]

The underlying point of this comparison is the same as in Rousseau: "A will cannot be represented: it is either the same will or it is different." Slaveholders view slaves as instruments of their will: "I don't like parting with any of my hands," says Mr. Shelby to the slave trader Haley in *Uncle Tom's Cabin* (1852), unconsciously equating his slaves' hands with his own.[15] But slaves have wills of their own, and the seemingly "smartest and most trusty fellow" is likely to be merely the most skilled in pleasing and deceiving his overseer to benefit himself.[16] If slavery is thus based on a false theory of delegation, so is the U.S. government, according to Douglass. In both instances the overseers' "great confidence" in their deputies is unfounded. If the slave driver ultimately cannot replace the slave's will with his own, neither can the government's overseers — the people — impose theirs on "the office-seekers in the political parties [who] seek to please and deceive" them, however vigilant the people may be. The injustice of slavery consists in one person's effort to destroy the will of another and replace it with his or her own. In affirming the irreducibility of one will to another, the argument against slavery quite naturally becomes a critique of representative government as well.

The slavery issue thus posed not only a practical threat but also a conceptual one to representative institutions. As a form of delegation that was publicly debated and denounced throughout the North, slavery threatened to erode public confidence in the system of political delegation that not only fostered its existence but also seemed strangely to resemble it. In "Resistance to Civil Government" (1848) Thoreau is thus able to use slavery and the Mexican War that was intensifying debate over it as starting points for a wide-ranging critique of delegated government. "The objections which have been brought against a standing army . . . may also be brought against a standing government," he states near the beginning of his lecture (*W*, 226). In the army, he observes, one delegates one's will and conscience to one's superiors, with the possible result that "you may see a file of soldiers . . . marching in admirable order over hill and dale to the wars, against their wills, aye, against their common sense and consciences" (227). According to Thoreau, men "who serve the State thus, not as men mainly, but as machines, with their bodies" deserve "no more respect than men of straw. . . . Yet such as these even are commonly esteemed good citizens" (228). The bedrock of democracy is supposed to be individual liberty. Why, then, should a democratic society honor those who resign their wills and consciences to others?

Thoreau's answer is that the resignation of individual will and conscience is integral to the operation of American democracy. After all, citizens surrender their wills and consciences not only when serving in the army but when consenting to let others represent them in the standing government:

> All voting is a sort of gaming, like chequers or backgammon, with a slight moral tinge to it, a playing with right and wrong, with moral questions; and betting naturally accompanies it. The character of the voters is not staked. I cast my vote, perchance, as I think right; but I am not vitally concerned that that right should prevail. I am willing to leave it to the majority. . . . Even voting *for the right* is *doing* nothing for it. It is only expressing to men feebly your desire that it should prevail. A wise man will not leave the right to the mercy of chance. . . . There is but little virtue in the action of masses of men. When the majority shall at length vote for the abolition of slavery, it will be

because they are indifferent to slavery, or because there is but little slavery
left to be abolished by their vote. *They* will then be the only slaves. (230–31)

Elections are supposed to constrain the government, *not* the voter, who, in
theory, exercises his or her sovereignty through the vote. For Thoreau as
for Rousseau, however, the truth is the opposite: voting is a way of *resigning* one's sovereignty to another, not a way of asserting it. The paradox of
representative government is that it appears to limit the citizen's legitimate
exercise of sovereignty to the act of delegating it. And not necessarily to the
person of one's choosing, since voting, like gaming and betting, presumes
one's willingness to abide by an outcome beyond one's control: "I am willing
to leave it to the majority." It's hardly clear, therefore, that voting constitutes
a moral act at all. "Voting *for the right*," Thoreau states, is "*doing* nothing for
it." No wonder American citizens esteem the soldier's obedience to his superiors as a mark of good citizenship: *his* surrender of sovereignty is merely
a token of the voting citizenry's surrender to its representatives. For Thoreau
that surrender, in turn, brings slavery to mind.

Thoreau's critique of representation assumes, as does Rousseau's, that the
people's representatives cannot be expected to act in a disinterested fashion.
"A will cannot be represented." Even should they want to, representatives
cannot magically suspend their own wills in order to become the vessels of
the citizens'. But if disinterestedness cannot be expected from a representative body, where can one expect to find it? Rousseau's answer is the general
will of the citizens, which, constituted as it is of the common interests of the
people, cannot but be impartial. Thoreau, who does not inhabit Rousseau's
ideal republic, is skeptical of this: "There is but little virtue in the action of
masses of men." Only a "very few . . . serve the State with their consciences"
as well as their minds and bodies, and they "necessarily resist it for the most
part" (228). It is in these people—"*men*" he calls them with emphasis—
that disinterested virtue can be found. Whereas Rousseau locates virtue in
the common interest, Thoreau finds it in the person unencumbered by any
material, social, or familial attachments that could interfere with his devotion to pure moral principle: "It will not be worth the while to accumulate
property; that would be sure to go again. You must hire or squat somewhere,
and raise a small crop, and eat that soon. You must live within yourself,
and depend upon yourself, always tucked up and ready for a start, and not

have many affairs" (237). This austere prescription for civic virtue explains Thoreau's difficulty in locating the kind of conscientious people he is looking for. "How many *men* are there to a square thousand miles in this country? Hardly one," he laments. "Our statistics are at fault: the population has been returned too large" (231). The more serious problem with Thoreau's definition of the principled civic leader, however, is his determination that his or her principles must not derive from the social body but solely from within. If the principled person's principles have no popular foundation, what is the basis for their authority?

The nature and magnitude of the problem can best be illustrated by contrasting Thoreau's view of the virtuous individual with James Madison's defense of a powerful federal government as the best means of securing virtuous public officers. Thoreau believes public virtue can be achieved only through the individual's withdrawal from the network of social relations that might bring his or her private interests into conflict with his or her principles. Without property or family, Thoreau's individual *has* virtually no private interests and therefore no incentive to swerve from his or her principles. Public virtue is a function of principle combined with individual autonomy radically conceived. Madison believes that the best way to purge public life of the many and conflicting private and provincial interests that dominated state legislatures in the post-Revolutionary period is decisively to subordinate those local bodies to a federal representative body. The members of such a body would be elected from districts so large, Madison reasons, that the narrow, selfish interests of individuals, towns, counties, and cities would cancel one another out in the electoral process, leaving only the general interest to prevail. The purpose of a representative body, Madison states, is "to refine and enlarge public views, by passing them through the medium of a chosen body of citizens, whose wisdom may best discern the true interest of their country, and whose patriotism and love of justice, will be least likely to sacrifice it to temporary and partial considerations." Since a "greater number of citizens and extent of territory . . . may be brought within the compass of Republican, than of Democratic [i.e., direct] government . . . factious combinations are less to be dreaded in the former than in the latter." According to Madison, therefore, the greater number of citizens and extent of territory the better: "Extend the sphere, and you take in a greater variety of parties and interests; you make it less probable that a majority of the whole will have a common motive to invade the rights of other citizens; or if such a common motive exists, it will be more difficult for all who feel it to discover their own strength, and to act in unison with each other."[17]

Whereas Thoreau prescribes individual withdrawal from social relations as the only way to protect principle from what Madison calls "temporary and partial considerations," Madison himself prescribes withdrawing *the government* as much as possible from the locales where narrow personal and parochial interests necessarily prevail over those of the nation as a whole. For him individuality is not so much a virtue as *a problem to be overcome* in pursuit of the common good. This may make Madison sound like an autocrat, but he isn't one. He fully accepts the idea that the government's working definition of the national interest must be authorized by the people of the nation.[18] His new national government is intended as a mechanism for allowing people's common interests as a nation to prevail over the narrower and often contrary interests of individual people and groups. He wants *not* to sever the government from the people but only to distance it from the states, not to dilute popular authority but to enhance it.

By the mid-nineteenth century, however, Madison's scheme appeared to have been foiled. The national government, which was supposed to transcend local interests, was breaking down along sectional lines; Congress was increasingly the setting for a conflict between two massive but nevertheless transparently regional interest groups.[19] In 1848 Thoreau could see no hope of principle prevailing there. Instead of seeking to ground principle in what is common to individuals as citizens, he therefore sought to base it upon that within the individual which transcends both individuality *and* the State. In expounding his definition of principle, Thoreau returns us to the issue of possession: "Action from principle,—the perception and performance of right,—changes things and relations; it is essentially revolutionary, and does not consist wholly with anything that was. It not only divides states and churches, it divides families; aye, it divides the *individual*, separating the diabolical in him from the divine" (232–33). While Thoreau disdains the State, he understands that individual principles require common validity in order to count as anything more than private interests. He solves this problem by arguing that principle is "divine," which is to say *not individual at all* but rather universal. In the process of trying to ground principle in the individual over against the State, Thoreau thus ends up dividing individuality itself. Individuals who act upon principle, it turns out, are themselves delegates of a sort: they represent a divine will through their actions. Setting out to critique representation, Thoreau replaces one form of it with another.

Thoreau's example may be taken as a caution: representational thinking of some sort often subsists within even the most withering critiques of representative institutions. The idea of delegation seems to be deeply involved with our definitions of legitimate authority and its difference from the mere exercise of raw power. As we have seen, in poems like "A Song for Occupations" Whitman appears to adopt a hard line against mediation in general, going so far as to assert that even the poem is "no agent or medium" but "the value itself." And his 1856 manifesto "The Eighteenth Presidency!" certainly matches, if not exceeds, "Resistance to Civil Government" in its vituperation against the electoral process and its beneficiaries:

> To-day, of all the persons in public office in These States, not one in a thousand has been chosen by any spontaneous movement of the people, nor is attending the interests of the people; all have been nominated and put through by great or small caucuses of politicians, or appointed as rewards for electioneering; and all consign themselves to personal and party interests. Neither in the Presidency, nor in Congress, nor in the foreign ambassadorships, nor in the governorships of The States, nor in legislatures, nor in the mayoralties of cities, nor the aldermanships, nor among the police, nor on the benches of judges, do I observe a single bold, muscular, young, well-informed, well-beloved American man, bound to do a man's duty, aloof from all parties, and with a manly scorn of all parties. Instead of that, every trustee of the people is a traitor, looking only to his own gain, and to boost up his party. The berths, the Presidency included, are bought, sold, electioneered for, prostituted, and filled with prostitutes. (*NUPM*, 6:2122)

This is one of the milder passages in a tract that also calls the delegates to the Democratic and American Party conventions "the lousy combings and born freedom-sellers of the earth" and claims that President Pierce "eats filth and excrement for his daily meals, likes it, and tries to force it on The States" (2123–24). Madison wanted to construct a government that was relatively immune to the influence of "temporary and partial considerations";

Whitman sees the government in 1856 as a hostage "to personal and party interests" and therefore indifferent to "the interests of the people." The solution he envisions, however, is not to withdraw from the State, as Thoreau recommends, but rather to make the State approximate direct democracy as closely as possible:

> I expect to see the day when the like of the present personnel of the governments, federal, state, municipal, military, and naval, will be looked upon with derision, and when qualified mechanics and young men will reach Congress and other official stations, sent in their working costumes, fresh from their benches and tools, and returning to them again with dignity. . . . There is more rude and undeveloped bravery, friendship, conscientiousness, clear-sightedness, and practical genius for any scope of action . . . now among the American mechanics and young men, than in all the official persons in These States. . . . I would be much pleased to see some heroic, shrewd, fully-informed, healthy-bodied, middle-aged, beard-faced American blacksmith or boatman come down from the West across the Alleghanies, and walk into the Presidency, dressed in a clean suit of working attire, and with the tan all over his face, breast, and arms; I would certainly vote for that sort of man, possessing the due requirements, before any other candidate. (2121)

The Jeffersonian ideal of the republican yeoman here becomes the Whitmanic ideal of the republican artisan. Unlike the dependent "office-vermin, kept-editors, clerks, [and] attaches" of the political parties, the "free workpeople" whom Whitman would like to see running the government are independently employed, earning their own livings with their own hands, apparently even during their tenure in government. Like Jefferson's yeomen, they can therefore afford to resist party pressures and forgo "the drip and spoil of politics" in order to act purely on their "principles, the true glory of a man" (2122–23).[20] Whitman here presents the Republican ideal of free labor as a model not only for the economy but for popular government itself. Further, he seeks to blur the distinction between government and the people by envisioning the work of legislating as essentially continuous with the work routine of some, if not all, skilled laborers. This is presumably the significance of his insistence that these artisan legislators should attend to their public duties dressed "in their working costumes." The work of the government and the work of the people are to be understood as one.

II   But what is [the dancer's] charm for the spectators other than
       this, that she dances for them, or they dance in her feet, not
       being,—fault of some defects in their form or education,—
       able to dance themselves? We must be expressed.
       —Ralph Waldo Emerson, "The Poet and the Times," 1842

But if the "free work-people" of the United States are everything Whitman
says they are, why, in his view, are they not already running their government? One can find a partial answer to this question in Whitman's rather
convoluted explanation to his working-men readers of the nativist American
Party's name:

> [They] are using the great word Americanism without yet feeling the first as-
> piration of it, as the great word Religion has been used . . . by men that made
> indiscriminate massacres at night. . . . To the virtue of Americanism is hap-
> pening to-day, what happens many days to many virtues, namely, the masses
> who possess them but do not understand them are sought to be sold by that
> very means to those who neither possess them nor understand them. What
> are the young men suspicious of? I will tell them what it stands them in hand
> to be suspicious of, and that is American craft; it is subtler than Italian craft;
> I guess it is about the subtlest craft upon the earth. (2128)

What the people lack, according to Whitman, is an understanding of their
own merit, and this lack of understanding makes them vulnerable to being
"sold," like slaves, to the political parties. Their "virtue" seems to be so instinctive or latent that it can only be made conscious through some kind of
supervening expression.

Enter the "Voice of Walt Whitman to each Young Man in the Nation,
North, South, East and West" (2120). In his preface to the 1855 edition of
Leaves of Grass Whitman writes of the poet that "the others are as good as
he, only he sees it and they do not" (l. 165). The poet's role, then, is to provide a medium through which the people's merit can become visible—or
audible—to them. In "Song of Myself" Whitman writes, "It is you talking
just as much as myself, I act as the tongue of you, / Tied in your mouth,
in mine it begins to be loosen'd" (ll. 1248–49). To say that the poet's role is
to provide a *medium* through which the people can hear themselves speak,
however, is to say that the poet is not an opponent of representation but is
himself representative.[21] And to say this is to raise two further questions: If

the poet is representative, why, then, does Whitman present his poetry as "no agent or medium" but "the value itself"? And if, according to Whitman, political representation at the time he is writing merely amounts to the surrender of sovereignty by the people to the government, thus necessitating a poetic remedy, how does *poetic* representation avoid turning into another usurpation of popular sovereignty?

Let us try to answer the second question first by returning to Emerson's essay "The Poet":

> There is no man who does not anticipate a supersensual utility in the sun, stars, earth, and water. These stand and wait to render him a peculiar service. But there is some obstruction . . . which does not suffer them to yield the due effect. . . . Every touch should thrill. . . . Yet, in our experience, the rays or appulses have sufficient force to arrive at the senses, but not enough to reach the quick, and compel the reproduction of themselves in speech. The poet is the person in whom these powers are in balance, the man without impediment . . . who traverses the whole scale of experience, and is representative of man, in virtue of being the largest power to receive and to impart. (*EL*, 448)

"Power" usually means the capacity to effect one's will. The power of the poet, by contrast, consists of an ability to serve as the passive instrument through which the act of poetic speech occurs. As Emerson puts it in "The Poet and the Times," "Nature[,] who gave to poets this high representative function . . . wished them to stand for the Intellect and not for the Will." [22] Restrained by his inspiration from expressing his own will, the poet embodies the principle of speaking for another: "The poet pours out verses in every solitude. . . . [B]y and by he says something which is original and beautiful. That charms him. He would say nothing else but such things. In our way of talking, we say, 'That is yours, this is mine;' but the poet knows well that it is not his; that it is as strange and beautiful to him as to you" (466). Because the poet's words are "not his," by speaking them he performs a representative function. The poet's power is thus not a personal attribute but "a great public power" exceeding "his privacy of power as an individual man" (459). If this power marks the poet as an exceptional person belonging to what Emerson calls "a new nobility," however, it does so only by disrupting his individuality (467). [23] "The man who is his own master knocks in vain at the doors of poetry," he writes, paraphrasing Plato. [24] By suspending the individual's self-control, and therefore the exercise of *self-interest,* poetic inspiration makes truly representative expression possible. Thus the poet "stands among partial men for the complete man, and apprises us not of his wealth, but of the commonwealth" (448). Like the virtue of the people in "The Eighteenth Presidency!," the complete man for Emerson exists *only latently or potentially;* his realization depends upon the intercession of the poet, who is not the complete man himself but is able to *stand for* the complete man by virtue of poetic possession.

For Emerson the complete man thus never emerges by or as himself but *only as he is represented.* Actual individuals are mere "partial men," consumed—like Madison's factions and Whitman's party hacks—by their own partial interests. They require to be passed through a medium that can refine and enlarge their views. The government having failed in this regard precisely for a lack of disinterested representatives, poetry steps in with representatives of its own.

We have already seen in chapter 2 that Whitman shares Emerson's view of the poet as possessed by an external force that speaks through him. And we have also seen that Whitman's favorite metaphors for poetic possession include rape and orgasm—graphic examples of the suppression and suspension of the will. His vision of poetic invention as involuntary thus removes the problem of the representative's individual partialities as causes of concern; after all, to be a poet is to have one's individuality suppressed (to use James' term) or sacrificed (to use Emerson's). In "Song of the Answerer" Whitman begins to suggest the political implications of this view. "Every existence has its idiom, everything has an idiom and tongue," he writes (1. 31). Yet the idiom of each individual existence is unique in itself and therefore incommunicable to others. Whitman here envisions each of us as though we inhabited our own solitary locale in which a dialect intelligible only to ourselves were spoken, or as though each of us were our own professional group with our own incomprehensible jargon. The idioms of individuals are thus rather like the virtue of the American people: they require some kind of supervening language to unite them. As in "The Eighteenth Presidency!," that language is Whitman's:

> A young man comes to me bearing a message from his brother,
> How shall the young man know the whether and when of his brother?
> Tell him to send me the signs.

And I stand before the young man face to face, and take his right hand in
   my left hand and his left hand in my right hand,
And answer for his brother and for men, and I answer for him that answers
   for all, and send these signs.

Him all wait for, him all yield up to, his word is decisive and final,
Him they accept, in him lave, in him perceive themselves as amid light.
. . . .

He resolves all tongues into his own and bestows it upon men, and any man
   translates, and any man translates himself also,
One part does not counteract another part, he is the joiner, he sees how they
   join.
      (ll. 3–33)

The role of individual idioms here is analogous to that of "parties and interests" for Madison, the role of poetry to that of his federal government. Even
Whitman's use of the term "idiom," with its evocation of provincial insu-
larity, suggests Madison's concern that provincial interests might obstruct
the pursuit of national ones. In "Song of the Answerer," however, poetry
and not the federal government is the medium that enlarges and refines
public views. Indeed, poetry turns isolated people and their idioms into *the
People*. Like "the complete man" in Emerson, the People, conceived as a coherent national body, is entirely the product of representation in "Song of
the Answerer": only the tongue of the poet enables discordant individuals
and idioms to "join." In fact, the poet himself enacts this joining physically
as well as verbally in the poem. Substituting himself for the absent "brother"
whose message the "young man" has brought him for translation, the poet
holds the young man hand in hand and "face to face" as he "answer[s] for his
brother and for men." The union of poet and brother establishes democratic
fraternity *by proxy;* the People is an effect of poetic mediation. "The genius
of the United States is not best or most in its executives or legislatures,"
Whitman writes in the preface to the 1855 edition of *Leaves of Grass*, "but
always most in the common people" (ll. 27–30). Yet the common people *do*
need to be represented: "Their Presidents shall not be their common referee
so much as their poets shall" (ll. 119–20).

Whitman thus departs slightly from Emerson in making the People an
outgrowth of poetry instead of something strictly internal to the experiences
of making and reading poetry. He departs from Emerson more significantly,

however, in his descriptions of poetry's sources. Whereas Emerson generally presents the force that inspires the poet as either natural or supernatural, Whitman frequently presents that force as a person or a group of people. Thus the "dæmons" that hem in the poet in Emerson's essay become a rather more real group of "prurient provokers" in "Song of Myself." So, too, the "impressions of nature," which the "majority of men" cannot reproduce in their speech (*EL*, 448) but which the poet can, become the messages from one person to another that the poet "resolves . . . into his own" tongue and "bestows . . . upon men" in "Song of the Answerer." For Emerson the source of inspiration is usually impersonal; for Whitman it is generally personal — or is made so through personification.

We now have an answer to the question of how poetry succeeds where government fails in its responsibility to provide true representation: poetry succeeds because in poetry *delegation is a condition of utterance.* "The inexorable rule in the muses' court [is] *either inspiration or silence,*" and inspiration means speaking not as oneself but as another. But this answer only makes our other question more pressing: If Whitman thinks the poet is representative, why does he nevertheless say that his poetry is "no agent or medium"?

This question can be divided into two more specific ones. First, why does Whitman write as though his poems actually make the People present instead of just representing them? Second, why does he insist that his poems make *him* present instead of just standing for him? These questions, in turn, can only be answered once we look more closely at *how* Whitman seeks to make himself and others present in his poetry.

Let us begin with his presentation of others. As we have seen, the 1855 version of "A Song for Occupations" opens with a bold effort on Whitman's part to subsume the reader's awareness of the printed page into the fiction of his own personal presence. In attempting to do so, he addresses his readers in the plural as lovers, entreating them to approach and embrace him:

Come closer to me,
Push close my lovers and take the best I possess,
Yield closer and closer and give me the best you possess.
    (*LG* 1855, ll. 1–3)

By repudiating the representational medium that both joins him with and separates him from his readers, Whitman seeks to turn the poem into a vehicle of loving mutuality in which the readers are present to him, he to them, *and also they to themselves.* That is, one effect of the opening lines is to incorporate the readers into the poem as objects of their own observation. In fact, what follows is largely a portrait of the lives of Whitman's ideal readers, the "free work-people" of America:

> The usual routine . . . . the workshop, factory, yard office, store, or desk;
> The jaunt of hunting or fishing, or the life of hunting or fishing,
> Pasturelife, foddering, milking and herding, and all the personnel and
>   usages.
>   (ll. 110–12)

Yet the opening's apparent repudiation of the print medium masks its other, more conventional, function: Whitman's plea to his lovers is also an *invocation.* As such, it seeks not so much to deny representation as to initiate it. The poet's summoning of his lovers (which is to say *us*) is merely a prelude to their representation in the poem, which, by presenting them to themselves, permits their self-recognition as a group. Whitman's repudiation of the print medium in favor of those it represents thus enables the poem to fulfill its representative function. In "A Song for Occupations," then, Whitman seeks to make the People present for the same reason that poets before him sought the presence of *their* muses: in order to speak for them.

Something similar might be said about Whitman's greatest catalogue, section 15 of "Song of Myself":

> The pure contralto sings the organloft,
> The carpenter dresses his plank . . . . the tongue of his foreplane whistles its
>   wild ascending lisp . . .
> .   .   .   .
> The duck-shooter walks by silent and cautious stretches . . .
> .   .   .   .
> The nine months' gone is in the parturition chamber, her faintness and
>   pains are advancing;
> The pavingman leans on his twohanded rammer — the reporter's lead flies
>   swiftly over the notebook — the signpainter is lettering with red and gold,
> The canal-boy trots on the towpath — the bookkeeper counts at his desk —
>   the shoemaker waxes his thread,

> The conductor beats time for the band and all the performers follow
>   him . . .
> .   .   .   .
> The drover watches his drove, he sings out to them that would stray,
> The pedlar sweats with his pack on his back—the purchaser higgles about
>   the odd cent . . .
> .   .   .   .
> The crew of the fish-smack pack repeated layers of halibut in the hold,
> The Missourian crosses the plains toting his wares and his cattle,
> The fare-collector goes through the train—he gives notice by the jingling
>   of loose change,
> The floormen are laying the floor—the tinners are tinning the roof—the
>   masons are calling for mortar,
> In single file each shouldering his hod pass onward the laborers . . .
> .   .   .   .
> Off on the lakes the pikefisher watches and waits by the hole in the frozen
>   surface,
> The stumps stand thick round the clearing, the squatter strikes deep with
>   his axe,
> The flatboatmen make fast toward dusk near the cottonwood or pekantrees,
> The coon-seekers go now through the regions of the Red river, or through
>   those drained by the Tennessee, or through those of the Arkansas . . .
> .   .   .   .
> The city sleeps and the country sleeps,
> The living sleep for their time . . . . the dead sleep for their time,
> The old husband sleeps by his wife and the young husband sleeps by his
>   wife;
> And these one and all tend inward to me, and I tend outward to them,
> And such as it is to be of these more or less I am.
>   (257–325)

This passage has generally been hailed as an extraordinary demonstration
of the democratic inclusiveness of Whitman's art.[25] Here, it seems, the presence of the poet gives way entirely to that of the People; and when the poet
finally surfaces after sixty-seven lines devoted to others, he does so apparently as just another among the mass of individuals and groups presented—
one more item in the catalogue of American life. Further, like "A Song for
Occupations" albeit more subtly, this passage seeks to link worker, work, and

product into an undivided, self-sufficient unit. Whitman's people *are* what they *do* here, a point he gets across by the way he names them: carpenter, drover, peddlar, shoemaker, performer. He even goes to some lengths to create odd and quite wonderful compound words to express his identification of people with their mode of labor: duck-shooter, nine month's gone, canal-boy, floormen, pikefisher, flatboatmen, coon-seekers. Personal and group identity are entirely a function of one's work in this passage. Whitman makes the same point by repeating variations on a single word in his descriptions of people working: "The drover watches his drove"; "The floormen are laying the floor — the tinners are tinning the roof." Tinner; tinning; tin: person, work, and materials all make up a self-enclosed unit of activity. So, too, for that matter, do Whitman's lines, each constituting an independent clause or set of independent clauses, each devoted to its own vignette, whole unto itself, and unreliant on those that precede and follow it for grammatical or narrative coherence. The ideology of free labor appears to have found its ideal poetic form.

Yet the very autonomy of each line and vignette also means that the individual lines (and the individual persons and groups presented in them) share nothing in common except the formal independence that separates them. Whitman emphasizes this fact by defining the people he presents so completely by their work, and by making them appear to be so thoroughly absorbed in it, that they demonstrate no awareness of anyone or anything beyond the labor in which they are immediately engaged. Each scene is its own little world apart from — and seemingly oblivious to — all the others surrounding it. By itself, free labor ideology seems atomizing in this passage precisely because it imagines each individual or group of workers as completely self-reliant.

Except, it turns out, for the poet. While the people in each scene seem unconnected to those in other scenes, they "one and all tend inward" to the poet, and he "tend[s] outward to them." The passage's many individuals and groups thus achieve unity with one another not by themselves but only through Whitman's identification with all of them. And this, in turn, means that the poet is *not* just another of the people presented in the passage; in his capacity to unite an otherwise heterogeneous collection of people into a tableau of the People, he is actually unique among those with whom he identifies. Thus, Whitman says of himself *not* that he is *one* of these people

but simply that he is "*of* these": "Such as it is to be of these more or less I am."
Through decades of revision, Whitman never altered this line, despite the
evident awkwardness of the phrasing. The very fact that he is *of* the others
indicates that he is not *one of* them since none of them are *of* one another.
The only figure in the catalogue who is not independent of the others — the
only figure who is not *one* — he is also the only figure capable of representing
the others to themselves and each other as a People through poetry.[26]

III   Lord! what a scramble there'll be for arms and legs, when we old
       boys come out of our graves on the Judgement Day; wonder if we
       shall get our own again? If we do, my leg will have to tramp up from
       Fredericksburg, my arm from here, I suppose, and meet my body,
       wherever it may be.
       —Louisa May Alcott, *Hospital Sketches*, 1863

As in "A Song for Occupations," Whitman seeks to make people present in
section 15 of "Song of Myself" in order to represent them as the People.
For him the existence of a democratic People depends upon representation,
and poetry is the only means by which genuine representation can be realized. Madison's plan to unify the states under a strong national representative body was born of the disunity fostered by the *Articles of Confederation*.
Whitman's plan to unify the citizens through a national representative literature was born of the federal government's failure, in the period leading
up to the Civil War, to meet the goals that Madison and the other members
of the Continental Congress had set for it.[27] The election of Lincoln in 1860
and the onset of the war in 1861 did not cause Whitman to change his poetic
mission fundamentally, but it did cause him to alter it in significant ways.
The election of Lincoln, whom Whitman supported unwaveringly throughout the war, restored Whitman's faith in the office of the presidency, which,
as we have seen, had previously been the target of some of his most searing
invective.[28] This renewal of Whitman's faith in federal authority did not extend without qualification to the Congress, however, partly because, unlike
Lincoln, who came into office as the result of a national election, the wartime Congress represented only those states that had chosen to remain in
the Union. Whitman's fervent Unionism, entailing as it did that he, like Lincoln,[29] continue to assert the Confederate states' membership in the Union,
thus appears to have prevented him from accepting the wartime Congress

as an adequately national body. (He also continued to express contempt for congressional party politics, a scorn Lincoln may have escaped in part because he led Whitman's own party.)[30] But the war also brought Whitman to Washington, initially in search of a brother reported wounded in Virginia, and there he found an institution that, unlike the Congress, really did contain, as he put it, "representatives . . . from all the States" (*PW*, 1:42): the military hospitals that had sprung up all over the capital to receive wounded from the campaigns in Virginia.[31] These hospitals, which Whitman visited daily throughout the war, encapsulated for him the citizenry that he had previously ranged all over the continent in his poetry to gather. Furthermore, they presented that citizenry to him as divided, physically shattered and desperately in need of assistance. They therefore quickly became as essential a literary resource for him as he was a help to them. In an 1863 letter to Emerson he grieves for "America, already brought to Hospital in her fair youth," and states his plan, already underway, to "write a little book out of this phase of America" (*C*, 1:69). In short, while the war gave Whitman a new reason to question the national authority of representative institutions (the presidency aside), the hospitals gave him a new source of authority for a national representative literature. With this political significance of the hospitals in mind, I would now like to examine how Whitman made political use of his service there — first by revisiting the self-portrait from the war period he provides in his letters.

As we saw in chapter 2, Whitman presents himself in his wartime correspondence as "filled from top to toe" with the hospitals (*C*, 1:75) — and as "fat," "red," and "running over" (164), seemingly as a result. We have already detected two overlapping sexual scenarios in Whitman's perception of himself as expanding, reddening, and overflowing because of his contact with the wounded: male homosexual penetration ("filled"), excitation ("fat" and "red"), and ejaculation ("running over") on the one hand, and insemination ("filled"), gestation "(fat"), and parturition ("the consummated book") on the other. And we have also discovered (as the second of these scenarios indeed assumes) a poetic corollary for both these scenarios in the doctrine of poetic inspiration. This self-portrait suggests yet another scenario, however, as a further example from Whitman's correspondence will show.

Writing to his mother from Washington in April 1863, he attempts to allay familial fears that, in his brother's words, "the immense number of unfortunate and heart-working cases [have] given you a sober and melancholy look." His assertion of well-being is similar to those I have already examined in other letters from this period in all but one respect: "Jeff writes he wonders if I am as well and hearty, and I suppose he means as much of a beauty as ever—whether I look the same—well, not only as much, but more so—I believe I weigh about 200 and as to my face, (so scarlet,) and my beard and neck, they are terrible to behold—I fancy the reason I am able to do some good in the hospitals, among the poor languishing & wounded boys, is that I am so large and well" (89). Here, as elsewhere, Whitman's body seems to expand in response to his contact with the wounded, and this expansion is accompanied by the redness he boasts of in other letters. In this letter, however, his face is not only "scarlet" but, as he self-mockingly puts it, "terrible to behold." Taken together, "scarlet" and "terrible to behold" might just as easily describe a wound as Whitman's face. In fact, the terrors of beholding the wounded are a frequent theme in his war writings. "It is the most magnetic as well as terrible sight" he writes of the "lots of poor wounded and helpless men" depending on his "soothing or talking to them" in a letter to his mother from the same year (*PW,* 2:622). "You must be on your guard where you look," he warns in another passage on "Bad Wounds" from *Specimen Days:* "Amputations are going on—the attendants are dressing wounds. . . . I saw the other day a gentleman, a visitor apparently from curiosity, in one of the wards, stop and turn a moment to look at an awful wound they were probing. He turn'd pale, and in a moment he had fainted away and fallen on the floor" (1:53).

By describing his face as "scarlet" and "terrible to behold," Whitman presents himself not simply as the image of health, as he seems primarily to have intended, but also, less reassuringly, as an image of the wounded. Indeed, his portrayal of himself in his letters as "red" and "running over" likens him to the wounded, bleeding soldiers at the same time as it expresses his desire for them. After all, "Spirit Whose Work Is Done" indirectly portrays the soldiers as "red," and the letters regularly describe them as "bloody." *The very terms of Whitman's self-description thus point to his embodiment of others.* "Filled" with scenes of the wounded, he envisions himself as resembling them.

He makes the political significance of this resemblance clear in the letter to his brother, (discussed in chapter 2), where he contrasts the "unAmerican and inappropriate" interior of the Capitol both to those of the hospitals and to his own: "Filled as I am from top to toe with scenes and thoughts of *the hospitals* (America seems to me now, though only in her youth . . . brought *already here* feeble, bandages and bloody *in hospital*) . . . all the poppy-show goddesses and all the pretty blue & gold in which the interior Capitol is got up, seem to me out of place beyond anything I could tell" (*C*, 1:75). When Whitman is filled with the hospitals, which themselves house "America," containing as they do "representatives . . . from *all* the States," he achieves in his own person a fullness of representation that the Congress, which meets in the Capitol, is itself unable to match at this time. In short, Whitman here proposes not only the hospitals but *himself* as an alternative to the Capitol and, by implication, the representative body it houses. And that claim—to embody the whole People in a manner that the legislature does not—is grounded in a logic, at once sexual and poetic, that stipulates self-surrender as the condition for representative authority. "When a man assumes a public trust, he should consider himself as public property," Jefferson remarks.[32] Whitman conceives his poetics of possession as a means of fulfilling that ideal.

This same process is apparent in "Spirit Whose Work Is Done." For if the spirit in that poem stands for the wounded, the speaker's request that it "fill" him with "currents convulsive" suggests the spasms of a wounded body as well as those associated with orgasm. The convulsions of the poet in *Drum-Taps*, then, are more than signs of inspiration or homosexual pleasure; as evidence of injury, they identify him with the soldiers. The poet's injury indicates not merely the disruption of identity caused by inspiration per se but, more specifically, his adoption of the injuries of those who inspire him. "I do not ask the wounded person how he feels, I myself become the wounded person," Whitman writes in "Song of Myself." "My hurts turn livid upon me as I lean on a cane and observe" (ll. 845–46). Whitman carries this identification out in a short paragraph entitled " 'Convulsiveness' " near the end of the Civil War portion of *Specimen Days*. There he acknowledges, after having "look'd over the proof-sheets of the preceding pages," that they might "prove, at best, but a batch of convulsively written reminiscences." He justifies this apparent flaw, however, by arguing that the form of his "reminiscences" mirrors the events that produced them: "They are but parts of the actual distraction, heat, smoke and excitement of those times. The war itself, with the temper of society preceding it, can indeed be best described by that very word *convulsiveness*" (*PW*, 1:122). By calling his "diary" "convulsively written," Whitman simultaneously characterizes the act of writing it as involuntary and associates this loss of control with being injured. In addition to being a metaphor for the automatism of inspired composition, however, Whitman's "convulsiveness" also represents that of wartime American society as a whole. As in "Spirit," in other words, his "convulsiveness" is a token of his representativeness.

As I noted in chapter 2, Whitman sometimes describes his inspiration by the wounded as a form of ingestion. In a paragraph in *Specimen Days* entitled "Soldiers and Talks," Whitman describes the stories he hears from the wounded as a kind of food: "I often have talks with them, occasionally quite long and interesting. One, for instance, will have been all through the peninsula with McClellan—narrates to me the fights, the marches, the strange, quick changes of that eventful campaign, and gives glimpses of many things untold in any official reports. . . . [T]he superfluous flesh of talking is long work'd off him, and he gives me little but the hard meat and sinew" (62–63). Whitman here so thoroughly identifies the soldier's story with his person that hearing one becomes equivalent to swallowing the other. At least one such "talk" provided the inspiration for a poem in *Drum-Taps*. In a notebook he kept while working in the hospitals, Whitman entered a brief prose sketch with the heading "Scene in the woods on the Peninsula—told me by Milton Roberts ward G (Maine)" (*NUPM*, 2:651). According to an entry in another hospital notebook, Roberts was a patient in Armory Square Hospital in 1863, where his left leg was amputated (571). The scene he described to Whitman probably occurred in June of the previous year, during the Seven Days' Battles between Lee and McClellan on the Virginia Peninsula.[33] When Whitman mentions a patient in "Soldiers and Talks" who has been "all through the peninsula with McClellan," he may well have had Roberts in mind. The sketch recounts in the first-person voice of Roberts a night march during which he and his fellow soldiers come upon an "opening in the woods." Here they find an "old church used impromptu for a hospital for the wounded of the battles of the day thereabouts." The passage then closes with a description of the "surgeons operating" in the "darkness dimly lit with candles" and the "crowds of wounded, bloody & pale" lying in and outside the building (651).

Whitman's description of the wounded as "bloody & pale" once more invites comparison with the alternately "red" and "pale" spirit whom he asks for inspiration in "Spirit Whose Work Is Done." The analogy seems particularly apt in this case, given that the sketch itself was inspired by the story of a wounded soldier, and that Whitman uses the first person in his narration, thus identifying himself with the soldier as he does metaphorically in "Spirit." In other words, Whitman enacts in the sketch the incorporation of the soldier implied in "Soldiers and Talks": he not only records his story but assumes his identity. The sketch thus exemplifies in a remarkably literal way how the inspiration of the soldiers could make Whitman's writing "not his," as Emerson says of the poet's.

Whitman's identification with Roberts is even more marked in the poem to which the sketch gave rise, "A March in the Ranks Hard-Prest, and the Road Unknown," where he assumes the soldier's voice without indicating, as he does in the heading to the sketch, that this voice is not his own. But in "A March in the Ranks" Whitman not only narrates the story as though he were the soldier but also enacts an internalization of the "bloody & pale" soldiers within the narrative itself. As in the sketch, the speaker's troop halts during the night at a church crowded with wounded:

> A march in the ranks hard-prest, and the road unknown,
> A route through a heavy wood with muffled steps in the darkness,
> Our army foil'd with loss severe, and the sullen remnant retreating,
> Till after midnight glimmer upon us the lights of a dim-lighted building,
> We come to an open space in the woods, and halt by the dim-lighted
>   building,
> 'Tis a large old church at the crossing roads, now an impromptu hospital,
> Entering but for a minute I see a sight beyond all the pictures and poems
>   ever made,
> Shadows of deepest, deepest black, just lit by moving candles and lamps,
> And by one great pitchy torch stationary with wild red flame and clouds of
>   smoke,
> By these, crowds, groups of forms vaguely I see on the floor, some in the
>   pews laid down,
> At my feet more distinctly a soldier, a mere lad, in danger of bleeding to
>   death, (he is shot in the abdomen,)
> I stanch the blood temporarily, (the youngster's face is white as a lily,)
> Then before I depart I sweep my eyes o'er the scene fain to absorb it all,

Faces, varieties, postures beyond description, most in obscurity, some of
  them dead,
Surgeons operating, attendants holding lights, the smell of ether, the odor of
  blood,
The crowd, O the crowd of the bloody forms, the yard outside also fill'd,
Some on the bare ground, some on planks or stretchers, some in the
  death-spasm sweating,
An occasional scream or cry, the doctors shouted orders or calls,
The glisten of the little steel instruments catching the glint of the torches,
These I resume as I chant, I see again the forms, I smell the odor,
Then hear outside the orders given, *Fall in, my men, fall in;*
But first I bend to the dying lad, his eyes open, a half-smile gives he me,
Then the eyes close, calmly close, and I speed forth to the darkness,
Resuming, marching, ever in the darkness marching, on in the ranks,
The unknown road still marching.
      (ll. 10–25)

The sketch's "crowds of wounded, bloody & pale" appear here in the eerie
exclamation "O the crowd of the bloody forms." The phrase is eerie in part
because while "bloody" renders the wounded acutely visible, "forms" renders them indistinct and abstract. While we might be inclined to attribute
the abstraction of "forms" to the speaker's difficulty in seeing—most of the
wounded, he tells us, lie "in obscurity"—the fact that he can tell they are
"bloody" calls this reading into question. The abstraction of "forms" seems
due less to the speaker's inability to see the soldiers clearly than to his sense
that their injury is emptying their bodies of content. In this account, the
fact that the soldiers are "bloody" is actually a sign of their growing abstraction: the more blood that appears on the outside of their bodies, the
more their bodies appear to be mere empty "forms." Their bloodiness makes
manifest the gradual departure of their spirits from their bodies. Because
of their depletion, these "forms" seem to be less like people than outlines or
images of them. This suggestion of discontinuity between body and person
is slightly stronger in the original 1865 version of the phrase, "O the crowd
of the bloody forms *of soldiers*" (*V,* 2:494). Here Whitman at once identifies
the forms as belonging to the soldiers and subtly discriminates between one
and the other: he sees not a crowd of bloody soldiers but a "crowd of bloody
forms" *of* them.

The speaker's relation to these forms is largely mediated by the single figure of the "lad" he finds "bleeding to death" at his feet. Like the wounded in the prose sketch for the poem, the lad is both "bloody & pale"; his loss of blood, Whitman tells us, has turned his face "white as a lily." While the lad thus resembles the inspiring "spirit" of "Spirit Whose Work Is Done," the narrator, "fain to absorb" the "scene," clearly resembles Whitman, "filled . . . with scenes and thoughts of *the hospitals.*" These analogies suggest a causal relation between the lad's "bleeding" and the speaker's absorption, one figured in the stanching of the lad's wound by the speaker. In "Song of the Banner at Daybreak"—a bellicose *Drum-Taps* poem drafted before he began visiting the wounded and possibly before the war even began— Whitman in fact depicts inspiration as the filling of his body with other people's blood. "My limbs, my veins dilate," the "Poet" exclaims; "The blood of the world has fill'd me full—my theme is clear at last" (464). The speaker in "A March in the Ranks" suggests something similar when, directly after "stanch[ing] the blood temporarily," he sweeps his eyes "o'er the scene fain to absorb it all." "It" here refers most immediately to the scene inside the church, but it can equally refer to the blood mentioned in the previous line; and this ambiguity, though slight, adds to the reader's sense that the bleeding and absorbing are connected. In fact, given that the scene the speaker is "fain to absorb" is itself dominated by "bloody forms"—that of the lad among them—the difference between absorbing the scene and absorbing the blood seems virtually nonexistent.

The speaker's purpose in stanching the lad's wound is not to absorb the blood, however, but to stop it from flowing. By stanching the blood, the speaker seems to obstruct any connection between the emptying of the lad's body and his own absorption of the scene. The two events, while presented consecutively, nevertheless appear to be discrete. But by stopping up the soldier's wound, the speaker also fills a logical gap in the narrative—the gap separating the symmetrical events of bleeding and absorbing. The stanching of the wound establishes a continuity between these otherwise distinct events at the same time it differentiates them, and this continuity, in turn, inevitably suggests causality. By interrupting the flow of blood out of the soldier, the speaker paradoxically opens a conduit between the soldier's body and his own.

This balancing of continuity and disjunction defines the delicate relationship between soldier and speaker. Near the end of the poem, when he "bend[s] to the dying lad," the speaker again seems to "absorb" him: "his eyes open, a half-smile gives he me / Then the eyes close, calmly close, and I speed forth to the darkness." The shift here from "his eyes" to "the eyes" marks the departure of the lad's spirit from his body. The eyes are no longer "his" because he no longer inhabits them. As in the case of the "bloody forms," the body becomes different from the person. But the disappearance of the possessive pronoun also creates ambiguity: "*the* eyes" could refer to the speaker's eyes. This blurring of the distinction between the two figures continues when, immediately after the eyes close, the speaker "speed[s] forth to the darkness." The darkness encountered by the speaker appears to follow from the closing of the eyes. The sequence of events traces a continuity between the lad and the speaker in which the ambiguity of "the eyes" serves as the link. However, this ambiguity is possible only because the lad's eyes are no longer his. Only the lad's absence from his body fully establishes his continuity with the speaker; their correlation depends on his death. Here, as earlier in the poem, Whitman simultaneously identifies himself as speaker with the lad and predicates this identification on their difference. By doing so he manages to present himself as both physically continuous with the lad and as his substitute. These two claims — to embody the lad and to substitute for him — seem contradictory: the first associates the speaker with another person's presence, the second with his absence. But by making the lad's absence the premise for their correlation, Whitman establishes the authority to represent the lad himself (he embodies the lad) as well as the circumstances that require him to do so (the lad is absent). Together, the conflicting claims to embody another and to substitute for him thus comprise Whitman's account of being representative.

The process by which the speaker becomes representative is also that by which he becomes inspired. When Whitman describes himself as "resuming" in his "chant" everything he "absorb[s]" at the hospital, he delineates a chain of cause and effect that stretches from the bleeding lad to himself as the absorbing speaker to the utterance of the poem itself. In this context, it is particularly significant that the lad's bleeding, like that of the other soldiers, indicates a gradual departure of his spirit from his body. It is as though Whitman wished to suggest that by absorbing the scene he is absorbing the spirits of the bleeding, dead, and dying men who comprise it — in particular that of the lad. In this reading, the lad's death is quite literally Whitman's inspiration: just as he seems to absorb the blood he stanches, so he appears to internalize the spirit whose departure from the lad the blood signals. This transfer of spirit from the dying lad to Whitman is suggested as well by the "half-smile" the lad "gives" the poet. Coming as it does between the moment when the lad opens his eyes and the one when, by closing, his eyes become no longer his, the "half-smile" coincides exactly with the departure of the lad's spirit from his body. Further, the fact that the lad "*gives*" this "half-smile" to Whitman makes explicit the idea that something is being relayed from the lad to the poet. That this something should be transmitted through the lad's mouth connects this moment in the poem to scenes of inspiration we have examined elsewhere, of which it would appear to be a subtle but nonetheless recognizable variation. Finally, the fact that it is a "*half*-smile" indicates its liminality, as though when it occurs the lad's spirit is already halfway out of his body and on its way to Whitman.

The reading of this silent interchange between lad and poet as a scene of inspiration is reinforced by the passage's similarity to a famous scene in another war poem that Whitman was reading at the time he composed *Drum-Taps.* I have in mind the death of Dido in Book 4 of Virgil's *Aeneid.* In this passage Dido, having run herself through with a sword in despair over her beloved Aeneas' departure from Carthage, lies expiring as her sister, Anna, rushes to her side to comfort her *and to inhale her spirit.* For the inhaling of the last breath of the dying, which was thought to convey the soul out of the body, was a familial custom among the Romans of Virgil's time. At the start of the scene in the *Aeneid,* Anna is speaking. The prose translation is the one Whitman read:

> Let me bathe her wounds with water, and catch with my lips, if there be yet any straggling remains of breath. This said, she mounted the high steps, and in her bosom embracing, cherished her expiring sister with sighs, and dried up the black blood with her robe. She, essaying to lift her heavy eyes, again sinks down. The wound, deep fixed in her breast, emits a bubbling noise. Thrice leaning on her elbow, she made an effort to raise herself up; thrice she fell back on the bed, and with swimming eyes sought the light of heaven, and having found it, heaved a groan.
>
> Then all-powerful Juno, in pity to her lingering pain and uneasy death, sent down Iris from heaven, to release the struggling soul and the tie that bound it to the body.[34]

The differences between this passage and Whitman's poem are obvious; but there are also several striking similarities. The most important of these is, of course, that between Anna's effort to catch her sister's last breath and the speaker's absorption of the lad's last smile. The fact that both Dido and the lad die of abdominal wounds is noteworthy as well, as is the fact that Virgil's Anna and Whitman's speaker each try unavailingly to stanch the flow of blood from the wound of the person each attends. Finally, Whitman's role in "A March" seems to share characteristics not just with Anna's role but also with Aeneas'. Like Anna with her sister, he attends the dying lad, stanches his wound, and absorbs his spirit; yet like Aeneas, he troops into the scene as a vanquished soldier and troops out leaving death behind him. Like Anna, he embodies the spirit of the dead; like Aeneas, he distances himself from them.

Whitman also stresses the connection between his absorption of the scene and the chant that results by embedding the utterance of the poem *within* the action it actually *recounts*, preceding and following it with present-tense narration, as though chant and scene were simultaneous when really they are not. The chant thus seems to be the immediate result of Whitman's internalization of the wounded, whom it conversely again makes immediate: "I see again the forms, I smell the odor." This illusion of simultaneity is complicated, however, by the phrase in which Whitman actually describes speaking the poem: "These I resume as I chant." By describing the utterance of the poem as an act of resumption, Whitman characterizes it as discontinuous with the scene that produces it. Like Whitman himself, the chant denotes the disappearance of the soldiers it also claims to make present.

"A March in the Ranks" is one of a group of major *Drum-Taps* narratives—including "Vigil Strange I Kept on the Field One Night," and "The Wound-Dresser"—that is centrally concerned with intimate transactions occurring between the poet-speaker and the soldiers. In each of these poems something intangible is transferred from soldier to poet. Each of these exchanges has a powerfully erotic aura. Each is silent. And each establishes a continuity between soldier and poet at the same time that it also replaces the former with the latter.

This structure, which I shall call *transferential* for lack of a better term, can be seen at its most basic in the enigmatic poem "O Tan-Faced Prairie-Boy":

O tan-faced prairie-boy,
Before you came to camp came many a welcome gift,
Praises and presents came and nourishing food, till at last among the
    recruits,
You came, taciturn, with nothing to give—we but look'd on each other,
When lo! more than all the gifts of the world you gave me.

This little poem is testimony to Whitman's genius for making everything hang upon what he doesn't tell us. In the context of this man-boy bond, the silence of both figures concerning the nature of the gift generates inevitable erotic speculation. While the gift is unidentified, the act of giving itself and the silence of the transfer—here effected through a look—clearly connect the poem to "March in the Ranks." Further, the apostrophic form, verging on open invocation, links the boy implicitly to inspiration. Yet the fact that what the boy gives is both inaudible and intangible creates an apparent need—certainly, on the reader's part, a strong desire—for supplemental enunciation. On the one hand, the poem is that enunciation: it translates the "taciturn" boy's gift into poetry in much the same way that Emerson's poet expresses for others what for them is inexpressible. In this sense the poem might be said to speak for the boy—to say what he does not say—and therefore to *embody* him. On the other hand, the poem gives no explanation: instead of a description of the gift—or, rather, the thing "more than all gifts"—we get the poem it occasions. In this sense the poem might be said to *replace* the boy's contribution to the poet in the very act of expressing the ineffable transaction between them.

An intimate exchange between soldier and poet in which something intangible is silently transferred from the former to the latter; an erotic atmosphere; an embodiment of the soldier by the poet that is also a replacement of the soldier: this is the transferential structure in a nutshell. And as we have begun to see, for Whitman it is also *the structure of poetry's popular authority*. The transfer both inspires the poet and authorizes him to speak for the other party. Its silence indicates the need for expression through a representative. (One need only think of the silence of the disenfranchised Northern workers for whom Whitman speaks in "The Eighteenth Presidency!" or of Union soldiers for whom Whitman writes letters during the war because they are "not sure of themselves" or "too sick" to do it themselves [*WWC*, 3:578].) The transfer's eroticism, whether muted or overt, testifies to the poet's bond with those for whom he speaks and also to the selfless nature of his utterance, which takes on something of the automatism of sexual desire itself. The poem's substitution for the soldier demonstrates both the foundation of representative authority and its limitation: the representative is empowered only by substituting for others, yet for this very reason he cannot truthfully claim to *be* the authority he embodies.

It is easy to see why the transferential structure should be central to the major poems of *Drum-Taps:* it constitutes the poems' claim to democratic authority. It does so, however, not by addressing the issue directly. In fact, these poems rarely thematize it as such.[35] Instead, they are designed to *enact* it. If we are to understand Whitman's views on the relationship between poetry and popular authority, we must look beyond his pronouncements on the subject, useful though they are, to the representational procedures he actually employs. These are quite varied even within the transferential poems of *Drum-Taps.* In "Vigil Strange I Kept on the Field One Night," Whitman uses familiar topoi, such as kisses, as well as new ones:

> Vigil strange I kept on the field one night;
> When you my son and my comrade dropt at my side that day,
> One look I but gave which your dear eyes return'd with a look I shall never
>   forget,
> One touch of your hand to mine O boy, reach'd up as you lay on the ground,
> Then onward I sped in the battle, the even-contested battle,
> Till late in the night reliev'd to the place at last again I made my way,
> Found you in death so cold dear comrade, found your body son responding
>   kisses (never again on earth responding,)
> Bared your face in the starlight, curious the scene, cool blew the moderate
>   night-wind,
> Long there and then in vigil I stood, dimly around me the battlefield
>   spreading,
> Vigil wondrous and vigil sweet there in the fragrant silent night,
> But not a tear fell, not even a long-drawn sigh, long, long I gazed,
> Then on the earth partially reclining sat by your side leaning my chin in
>   my hands,
> Passing sweet hours, immortal and mystic hours with you dearest
>   comrade — not a tear, not a word,
> Vigil of silence, love and death, vigil for you my son and my soldier,
> Vigil final for you brave boy, (I could not save you, swift was your death,

I faithfully loved you and cared for you living, I think we shall surely meet
   again,)
Till at latest lingering of the night, indeed just as the dawn appear'd,
My comrade I wrapt in his blanket, envelop'd well his form,
Folded the blanket well, tucking it carefully over head and carefully under
   feet,
And there and then and bathed by the rising sun, my son in his grave, in
   his rude-dug grave I deposited,
Ending my vigil strange with that, vigil of night and battlefield dim,
Vigil for boy of responding kisses, (never again on earth responding,)
Vigil of comrade swiftly slain, vigil I never forget, how as day brighten'd,
I rose from the chill ground and folded my soldier well in his blanket,
And buried him where he fell.

The kisses in "Vigil" suggest a transfer comparable to that effected by the
lad's half-smile in "March in the Ranks" and the overtly inspirational kiss
of "Spirit Whose Work Is Done." Similarly, when the comrade reaches up
to touch the speaker's hand upon being shot, he can be seen as eliciting the
substitution of someone else's hand for his own. Further, the poem's "moderate night-wind" echoes a description of the wind blowing through the leaves
in another *Drum-Taps* poem, "Come up from the Fields Father":[36]

Lo, 'tis autumn,
Lo, where the trees, deeper green, yellower and redder,
Cool and sweeten Ohio's villages with leaves fluttering in the moderate
   wind.
      (ll. 3–5)

"Leaves" in *Drum-Taps* as elsewhere in *Leaves of Grass* are, of course, Whitman's prime metaphor for his poems. The moderate wind, on the other hand,
recalls the inspiring breeze of the opening line of *The Prelude:* "O there is a
blessing in this gentle breeze."[37] It therefore seems reasonable to associate
the gentle wind in both Whitman poems with the inspiring wind of the English Romantics. Finally, when the speaker, after looking at the body from
above, sits down next to it, the resulting scene uncannily resembles one in
which Whitman describes himself as having frequently written during the
war: "I commenced at the close of 1862, and continued steadily through '63,
'64, and '65, to visit the sick and wounded of the army, both on the field and

in the hospitals in and around Washington city. From the first I kept little notebooks for impromptu jottings in pencil to refresh my memory of names and circumstances, and what was specially wanted, &c. In these I brief'd cases, persons, sights, occurrences in camp, by the bedside, and not seldom *by the corpses of the dead*" (*PW,* 1:2n.; my emphasis). Seated by the corpse of his dead comrade, the speaker in "Vigil" is thus in position to write.

He does not write, however — at least not literally. In place of a direct portrayal of the act of writing, we receive the curiously overdetermined account of the position that the speaker assumes next to the body of his dead comrade: "long, long I gazed, / Then on the earth partially reclining sat by your side leaning my chin in my hands." What makes this account overdetermined is that the speaker describes himself as simultaneously sitting by the side of the corpse (hence the resemblance to the scene of writing) and "reclining" or lying down next to it. That is, his description places him both in the position of the writer seated "by the corpses of the dead" and of the corpse itself lying on the ground at his side. While not exactly inconsistent ("partially reclining" may be read as similar to sitting), the phrase "reclining sat" seems to obey a logic other than the merely descriptive. For by placing the speaker's body both in the position of the writer and of the corpse, the poem simultaneously identifies the speaker with the writer and associates the activity of writing with putting one's own body in the position of another.

The position of the speaker in "Vigil" thus conveys the same mixture of continuity and disjunction between speaker and soldier as does the stanching of the soldier's wound in "March in the Ranks." At the same time that Whitman's persona likens himself to his dead comrade, he also marks that likening as a mimetic act, thereby differentiating himself from the comrade whose place he assumes. It is in "The Wound-Dresser," however, that the play between continuity and disjunction, presence and substitution, receives its definitive treatment. It is there, too, that the eroticism of the soldier-poet bond is directly tied to the issues of poetic agency and popular authority.

"The Wound-Dresser" is split into two scenes. In the first, which frames the major part of the narrative, the speaker, now an "old man," is asked by "young men and maidens" (l. 3) to recount his war experiences, which are presented as being long passed, although the poem was in fact written during the war. In the second he "resum[es]" (l. 2) his hospital duties while narrating them, inviting the reader to "follow without noise and be of strong heart" (1. 24). The first scene amplifies the discontinuity between poetic utterance and content suggested by the word "resume" in "A March in the Ranks" by projecting the moment of utterance years forward from the actual time of composition. (A less dramatic version of the same effect can be found in "Vigil," when the speaker, after having "bared" his fallen comrade's "face in the starlight," states "curious the scene," thus removing the reader and himself from the events at hand in order to portray them as composing something on the order of a representation.) [38] By expanding the moment of utterance only briefly mentioned in "March in the Ranks" into an entire scene in "The Wound-Dresser," Whitman thus openly dramatizes the discontinuity between poetic utterance and what it represents:

> An old man bending I come among new faces,
> Years looking backward resuming in answer to children,
> Come tell us old man, as from young men and maidens that love me,
> (Arous'd and angry, I'd thought to beat the alarum, and urge relentless war,
> But soon my fingers fail'd me, my face droop'd and I resign'd myself,
> To sit by the wounded and soothe them, or silently watch the dead;)
> Years hence of these scenes, of these furious passions, these chances,
> Of unsurpass'd heroes, (was one side so brave? the other was equally brave;)
> Now be witness again, paint the mightiest armies of earth,
> Of those armies so rapid so wondrous what saw you to tell us?
> What stays with you latest and deepest, of curious panics,
> Of hard-fought engagements or sieges tremendous what deepest remains?
>   (ll. 1–12)

Yet in the second, intentionally more powerful, scene Whitman insists even more strongly than in "March" on the simultaneity of his language with the events it describes. At the scene's opening, for example, he explicitly pulls the reader with him through the hospital doors, which now demarcate the boundary between the space outside the poem and that within it. The reader's passage through the doors thus signifies the abolition of that boundary and consequently the immediacy of the scene narrated:

> But in silence, in dreams' projections,
> While the world of gain and appearance and mirth goes on,
> So soon what is over forgotten, and waves wash the imprints off the sand,

With hinged knees returning I enter the doors, (while for you up there,
Whoever you are, follow without noise and be of strong heart.)
    (ll. 20–24)

While the hospitals continue to exist only in "dreams' projections" in the first line of this passage, the world of the *present* has become mere "appearance" by the next. (The following line, however, which compares the events of the war to sand "imprints" washed away by the waves, again suggests an intimate bond between the apparently conflicting processes of making the war's wounded present and effacing them.) Extending his analogy between his own and the reader's movement through the poem and their passage through the doors of the hospital, Whitman even likens the movement of his lines toward and away from the right margin to his movement up and down the aisles of the hospital:

Bearing the bandages, water and sponge,
Straight and swift to my wounded I go,
Where they lie on the ground after the battle brought in,
Where their priceless blood reddens the grass the ground,
Or to the rows of the hospital tent, or under the roof'd hospital,
To the long rows up and down each side I return,
To each and all one after another I draw near, not one do I miss,
An attendant follows holding a tray, he carries a refuse pail,
Soon to be fill'd with clotted rags and blood, emptied, and fill'd again.
    (ll. 25–33, my emphasis)

The reader, who has been told to "follow" the speaker through the hospital, here becomes embodied within the world of the poem as the attendant, who "follows" the speaker with pail and tray. "Draw[ing] near" to each wounded soldier, the speaker enacts the passage's mission to achieve an effect of physical immediacy.

Meanwhile, the poem's claim to that immediacy — that is, to identity with the wounded it represents — is conveyed by two metaphors for Whitman's poetry. The first is that of the grass, the metaphor of his book's title, which is here "redden[ed]" by the "priceless blood" of the soldiers.[39] This line alludes to Whitman's inauguration of the grass metaphor in section 6 of "Song of Myself":

Tenderly will I use you curling grass,
It may be that you transpire from the breasts of young men,
It may be that if I had known them I would have loved them.
     (ll. 111–13)

Whitman's allusion to this passage strengthens our sense that the blood being spilled in "The Wound-Dresser" is meant to be perceived by us as a kind of nourishment for the grass, which is to say that the grass-poem metaphor here functions, as in its first appearance, to portray the poem as an organic outgrowth of the young men.

The passage's second metaphor for Whitman's poetry is the pail of blood-clotted rags carried by the reader-attendant. In *Specimen Days* Whitman describes such a pail in terms that suggest its potential as a metaphor for narrative. "He had been getting along pretty well till night before last," Whitman writes of a wounded Wisconsin officer, "when a sudden hemorrhage that could not be stopt came upon him, and today it still continues at intervals. Notice the water-pail by the side of the bed, with a quantity of blood and bloody pieces of muslin, nearly full; *that tells the story* (*PW*, 1:64; my emphasis). The bucket of bloody rags in "The Wound-Dresser" may also be associated with the notebooks Whitman carried with him on his visits to the hospitals, and which he describes in *Specimen Days* as "blotch'd here and there with more than one blood-stain" (1:2n.).[40] Carried significantly by the reader figure, however, the pail of bloody rags may refer more directly to *Drum-Taps* itself, which Whitman describes in another poem in the collection as "a cluster containing . . . blood-dripping wounds" ("Lo, Victress on the Peaks," l. 8). In any case, the function of the metaphor is similar to that of the grass: to connect the poem directly — even physically — with the men it describes.

Perhaps the poem's most powerful strategy for achieving an effect of immediacy is its most obvious one — its continuous, direct insistence that to read the page *is* to see the injuries the poem depicts:

The crush'd head I dress, (poor crazed hand tear not the bandage away,)
The neck of the cavalry-man with the bullet through and through I
     examine,
Hard the breathing rattles, quite glazed already the eye, yet life struggles
     hard,

(Come sweet death! be persuaded O beautiful death!
In mercy come quickly!)

From the stump of the arm, the amputated hand,
I undo the clotted lint, remove the slough, wash off the matter and blood,
Back on his pillow the soldier bends with curv'd neck and side-falling head,
His eyes are closed, his face is pale, he dares not look on the bloody stump,
And has not yet look'd on it.

I dress a wound in the side, deep, deep,
But a day or two more, for see the frame all wasted and sinking,
And the yellow-blue countenance see.
        (ll. 40–53)

The insistence on the immediate presence of the wounded to poet and reader
is implicit here in the graphic descriptions and compulsive focus on eyes
and sight: "I examine," "quite glazed already the eye," "he dares not look."
It becomes explicit in the repeated command to the reader, see, see.[41] The
effect of this insistence is enhanced by the near-total lack of possessive pronouns in the passage, which, like the phrase "bloody forms" in "March,"
seems eerily to bring the wounded bodies closer to the reader by dissoci-
ating them from the soldiers to whom they actually (if tenuously) belong.
This catalogue thus turns Whitman's techniques of abstraction or disjunction to inverse effect—or, rather, it demonstrates once again that evoking
the *presence* of the People and replacing them with representation can be
interconnected, not contradictory, goals.[42]

In fact, as we have seen, evoking the People's presence for Whitman almost always involves observing their *need* for representation—all the more
so when the People have fallen into so maimed and divided a state as during
the Civil War. Thus the soldier who has lost his hand embodies a need that
the poet supplies with his own "impassive hand" (l. 58). In the hospitals the
People's need for surrogates often takes on a powerfully physical reality, as
in the case of one Frank H. Irwin of the 93rd Pennsylvania, to whose mother
Whitman writes a letter: "The wound was in the left knee, pretty bad. He
was sent up to Washington, was receiv'd in Ward C, Armory Square hospital, March 28—the wound became worse, and on the fourth of April the leg
was amputated a little above the knee. . . . I was in the habit of coming in

afternoons and sitting by him, and soothing him, and he liked to have me—
liked to put his arm out and lay his hand on my knee—would keep it so a long
while" (*PW*, 1:103; my emphasis).

In addition to this kind of physical substitution, however symbolic—representation, after all, *is* symbolic—the amputee in "The Wound-Dresser"
stands in need of another kind. He "dares not look on the bloody stump"
where his hand has been amputated, "and has not yet look'd on it." Indeed, his whole body appears to express a mute terror of beholding his injury: "Back on his pillow the soldier bends with curv'd neck and side-falling
head, / His eyes are closed, his face pale, he dares not look. . . ." The soldier's
inability to look at his own arm bespeaks a more than physical amputation; it
indicates an incapacity for self-knowledge that harks back to Whitman's remark in "The Eighteenth Presidency!" about the People's ignorance of their
own virtue. The amputation of the soldier's hand is a tragic consequence
of that ignorance, as is the national disunion it is undoubtedly intended to
represent. The war, it appears, has not only translated that inability into
physical disability but has also turned the People's lack of self-recognition
into a positive fear of it, since self-recognition as a People now entails recognition of the political disseverment of North and South.

If Whitman supplies the hand that the soldier now lacks, however, he
also provides the *sight* that the soldier dare not use: *he* "dares not look on
the bloody stump," but Whitman does and we as readers do with him. In
doing so, and in making us do so with him, Whitman supplies the recognition the soldier, token of the People, cannot or dares not supply for himself.[43]
That recognition is now one of dismemberment and disunion, which is why
the People's innocent lack of self-knowledge has been replaced by a fear
of self-knowledge. But the recognition, the compulsion Whitman imposes
on himself and on us to *look*, itself supplies a compensatory—and substitu-
tional—wholeness. If the soldier cannot complete the visual circuit between
himself and his maimed body, a circuit which would provide him with at
least some psychological unity even though it would require acknowledgment of his having lost a hand, the poet can complete that circuit *for him.* If
the People cannot acknowledge their division, and thus end up internalizing
it, the poet can provide the acknowledgment and thus offer a means of possible amelioration and reunification. Thus the poem's retrospective fiction

projects, albeit wishfully, a future reunified perspective on the war—one, it
is implied, that follows from the poet's work to supply the people with their
lost wholeness by proxy during the war.

Yet the role of wound-dresser—which is the role of supplying the People
with the wholeness they lack by embodying them—brings its own form
of internal division. Thus, when Whitman describes himself as moving
through the wards "with hinged knees and steady hand to dress wounds," his
limbs seem more to accompany him than to be part to him.[44] In other words,
the speaker's own limbs seem somewhat disjoined from their owner in the
same way the soldiers' do. "These and more I dress with impassive hand,"
he states later, "(yet deep in my breast a fire, a burning flame)" (l. 58). The
"burning flame" in the poet's "breast" takes us back to the inspiring penetration of his heart by his soul in "Song of Myself"; the "impassive hand"
to the hand of the twenty-ninth bather, which, while trembling rather than
"steady," seems to function, like the dresser's hand, more by dictation than
intention. But here the contrast between hand and heart evinces a compartmentalization more marked than any internal divisions the speaker exhibits
in these passages from "Song of Myself." Impassive yet burning, he seems to
embody the double structure of identification and dissociation that defines
his relationship to the People in this and other poems in *Drum-Taps*. This
internal division is evident in the poem's conclusion as well:

> Thus in silence in dreams' projections,
> Returning, resuming, I thread my way through the hospitals,
> The hurt and wounded I pacify with soothing hand,
> I sit by the restless all the dark night, some are so young,
> Some suffer so much, I recall the experience sweet and sad,
> (Many a soldier's loving arms about this neck have cross'd and rested
> Many a soldier's kiss dwells on these bearded lips.)
>   (ll. 59–65)

The poem ends by powerfully evoking the physical presence of the speaker
and, finally, of his lips—the vehicle, we are to understand, through which
his words are conveyed to us. Suddenly we know with certainty that the
"new faces" that greet the poet at the poem's opening are meant to be our
own. While Whitman earlier identified his language with the presence of
the wounded by comparing the reader's progress with him through the poem

to a walk through a hospital ward, here he identifies his writing with his own body. But "these bearded lips" embody more than just Whitman; on them "dwells" "many a soldier's kiss." The soldiers' kisses exemplify with remarkable economy the complex correlation of poetic inspiration, male-male desire, and popular authority that is the focus of this study. Plainly homoerotic, the kisses also seem to empower poetic utterance, for the lips that the soldiers once kissed are those that now speak the poem. And if the soldiers' kisses, here as elsewhere, provide Whitman with inspiration, they also authorize him to speak *for the soldiers.* Hence the importance of the word "dwells" in the final line of the poem: by claiming that the kisses somehow remain on his lips as he speaks, Whitman claims to incarnate the soldiers. This claim to make the soldiers present with his own lips, however, is predicated on their absence — an absence accentuated by the narrative frame to which Whitman here returns. In fact, with the return to the scene of the poem's utterance, the physical presence of the soldiers, so extensively elicited earlier in the poem, is displaced by that of Whitman himself, whose body seems to take on the powerful immediacy with which theirs were previously invested. At the same time that he claims a sort of physical continuity with the soldiers whose kisses dwell on his lips, Whitman replaces their presence with his own. (After all, what dwells on Whitman's lips is all that remains of them to the projected audience of the poem.) "I act as the tongue of you," he tells us in "Song of Myself." "Tied in your mouth, in mine it begins to be loosen'd." Your tongue in my mouth: in the context of "The Wound-Dresser," this hallmark statement of the poet's representative role sounds like a *kiss.* In the context of "Song of Myself," on the other hand, the kisses of "The Wound-Dresser" sound like a transfer of popular authority.

While "The Wound-Dresser" ends by evoking the presence of the lips that speak it, however, the presence of these lips is not precisely that of Whitman. For the demonstrative adjectives Whitman uses to equate his writing with the presence of his body are also *impersonal:* "this neck," "these bearded lips." The immediacy of Whitman's body to the reader, like that of the soldiers' bodies, seems to depend on its depersonalization. Indeed, if the poem's capacity to evoke the soldiers' bodies is an effect of the eerie way in which they appear to float free of their owners, the immediacy of Whitman's body rests on its capacity to stand for the people it isn't. And this capacity, in turn, demands that his body be dissociated from him. Why does Whitman insist that his poetry makes him physically present to us? Because he sees his body as a vehicle of representation — *like* his language, not different from it. The difference between poetic representation and the body of the poet disappears when that body is itself conceived as a representational medium. Of compulsions like his wartime "religion" of attending the wounded, Whitman thus says "it possesses itself of him, *makes him over into its image*" (*WWC*, 5:581; my emphasis). Yet the possession that turns him into an image of others also exacts a price: "My body? . . . it had to be sacrificed" (582). Romantic self-surrender enables Jeffersonian public virtue: by resigning ownership of his body to the public, Whitman claims popular authority for poetry. For Thoreau the source of principle is divine and the man of conscience is its instrument. For Whitman the source of principle is the general will — what he calls "the divine average" — and poetry is the only vehicle that can vouchsafe its expression.[45]

At the opening of this chapter I noted that Whitman's homosexuality has recently been seen either as conflicting with his claims to perform the representative role of national poet or — what amounts to the same thing — as subversive of that role and the nationalism it implies. One purpose of this section has been to demonstrate that Whitman's desire for the "American young men" he nursed during the war neither conflicts with his claims to representative status nor subverts his nationalism. In fact, the sexual dimension of Whitman's relationship with the soldiers is, in his view, integral to his ability to stand for them, and by standing for them he represents the nation.

IV

Yet the demonstrative adjectives of "The Wound-Dresser" can also be read as drawing attention to Whitman's *words* — *look at these, look at this* — not only to the neck and lips they seek to conjure. In fact, the effort to nullify the reader's awareness of the linguistic medium through an appeal to the visual immediacy of what is represented always entails the possibility that this awareness will be *heightened* since reading itself is a visual activity.[46] As we have seen, Whitman's evocation of his presence at the end of the poem is actually grounded in his sense of his own equivalence to language as a vehicle of representation. Further, this evocation of his representative function, like the evocation of the status of his language as a medium, has the effect of distancing us from the objects of representation—the soldiers— who were previously brought so near to us. Drawing attention to himself as medium and drawing attention to his language thus produce the same result: to present us with the representative, not the represented. As we have also seen, this purpose is an integral part of Whitman's poetics of popular representation, both distinguishing the representative as such and delimiting his authority by acknowledging his difference from the People.

The transferential narratives of *Drum-Taps* display both sides of Whitman's poetic strategy for popular representation, but, focusing as they do on the interchange between poet figure and soldier, they emphasize identification more strongly than disjunction. Another genre of *Drum-Taps* poem— the brief, imagistic vignette, which Whitman perfected during this period —provides some counterpoint to the more intimate narratives of the collection. For this reason, most of these shorter poems fall outside the overall concern of this study, which is the interlocking erotics, poetics, and politics of Whitmanic possession. Two of these poems are directly related to the issue of possession, however, and I would like to close this chapter with a discussion of them.

Like "Spirit Whose Work Is Done," "Reconciliation" was written at the close of the war; unlike "Spirit," it expresses a wish not to preserve the spirit of the war but rather to erase it:

> Reconciliation.

> Word over all, beautiful as the sky,
> Beautiful that war and all its deeds of carnage must in time be utterly lost,
> That the hands of the sisters Death and Night incessantly softly wash
>   again, and ever again, this soil'd world;
> For my enemy is dead, a man divine as myself is dead,
> I look where he lies white-faced and still in the coffin—I draw near,
> Bend down and touch lightly with my lips the white face in the coffin.

The poem is, of course, devoted to the passing of the war, a passing it seems concerned both to confirm—"I look where he lies . . . in the coffin"—and, if possible, to expedite. (By contrast, the fact that the work of "the sisters Death and Night" is described, like the hand washing of Lady Macbeth, as incessant, suggests some concern on Whitman's part about whether "deeds of carnage" are ever "utterly lost," while the word "lost" suggests a contrary urge to *preserve* in some form what is here described as in the process of being effaced.) The erasure of the conflict and carnage is accompanied here by the highlighting of the poetic medium. Thus the first line not only explicitly thematizes language ("Word over all") but also refers to the title, which is literally *the word over all the others in the poem*—"sky" to the poem's "soil'd world."[47] By describing the conflict's erasure as, in part, a linguistic process—the replacement of the carnage by the *word* "reconciliation"—the poem thus describes its own role in that process. In fact, the process of erasure seems to merge here into that of embodiment as we have seen it enacted in other poems in *Drum-Taps.* Thus the poet's kiss serves, here as elsewhere, to establish a degree of identity between himself and the soldier he kisses, whom he calls "a man divine as myself." As in "March in the Ranks," that identification is predicated on the death of the person with whom the poet identifies. But here the soldier is "my enemy" and his death represents the death of the Confederacy, upon whose disappearance, after all, national reconciliation depends. The poem is therefore deeply interested in the erasure of this figure as an autonomous entity and his incorporation into its representational structure. Thus Whitman portrays the rebel's death, which leaves him "white-faced," as preparation for his replacement by the word and the white face of the page on which it sits.

Like the other *Drum-Taps* poems I have examined, "Reconciliation" features a silent, physical exchange between poet and soldier. Its portrayal of the poet's replacement of the soldier with himself and his language, however, is more emphatic than its predecessors'. In this process, the poem underscores its representational status quite conspicuously, and this naturally involves an increased emphasis on the *poem* rather than the *speaker* as representative medium. In "Reconciliation" the poet's kiss is not the final act in the poem's process of embodiment and substitution, though it is the last act described in the poem. Rather, the subordination of both figures to the "word" is the end toward which this poem strives. The poem thus serves as a link connecting the transferential narratives of *Drum-Taps* to its vignettes, in which the speaker's role as medium is largely replaced by that of the word. While this shift generally coincides with a shift away from emphasizing the physical presence of the speaker, it need not vitiate the overall visual impact of the poem. Indeed, as "Look Down Fair Moon" demonstrates, the removal of the speaker from the scene can increase the scene's immediacy:

Look down fair moon and bathe this scene,
Pour softly down night's nimbus floods on faces ghastly, swollen, purple,
On the dead on their backs with arms toss'd wide,
Pour down your unstinted nimbus sacred moon.

The stunning force of this poem derives, first of all, from the unstated analogy it establishes in its first few words between the moon, which the poet
entreats to "look down" at the battlefield, and the reader, who *is* looking down
at the page when he or she reads the poem. In fact, readers must inevitably
take in the first two words of the poem as an imperative addressed to *them*
until they read on to find that their position above the page is subsumed
into that of the moon over the battlefield. (This is why Whitman uses the
verb "look"—a word for something readers do—instead of "shine," which
would immediately imply a subject other than the readers.) The "scene" of
the poem is thus endowed with the nearness of the printed page. Like the
invocation to "A Song for Occupations" and the command to the reader to
"follow" in "The Wound-Dresser," but more subtly and concisely than either,
this invocation exploits the reader's nearness to the page in order to invest
its illusion with immediacy. Still, nothing in the first line of the poem prepares us for the jolt of what follows. "Scene," after all, is neutral and un-
informative; to the extent that it connotes anything about what's to come,
it misleadingly suggests an image that, however real (we *are* looking right
down at it), will nevertheless be safely packaged as a *view* of something. Instead, we get the most jarring image of human bodies in all of Whitman's
poetry: "faces ghastly, swollen, purple." The shock results, in part, from the
nearness established in the previous line as well as the contrastingly gentle
image of liquid moonlight. But it also results from the fact that these things
that are so near to our faces are faces themselves—dead, hideously distorted
ones, yet faces like the ones facing them. The *poet's* role as embodiment of
the soldiers has been transferred to the *poem* and, consequently, Whitman
has been freed from the constraint of having to create images of the soldiers
that he can readily assimilate to himself. The image that results in "Look
Down Fair Moon," however, seems at once related to our own and impossible
to assimilate altogether.

Yet, for this very reason, it especially calls for some form of alleviating
sublimation. As we saw in "Reconciliation," the earth must somehow be
cleansed of such graphic, human evidence of conflict for a united People to

replace enemy peoples. "Faces ghastly, swollen, purple" cannot serve as face for a nation. As it turns out, the moon Whitman invokes to illuminate the faces of the dead also serves this seemingly contrary function. Like "the sisters Death and Night" in "Reconciliation," the moon is asked not only to illuminate but, in doing so, to "bathe" the battlefield, "pour[ing] . . . floods" down onto the dead. As in the transferential poems, the purpose of poetic representation here seems to be as much to displace people as to embody them. "Night's nimbus floods" appear to be called upon not only to confront us with the disfigured face of civil war but also to wash that face from our sight.

Whitman's use of the word "nimbus" suggests a synthesis of these clashing imperatives. The moon's "unstinted nimbus" neither simply illuminates nor merely eliminates the faces of the Civil War dead. Instead, it *transfigures* them, at once preserving them and transforming them into something new and distinct. "Him they accept, in him lave, in him perceive themselves *as amid light*," Whitman says of the people's response to the poet in "Song of the Answerer." Shelley grounded his famous declaration that "Poets are the unacknowledged legislators of the world" in the belief that the spirit that inspires them "is less their spirit than the spirit of the age" (*SPP*, 508). In his 1855 preface to *Leaves of Grass* Whitman gives this formula a not un-Shelleyan emendation: "The direct trial of him who would be the greatest poet is today. If he does not flood himself with the immediate age as with vast oceanic tides . . . *and if he be not himself the age transfigured* . . . let him merge in the general run and wait his development" (ll. 581–93, my emphasis). "Look Down Fair Moon" gives us an image of *poetry*—not the poet—as "the age transfigured." The moon's nimbus, invoked by the poet, becomes a transformative force. Madison proposed a new federal representative body in order "to refine and enlarge public views, by passing them through the medium of a chosen body of citizens." For Whitman this formula becomes one for passing what he sees as a people at war with itself through the more radically transfiguring medium of poetry.

At the outset of this chapter I argued that, unlike readings of Whitmanic sexuality, which view the space of poetic representation as one of "utopian potential," so-called political readings tend to present his poetry as an effort to abolish poetry's representational status, as though the treatment of politics somehow required a violation of the poetic medium. Implicit in this approach — and occasionally explicit as well — is the belief that just as Whitman rejects the idea of poetry as representation, so, too, he rejects *political* representation. Readings based on such assumptions are perforce largely thematic, rejecting as they do the idea of poetry as a *vehicle.*

My goal in this chapter has been twofold. First, I have tried to delineate how Whitman's politics involve no rejection of poetic or political representation but instead represent an effort to conceive of poetic representation as a means of overcoming the deficiencies of its political counterpart. In doing so I have primarily focused not on Whitman's political pronouncements in poetry and prose, which, though important, are also intermittent, but rather on his representational procedures, which are necessarily pervasive. I have also attempted, however, to keep the theme of popular authority very much in view; hence my emphasis on Whitman's Civil War writings, which feature him in constant interaction with the people he consistently identifies as the source of popular authority, America's young men.

These young men have also been central to the second part of my goal, which has been to show that Whitman's homosexuality is, in his view, essential to his claim to popular authority, not subversive of it, as the shape of recent scholarship would suggest. What binds them together is his belief that poetry is a form of *possession;* his views on male homosexuality and popular authority are both shaped in light of this conviction. Of his hospital service Whitman thus says, "What did I get? I got the boys, for one thing. . . . I gave myself for them: myself: I got the boys: then I got Leaves of Grass" (*WWC,* 5:581–82). As we have seen, he explains his devotion as a form of possession: "That . . . seized upon me, made me its servant, slave." Possessing because possessed by the soldiers, Whitman exemplifies the inspired state as described by James: "You must be *possessed,* and you must strive to possess your possession." For James, being a national poet means being possessed by "the idea of your country's greatness." What possesses Whitman is not an idea, however, but a population: "America, already brought to Hospital in her fair youth." By surrendering his body to possession by these reportedly inarticulate masses, who thereby become muses, he gets his poetry — and with it the voice of the People: "The boys: thousands of them: they were, they are, they will be mine" (582).

𝒫𝒮 CHAPTER 4

Lines of Penetration

I

Today's critical consensus on Whitman holds that his treatment of sexuality subverts the ideal of individual identity upon which political authority is currently believed to depend. Further, this consensus maintains that his subversion of the self allows him to express an egalitarian promise that is otherwise largely invisible and unrealized in the hierarchical culture of his period and in our own. This democratic vision is considered to be fundamentally antirepresentational, both because the integrity of the vision depends upon its utopian disengagement from the discursive universe of his time and because it perceives representation as the primary instrument for the construction of precisely those differences—between self and other, male and female, heterosexual and homosexual, government and people—that his poetry is designed to abolish. In this view, Whitman conceives of his poetry as either detached from the culture it reinvents instead of representing or as storming the culture from "without" in its determination to break down the barriers between literature and life, ideal and real.[1]

The reading of Whitman I have presented differs from this one on almost every point. Whitman does portray sexual desire in general and male homosexual desire in particular as violations of personal identity—indeed, he even celebrates them as such. But he does not undermine structures of cultural or political authority by doing so. On the contrary, by portraying sexual desire as an invasive, automating force, he identifies it with the oldest form of cultural authority in the Western tradition: inspiration. Since, in his view, his homosexuality is nothing other than the structure of male sexual desire made manifest, it therefore figures in his poetry as a *mark* of authority, not an affront to it. He thus presents his reader with a vision of male homosexuality as a relation of invasion and submission, not one of egalitarian eros. Nor can this vision be described as critical of Whitman's culture per se. For while it certainly reverses hygienic edicts, it employs established literary ones. Further, Whitman sees in erotic and poetic possession not a means of liberation from an oppressive system of political authority but rather a means of *authorizing* literature as a representative institution by *liberating representation* from the problems of personal, party, and regional interests that threaten to destroy representative government. In other words, the subversion of the self, which Whitman's critics maintain is his means of subverting authority, is actually the cornerstone of his effort to *redeem* the notion of representative authority from the forces of self-interest that he sees as its ultimate enemy. While his effort to establish literature as a representative institution rivaling the federal government clearly expresses a profound skepticism about that government's claim to represent the People, it also constitutes an attempt to shore up the notion of popular representation in general, not to replace it with direct democracy. Although Whitman sees the common people as the source of democratic authority, he also believes that only representative mediation can realize that authority.

In short, Whitman's critics are mistaken not in believing that he renounces what they see as a masculine, heterosexist model of identity but in assuming that this renunciation entails opposition to structures of cultural and political authority too. The truth is more often the opposite: the theory and practice of representative authority in the United States, as inaugurated by Madison, treats the self not as the foundation of state power but as a menace to republican legitimacy and stability. Together with Shelley and Emerson, but more systematically than either, Whitman contributes to the evolution and propagation of this fiction of authority by incorporating it into the Romantic theory of poetic invention. His unique contribution, however, is to blend the Federalist and Romantic critiques of the self with poetic and reformist ideas of sexual desire in such a way as to present male homosexuality as a token for the sacrifice of individuality upon which he believes legitimate authority depends.

This homoerotic inflection of poetic and political thought is particularly relevant to theoretical debates about the politics of sexuality today. If recent work on Whitmanic sexuality errs, it is because of its uncritical efforts to make him conform to a poststructuralist paradigm. My own reading suggests, however, that the poststructuralist project of attempting to subvert cultural and political authority by decentering the sexual subject is in need of critical reexamination. Indeed, from our present standpoint, the predominant view of the subject as constructed and contained by ideological forces looks like another version of Whitman's own fiction of popular authorization. According to Whitman, people can actualize their authority as the People only through the medium of poetic representation; according to today's theoretical axiom, people's agency is always a function of larger sociodiscursive processes. The difference is that whereas Whitman, like poets and political theorists before him, tries to legitimate authority by locating its source outside individuals, contemporary theorists of sexuality believe we can *defy* authority by the same means.

This chapter undertakes a critique of theoretical approaches to sexual politics from Derrida and Foucault to Judith Butler and Leo Bersani. (At the same time, I build upon Bersani's criticism of constructionist theory and Foucault's pragmatics of power.) One of my goals is to demonstrate how the current theory of sexuality reenacts nineteenth-century efforts to locate the agency of poetry and sex outside the self. But while Romanticism often posits the existence of transcendental selves that act through the poet, the poststructuralist critique of the subject — of which recent theoretical work on sexuality is largely an extension — rejects the existence of such transcendental selves at the same time it describes actual subjects as instruments of all-encompassing external forces. Attempting to disguise this apparent contradiction, theorists frequently resort to personifications. That is, instead of providing a theory of transcendent agency, they tend merely to adopt the rhetoric of it. Yet this rhetoric cannot mask the deeper contradiction attending the effort to derive the subject from its social and discursive contexts: by subtracting agency from the subject, poststructuralism effectively detaches the subject from the forces that are supposed to produce it. The passivity of the subject as conceived by poststructuralism makes it incapable of participating in the systems that constitute it, and, as we shall see, this escape from participation invariably becomes the foundation for resistance to those systems. The effort to decenter the subject thus becomes instead a method for confirming its innate integrity.

II

The project of decentering the sexual subject derives much of its impetus and many of its conceptual resources from the Derridean critique of logocentrism. Indeed, it seems fair to say that the logocentric ideal of the subject, as described by Derrida — the subject as inviolate and self-sufficient — more or less *is* the sexual subject that theorists of sexuality today seek to displace. For many, logocentrism has become both the foundation and the equivalent of masculinist heterosexism. To call this a shift in deconstruction's emphasis, however, would be slightly misleading; some of Derrida's most important early work concerns sexuality and politics.

This is particularly true of his reading of Rousseau in *Of Grammatology*. Here Derrida connects Rousseau's theory and experience of writing to his sex life (especially his habit of masturbating) and his views on political representation, among other things. The basis for these comparisons is what Derrida calls "the concept of the supplement" (*OG*, 144): Rousseau sees writing as a supplement to speech, masturbation as a supplement to intercourse, and representation as a supplement to the general will of the people, and his attitude toward each results from his ambivalence toward the idea of supplementarity in general. What makes him ambivalent, according to Derrida, is the "two significations" of the term (144). "The supplement adds itself, it is a surplus, a plenitude, the *fullest measure* of presence," yet "it adds only to replace" and therefore marks as absent or somehow deficient that to which it adds: "It intervenes or insinuates itself *in-the-place-of;* if it fills, it is as one fills a void. If it represents and makes an image, it is by the anterior default of a presence" (144–45). Rousseau therefore embraces writing as a practice in order to make himself known for who he is. As Derrida explains, it is "the restoration . . . of presence disappointed in itself in speech" (142). At the same time, however, Rousseau condemns writing for replacing speech and thereby causing "the degeneracy of culture and the disruption of the community" (144). Similarly, according to Derrida, Rousseau excuses his masturbation as a way of making his beloved present through imagination yet fears it as an act that replaces a real good with an imaginary one: "The enjoyment of the *thing itself* is thus undermined" (154). Finally, Rousseau approves of "the total alienation of each associate with all his rights to the whole community" in the constitution of the general will, which he calls a "collective and artificial body,"[2] but (as we saw in chapter 3) he rejects the idea that the general will can be represented:

> Now the general will risks becoming a transmitted power, a particular will, preference, inequality. The decree, that is to say writing, can be substituted for the law; in the decrees representing particular wills, "the general will becomes mute." . . . It is the moment when the *general will* which cannot err by itself, gives way to *judgment*, which can draw it into "the seductive influence of individual wills." . . . It is therefore absolutely necessary that the general will express itself through *voices* without proxy. It "makes law" when it *declares* itself in the voice of the "body of the people" where it is indivisible; otherwise, it is divided into particular wills, acts of magistracy, decrees. (297)

What Rousseau cannot recognize, according to Derrida, is that in each and every one of these cases, supplementarity actually *produces* the presence it replaces. Thus Derrida writes of Rousseau's anguish over his habit of masturbating that he "neither wishes to think nor can think that this [self-]alteration does not simply happen to the self, that it is the self's very origin. He must consider it a contingent evil coming from without to affect the integrity of the subject" (153). In fact, however, Rousseau's sexuality has been shaped from the beginning by the concept of the supplement. Rousseau masturbates, for example, instead of having intercourse with his lover, Thérèse, to avoid both the risk of conception and, according to him, the aggravation of his ill-health. Thérèse, in turn, is "a successor to mamma," his previous beloved, who in turn replaces the real mother he never knew, as Rousseau's name for her indicates. And this real mother, Derrida adds, "was also in a certain way a supplement, from the first trace, and even if she did not 'truly' die in childbirth" (156–57). Masturbation is merely the culmination of this logic of supplementarity — or, rather, the making manifest of it. And so too, it turns out, with political representation. "The system of the social contract, which founds itself on the existence of a moment anterior to writing and representation," states Derrida, "can, however, not avoid allowing itself to be threatened by the letter. That is why [it is] obliged to have recourse to representation" (297). Why must representation succeed direct democracy? Because for Rousseau, Derrida writes, direct democracy is itself "always the supplement of a natural order [that is] somewhere deficient"; and "the general will . . . is therefore the supplement of nature" (298). The social contract, which involves "the total alienation of each associate with all his rights to the whole community," is instituted in order for individuals to escape a state of nature, in which they could "no longer subsist" on their own, Rousseau writes.[3] Made possible by some given potential for alienation and substitution, it therefore cannot put an end to that potential upon which it is dependent. Political representation—the alienation of the general will to the delegate—is merely another manifestation of the potential for substitution that enables the social contract to occur in the first place. According to Derrida, it therefore makes little sense to oppose representation, as Rousseau does, on the grounds of its supplementarity.

The concept of the supplement, intended by Rousseau to describe and condemn political representation and masturbation, among other things, thus describes both the structure of the general will and that of male heterosexuality. Most important for Derrida, however, it also describes the structure of language within which these sexual and political phenomena necessarily take form—a structure he identifies by the term for Rousseau's other supplement, writing. The deconstruction of Rousseau's sexuality and political theory is therefore significant in ways that exceed the study of Rousseau. For the logic of supplementarity is not something invented or even intended by Rousseau so much as it is imposed upon him by a discursive system that shapes the contours of his discourse in ways he could never fully comprehend: "The writer writes *in* a language and *in* a logic whose proper system, laws, and life his discourse by definition cannot dominate absolutely. He uses them only by letting himself, after a fashion and up to a point, be *governed* by the system. *[Il ne s'en sert qu'en se laissant d'une certaine manière et jusqu'à un certain point gouverner par le système]*" (158, my emphasis).[4] Or, as Derrida puts it a few pages later, "the person writing is inscribed in a determined textual system" (160). The interest of the supplement, he explains, is that it thematizes the structure of that system: "*This theme describes the chain itself, the being-chain of a textual chain, the structure of substitution, the articulation of desire and language, the logic of all conceptual oppositions taken over by Rousseau*" (163). The issue is not, then, what Rousseau thinks about language, sex, or politics; according to Derrida, much of what he writes about these issues exceeds the bounds of his own thinking. The issue is instead what the textual system tells us about sexuality, about republics, and about itself *through Rousseau.* What it tells us, in Derrida's view, is that male heterosexuality is a state not of plenitude or self-presence but of fundamental deprivation for which every love object represents a compensation that can never be fully satisfactory, the deprivation being what constitutes the subject. This is the decentering of the male heterosexual subject. What it also tells us, in Derrida's view, is that direct democracy or government by the general will is necessarily a flawed and unstable form poised between the state of nature, to whose insufficiency it is a response, and delegated government, to which it inevitably gives rise, being itself a product of substitution. Finally, what it tells us about itself is that it is a system of substitutions that both enables such seemingly disparate phenomena as heterosexual desire and democratic political theory and also dictates that their structure more or less replicate its own.

These are some of the things that writing tells us through Rousseau. And the authority of Rousseau's example rests on the conviction that the lessons he offers, like those of the inspired poet, are indeed offered *through* him and not merely *by* him. To say that writing speaks through Rousseau, however, is not so much to decenter the subject of Rousseau's writings as to replace it with a new one, which is not a person or a people but a *personification:* the "textual system" itself. This personification takes up all the functions previously ascribed to the writer: it is the source of the text and its meanings. Whereas Romantic authors from Coleridge to Emerson and Whitman traditionally attribute authorship to beings that both transcend and animate human and literary forms, deconstruction attributes authorship to linguistic forms that both enable and exceed writers and their intentions. This reversal of form and content aside, the two theories are remarkably similar. Both figure the writer as a delegate for a personified force that he or she does not fully comprehend but that, on the contrary, comprehends the writer. Both link this linguistic automatism to the sexual subjection and feminization of the male writer. And both explicitly connect the status of writing as a form of delegated agency to political delegation, thus suggesting that the former somehow dictates or validates the latter.[5]

As we have seen, the theory of inspiration accounted for the apparently unintended aspects of a writer's work by positing the existence of another, transcendental author (God, nature, sexuality) who *did* intend them but affected its intentions through the involuntary medium of the writer. Current literary studies do not generally credit the existence of transcendental authors; it is worth noting, however, that the acceptance of their existence in earlier periods allowed for an entirely coherent explanation of poetic invention. As M. H. Abrams remarks of pre-Romantic versions of the doctrine, "The theory of a supernatural afflatus . . . fulfills all the requirements of a good hypothesis; it is simple, intelligible, and comprehends all the facts. That the poem is dictated to the poet by a visitor from without accounts for its spontaneity, involuntarism, and unfamiliarity; that the visitor is divine accounts for the accompanying ecstasy."[6] But what happens when, while maintaining belief in the text's apparent spontaneity, involuntarism, and unfamiliarity, one attempts to explain them without reference to a transcendental author? This is the question most pressingly raised by Derrida's reading of Rousseau. For Derrida here famously insists that the source of the text's involuntary elements is internal to the text itself: "There is nothing outside the text" (158). And yet if the "textual system" exceeds Rousseau's authorship and his works, then it is effectively outside the text, unless the text and the textual system are one, in which case the system cannot *govern* the text. By assuming a distinction between textual system and text, Derrida therefore revives the idea of transcendental author (the textual system) in the act of delimiting the role of the natural author (Rousseau).

Is there an alternative to the transcendental author offered in different ways by Romanticism and deconstruction? Derrida infers the existence of the "system" from the pervasiveness of the problem of supplementarity in Rousseau's writing, which suggests the outlines of an overarching logic or discursive "system." But even if such a system were to exist in Rousseau's writings, that would not in itself mean it was necessarily unintended or "unperceived by the writer," as Derrida states (158). He infers this from the contradictory use of the term "supplement," which he sees as evidence that Rousseau does not fully command the "patterns of language that he uses" (158). The apparent lack of authorial control leads Derrida to conclude that those patterns originate elsewhere or, rather, that they themselves constitute an originary system governing the author. This is to assume that for Rousseau to be fully the author of his text he must be aware not only of every word he writes but also of every plausible implication of every word.

Obviously, this is impossible. As Steven Knapp has shown, however, it is possible for an author to intend a *set* of meanings without necessarily intending every meaning belonging to the set: "Cognitive content can embrace 'implicatures' that belong to the 'set of assumptions' the writer has in mind, even if the writer does not have in mind each particular member of the set."[7] The presence of multiple, conflicting meanings of "supplement" in Rousseau's writings, then, need not imply the existence of a force additional to the writer at work. As long as those meanings make up parts of the set intended by the writer, they can be considered intentional — as can the "system" they compose.

III

If Derrida provides one major element of the current paradigm for the decentering of the sexual subject (decentering itself being a deconstructive term), Foucault provides another. While Foucault and Derrida differ in ways that have been much discussed, they also share certain basic assumptions that have enabled other theorists to synthesize major aspects of their philosophies into a more or less unified poststructuralist approach to sexuality.[8] One of Foucault's main contributions to this approach is his portrait of sexuality as "a historical construct":

> Sexuality must not be thought of as a kind of natural given which power tries to hold in check, or an obscure domain which knowledge tries gradually to uncover. It is the name that can be given to a historical construct: not a furtive reality that is difficult to grasp, but a great surface network in which the stimulation of bodies, the intensification of pleasures, the incitement to discourse, the formation of special knowledges, the strengthening of controls and resistances, are linked to one another, in accordance with a few major strategies of knowledge and power. (*HS*, 105–6)

As this passage suggests, Foucault's demotion of sexuality from natural given to historical construct coincides with his elevation of other phenomena — primarily power and knowledge — to the status of givens, if not quite of natural ones. When, in a 1977 interview, Foucault explains that "one has to dispense with the constituent subject, get rid of the subject itself . . . in order to arrive at an analysis which can account for the constitution of the subject within a historical framework," he has power and knowledge in mind as dominant components of that framework, regardless of historical period.[9]

While this historicizing of the sexual subject threatens to generate its own constituent personifications in the form of power and knowledge, Foucault appears to avoid this pitfall by describing power as a relationship between free and independent agents rather than an impersonal force that determines people's actions. In his essay "The Subject and Power," for example, Foucault writes that "what defines a relationship of power is that it is a mode of action which does not act directly or immediately on others. Instead it acts upon their actions" ("SP," 220). Power thus differs from "determination" in that while determination can have only "passivity" as its "opposite pole," power requires "that the 'other' (the one over whom power is exercised) be . . . maintained as a person who acts" (220). By "a person who acts" Foucault does not mean a person who is *made* to do something: "Where the determining factors saturate the whole there is no relationship of power" (221), only total determination. By "a person who acts" he means instead one for whom, when "faced with a relationship of power, a whole field of responses, reactions, results, and possible inventions may open up" (220). What distinguishes power, then, is that the person over whom it is exercised must be able to act as he or she chooses.

By defining power as "a mode of action on the actions of others," Foucault includes in his definition "an important element: freedom." Indeed, as he is quick to point out, power's identity as a social relationship depends on the fact that "Power is exercised only over free subjects, and only insofar as they are free." This freedom consists of "a field of possibilities in which several ways of behaving . . . may be realized." That is, freedom for Foucault means above all freedom of choice—freedom, within a particular power relationship, to choose from an array of possible responses. But as this formulation already implies, such freedom is never unconditional. For to say that power is "a mode of action upon the actions of others" is to say that for the person over whom power is exercised the range of possible actions is always limited—though never eliminated altogether—by the power relationship. (Hence Foucault also says that to exert power is "to structure the possible field of action of others" [221].) And since, as Foucault writes, "to live in society is to live in such a way that action upon other actions is possible—and in fact ongoing"—since the potential for a power relationship is "coextensive with every social relationship" — freedom is always exercised within and conditioned by power relations (222, 224). Thus, while one cannot say, given Foucault's definition of power, that the exercise of power destroys freedom of action, neither can one claim that the exercise of freedom occupies a position external to power relations. Power and freedom are never "mutually exclusive"; there is instead "a much more complicated interplay" between them (221).

Power and freedom are mutually inextricable; power relations are coextensive with society: dire as these formulations may sound to some, it does not follow that resistance to power is futile in either its immediate or long-term effects. "For to say that there cannot be a society without power relations," Foucault points out, "is not to say . . . that those which are established are necessary" (223). Indeed, any given power relation is inherently reversible by virtue of the "possibility of recalcitrance" that its subjects always possess, and without which "power would be equivalent to physical determination" (221). The fact that we can never completely escape having our actions conditioned by the actions of others, and that power relations are thus "rooted deep in the social nexus, not reconstituted 'above' society as a supplementary structure" (222), does not mean then that "power constitutes a fatality at the heart of societies, such that it cannot be undermined." Rather than being a cause of political impotence, our constant involvement in power relations — all of which are both threatening and potentially reversible — "makes all the more politically necessary the analysis of power relations in a given society, their historical formation, the source of their strength or fragility, the conditions which are necessary to transform some or abolish others" (223). The fact that power relations *as such* inhere in society does not change the fact that "there is no relationship of power without the means of escape" (225). It only means that escape from particular power relations never amounts to a total escape from power. To say, then, that power relations inhere in society is not to say that the freedom to act is absent, or that more freedom cannot be attained, but only that our freedom is never unlimited.

This definition of power relations seems to me entirely coherent.[10] And unlike the "textual system" of Derrida, it has the advantage of presenting a model of political relations that is independent of the representational fiction. For Foucault the assertion of popular authority in no way involves the resignation of one's will to another; unlike Derrida's writer, Foucault's subject does not have to surrender to a system in order to act. On the contrary, like Rousseau and Thoreau before him, Foucault views the resignation of one's will to another not as an exercise of power but merely as a form of submission. His view of power thus goes hand in hand with an extreme distrust of representative politics even when the representatives in question are writers and not politicians. With reference to the political events of May 1968, for example, Foucault states that "the intellectual discovered that the masses no longer need him to gain knowledge: they *know* perfectly well, without illusion; they know far better than he and are certainly capable of expressing themselves." The role of the democratic intellectual is thus not the Emersonian one of expressing for people what they cannot express themselves but instead one of opposing the cultural and political forces that discount the voices of the masses in favor of the intellectuals who are supposed to speak as their proxies:

> There exists a system of power which blocks, prohibits, and invalidates this discourse and this knowledge. . . . Intellectuals are themselves agents of this system of power—the idea of their responsibility for "consciousness" and discourse forms part of the system. The intellectual's role is no longer to place himself "somewhat ahead and to the side" in order to express the stifled truth of the collectivity; rather, it is to struggle against the forms of power that transform him into an object and an instrument in the sphere of "knowledge," "truth," "consciousness," and "discourse."[11]

While Foucault's description of power relations is thus consistent with the critiques of political representation we have seen in Rousseau and Thoreau, however, it is not at all consistent with his view of the subject as a historical construct.[12] For the description of power posits "the person who acts" as a condition for power's existence: "Where the determining factors saturate the whole there is no relation of power." Yet the constructionist view of the subject posits power as the *source* of the subject and its actions, in which case it must be precisely a determining factor. In other words, Foucault mistakes the idea that power and human interaction are mutually inextricable for evidence that the subject is *constructed* by power, which would then have to exist, like Derrida's textual system, independently of subjects and their actions. But simultaneity does not prove causality; on the contrary, it presupposes that neither of the two simultaneous phenomena precedes the other.

Whereas Foucault's description of power as relational characterizes it as a mode of human interaction, his description of the sexual subject's construction characterizes power as an impersonal force invading people's bodies and influencing their behavior. (The claim that power itself is plural—that the subject is constructed by a "multiplicity of force relations"—only magnifies the problem of personification instead of eliminating it.)

In fact, Foucault's personification of power as penetrating and sexualizing the body and its actions is remarkably similar to those of the sexual hygiene movement. In his introduction to *The History of Sexuality, Volume One,* for example, he describes his project as follows: "My main concern will be to locate the forms of power, the channels [*canaux*] it takes, and the discourse it permeates in order to reach the most tenuous and individual modes of behavior, the paths that give it access to the rare or scarcely perceivable forms of desire, how it penetrates and controls [*pénètre et contrôle*] everyday pleasure—all this entailing effects that may be those of refusal, blockage, and invalidation, but also incitement, and intensification: in short, the 'polymorphous techniques of power'" (*HS*, 11).[13] Antebellum sexual hygiene writers personified desire as an invasive and despotic force, implicitly likening its penetration of the body to rape. Foucault here does the same thing for power, personifying it as a stealthy rapist imposing its will on the unsuspecting subject. The whole scene of penetration, control, resistance, blockage, and incitement likens power's operation upon the subject to a sexual assault (with the provision that Foucault's subject, like Coleridge's coy maid, seems half-willing to be ravished). This scene undergoes different variations throughout the volume. Consider Foucault's description of the effort to control children's sexuality: "All around the child, indefinite *lines of penetration [lignes de pénétration]* were disposed" (42/58). Or of the "implantation of perversions": "It is through the isolation, intensification, and consolidation of peripheral sexualities that the relations of power to sex and pleasure branched out and multiplied, surveyed the body, and penetrated [*pénètrent*] modes of conduct" (48/66). Or the "deployment of sexuality": "The deployment of sexuality had its reason for being . . . in proliferating, innovating, annexing, creating, and penetrating [*pénétrer*] bodies in an increasing detailed way" (107/141). Or the fictitiousness of biological sex: "Sex is the most speculative, most ideal and most internal element in a deployment of sexuality organized by power in its grip [*ses prises*] on bodies and their materiality . . . sensations and pleasures" (155/205). Or consider the most striking example of all — his portrayal of the link between power and pleasure: "The power which thus took charge of sexuality set about contacting bodies, caressing them with its eyes, intensifying areas, electrifying surfaces, dramatizing troubled moments. It wrapped the sexual body in its embrace. There was undoubtedly an increase in effectiveness and an extension of the domain controlled; but also a sensualization of power and a gain of pleasure" (44).

This last claim about the sensualization of power is misleading. In Foucault's analysis of sexuality, as the preceding examples demonstrate, power behaves as a sexual agent *from the beginning*. His view of sexuality as a historical construct results in an image of power as a sexual assailant acting *upon* and *through* the bodies of those it penetrates and controls. Yet its actions are never really those *of* anyone involved. In this regard, the structure of sexual politics in Foucault is identical to the structure of sexual desire in the literature of sexual hygiene. In both cases sexuality entails the internalization of an external oppressor, and in each the metaphor for this process is sexual penetration. Most important of all, in both instances the sexual subject is always the victim of power and never its author. Foucault's critique of the deployment of sexuality thus begins to look like a hygienic critique of the involuntary nature of sexual desire per se.

Indeed, like the hygiene movement's onanist, Whitman's poet, and Derrida's writer, Foucault's sexual subject is not even the author of its own utterances. This is the point of his analysis of the history of confession, which he sees as part of a general "transformation of sex into discourse" (61). Foucault writes that "the obligation to confess is now relayed through so many different points, is so deeply ingrained [*incorporée*] in us, that we no longer perceive it as the effect of a power that constrains us" (60/80). Yet the agent of that internalization is power, which "spreads [sex] over the surface of things and bodies, arouses it, draws it out and bids it speak, implants it in reality and enjoins it to tell the truth" (72). Being a historical fiction, of course, sex has no great truth to tell. Nevertheless, the "immense labor to which the West has submitted generations" has not been without consequence; it has produced "men's subjection" (60). In this account, the voice of the person confessing is never really his or her own. The subjects of confession speak not for themselves but for power: they are at once its objects and its mouthpieces. The compulsion to achieve expression of that which is innermost to the self is actually an internalized form of coercion, and the more thorough the expression, the more complete the constraint. The person who speaks of his or her sex, in other words, speaks *involuntarily*. But this automatism is not the product of some intrinsic or *personal* drive demanding expression; rather, it is the result of power's possession of the speaker.

By portraying power as an autonomous force that acts upon people's bodies instead of a characteristic of people's interactions, Foucault's theory of sexuality suggests that power is not native to the body at all, that it always *befalls* people in the form of an external imposition. This view, in turn, enables him to invoke the body and what *is* native to it as the foundation for resistance to the regime of sexuality: "We must not think that by saying yes to sex we are saying no to power; on the contrary, we merely track along the course laid out by the general deployment of sexuality. We must shake off the urgency of sex if, through a tactical reversal of the various mechanisms of sexuality, we wish to array bodies, pleasures and knowledges, in their multiplicity and their possibility of resistance, against the grips of power. The foundation for a counterattack against the deployment of sexuality must be not sex-desire, but bodies and pleasures" (157, translation modified). We have come a long way here from the definition of power as "a mode of action on the actions of others." Now bodies and pleasures have an existence prior to power's imposition and potentially external to it. Yet it is Foucault's constructionism—his belief that we are the *products* of power relations and not just constant participants in them—that prepares the way for this vision of bodies and pleasures as a foundation for resistance. By construing the subject as a product of power, he exempts it from *exercising* power: the subject may be power's target or its instrument but never its author. This subject is not "the person who acts" whom Foucault makes the basis for power relations elsewhere.[14] The subject's exemption would appear to doom it to eternal oppression. But, in fact, this exemption constitutes its potential for liberation. For by separating the agency of power from people, Foucault suggests that power *is not a fundamental attribute of personal interaction*. Once this conceptual separation is achieved, it therefore becomes possible to consider the person as a potential foundation for *resistance* to power. Unable to act independently, we can thus *do no wrong*—and this, paradoxically, makes us a potential source of good. *Our subjection to power, unalloyed by participation in it, assures our capacity for virtuous resistance to it.* Foucault's constructionist theory of sexuality necessarily reproduces the essentialism it sets out to combat.

IV

Derrida and Foucault both set out to replace theories of discourse, sexuality, and politics that they believe are based upon flawed assumptions about the primacy of the individual self with theories that present the self as a product of systems of discourse and, in Foucault's case, of power. My thesis thus far has been that the unrecognized effect of these efforts is merely to replace one fiction — that of the radically autonomous self — with another, according to which people are or can be involuntary agents of a will greater than their own.

Poststructuralist theory holds that personal identity is at once a socio-discursive construct and a constraint. The project of resisting constraint is therefore inseparable from that of denaturalizing the subject. It was perhaps inevitable, therefore, that these theoretical precepts should eventually make homosexuality one of theory's primary themes. Detached from any procreative dictate yet, like desire in general, given rather than chosen, homosexual desire appears to embody the poststructuralist view of subjectivity as both artifact and imposition. Further, as an offense against the belief that heterosexuality is ordained by nature, homosexuality seems to incarnate the poststructuralist aim of denaturalizing the subject. Apparently both found and made, homosexuality therefore seems tailor-made to exemplify poststructuralist beliefs about subjectivity. It should come as no surprise, then, that homosexuality has become a major vehicle for the consolidation of poststructuralist theories concerning the subversion of the subject.

At present the most prominent participant in this effort is Judith Butler, whose work seeks to synthesize and radicalize the anti-essentialist axioms of poststructuralism in order to bring them to bear on the construction of gender, sexuality, and, in particular, homosexuality. Butler's range of theoretical reference is too wide to allow for a full accounting here; Derrida and Foucault play central roles in her thought, and it is against the background of their work that I propose to discuss her analysis of sexual subjectivity.[15]

Butler begins *Gender Trouble* by addressing what she sees as a crisis of representation within the feminist movement. "For the most part," she writes, "feminist theory has assumed that there is some existing identity, understood through the category of women, who . . . constitutes the subject for whom political representation is pursued" (*GT,* 1). Yet "the very subject of women is no longer understood in stable or abiding terms"; for "there is very little agreement . . . on what it is that constitutes, or ought to constitute, the category of women" (1). More recently, in *Bodies That Matter,* Butler has suggested the likelihood of a similar problem arising out of the recent uses of the term "queer": "The assertion of 'queer' will be necessary as a term of affiliation, but it will not fully describe those it purports to represent" (*BTM,* 230). She invokes these difficulties not because she wishes to propose more stable or inclusive terms but rather because she believes that these particular problems of representation indicate a general characteristic of identity categories: they establish the subjects they claim to represent only through "certain exclusionary practices" built into the process of representation itself (*GT,* 2). According to Butler, this means that the project of seeking representation for oppressed groups must be supplemented, if not replaced, by an analysis of how a concept like women "is produced and restrained by the very structures of power through which emancipation is sought" (2).

This is not to say that Butler thinks we should entirely abandon the hope for emancipation that representation has traditionally embodied for disenfranchised groups, nor that we should vacate the field of representational politics itself. "The juridical structures of language and politics constitute the contemporary field of power," she writes; for "there is no position outside this field, but only a critical genealogy of its own legitimating practices" (*GT,* 5). Butler thus appears to position herself some place between Derrida's untroubled acceptance of the representationalist fiction as an inevitable effect of supplementarity, on the one hand, and Foucault's dismissal of that fiction, on the other. As it happens, her demand for a critical genealogy of the representational fiction also seems to ally her to the kind of analysis I have attempted to perform in this study.

Butler's genealogy of sex and gender categories is recognizably Foucauldian in its overall logic. For example, Foucault argues that the sex we take for natural is actually the product of the historical process of sexuality's deployment (*HS,* 155). Butler similarly claims that the sexual body must be understood as the reification of gender norms and not, as other feminist theorists have held, as the natural ground upon which culture builds the artificial construct of gender: "The question is no longer, How is gender constituted as and through a certain interpretation of sex? (a question that leaves the "matter" of sex untheorized), but rather, Through what regulatory norms is sex itself materialized?" (*BTM*, 10). As Butler herself states, "That matter is always materialized has . . . to be thought in relation to the productive and, indeed, materializing effects of regulatory power in the Foucaultian sense" (9–10).

Yet her genealogy of sex also includes Foucault as an object of criticism. In *Gender Trouble*, for example, she notes that by habitually portraying the body as a passive medium upon which power inscribes itself, Foucault "appears to assume a materiality prior to signification and form" (130)—a charge she repeats in the title essay of *Bodies That Matter* when she writes that "at times it appears that for Foucault the body has a materiality that is ontologically distinct from the power relations that take that body as a site of investments" (33). As we have already seen, Foucault's tendency to describe the body as a passive target of power results from his constructionism: when he shifts from defining power as a kind of relationship between people's actions to defining it as something that *constitutes* people and their actions alike, he becomes liable to viewing people and their bodies as *external* and *subsequent* to power. In one sense this is inconsistent, for if power constructs the subject, then how can it be said to impose itself on the subject from without? In a limited sense, however, Foucault's portrayal of power penetrating and controlling the body from without is perfectly consistent with his constructionism. For by positing the sexual subject as the product of power, he effectively strips it *of* power—that is, of the capacity for independent action on which the exercise of power depends. And this, in turn, leads him to portray it variously as an inactive—which is to say merely physical—target of a power external to it and as the foundation for a "different economy of bodies and pleasures" untainted by power relations (*HS*, 159). Butler is correct in perceiving the inconsistency. Unfortunately, *she fails to perceive how this contradiction follows from Foucault's constructionism.* Instead, she sees it merely as a *lapse in constructionist rigor* and sets out to correct it by analyzing the body itself as a construct: "The critical inquiry that traces the regulatory practices within which bodily contours are constructed constitutes precisely the genealogy of 'the body' in its discreteness that might further radicalize Foucault's theory" (*GT*, 133).

The results of this effort in *Gender Trouble* are similar to those in Foucault. For example, Butler claims to reject "the figure of the body as mute, prior to culture, awaiting signification" — a figure she compares to "the feminine, awaiting the inscription-as-incision of the masculine signifier for entrance into language and culture" (147–48). Yet, like Foucault, she translates the constructionist subject's production by power into an image of its passive reception of a power distinct from it: "the body is not a 'being', but . . . a surface whose permeability is politically regulated" (139). To call the body a *surface* to which power is *applied* is precisely to treat it as dumb matter "awaiting signification." The constructionist decentering of the sexual subject thus seems to lead inevitably to a view of the body as *separate* from the power that constrains it. For without such a separation the constructionist subject's constitutive subjection to power would not be conceivable *as subjection,* that is, as a political problem. For the same reason, the sexual subject's decentering also leads, in Butler as in Foucault, to the personification of power. In the same breath that she tells us that "ontology is . . . not a foundation" — that is, that being can never be assumed to have a given shape — she also calls it a "normative injunction": in the beginning was the norm. Nor do we need to look far to find sources for these commandments. Butler eschews the idea that to speak of acts is necessarily to impute them to an agent: "My argument is that there need not be a 'doer behind the deed'" (142). Yet in practice this view merely leads to a proliferation of *personified* agents. Thus we are told that the "disciplinary production of gender effects a false stabilization of gender in the *interests* of the heterosexual construction and regulation of sexuality" (135, my emphasis), and that "the performance [of gender] is effected with the strategic *aim* of maintaining gender within its binary frame — an aim that cannot be attributed to a subject, but, rather, must be understood to found and consolidate the subject" (140, my emphasis). *Interest, aim:* these words imply subjects with intentions. However much Butler may protest against such implications, they are, after all, *her own.* For only through the imputation of an intentional subject can Butler establish that gender and sex are the results of political acts requiring political redress instead of random or, worse, natural events.[16]

It is presumably in response to such intractable difficulties as these that Butler tries to clarify her terms in *Bodies That Matter.* Here she brings Derrida to bear by identifying the principle that she believes to guide the process of identity construction — what she calls "performativity" — with his notion of supplementarity.[17] The construction of sexual identity thus becomes a "temporal process which operates through the reiteration of norms," and sex itself becomes the "sedimented effect of a reiterative or ritual practice" (*BTM*, 10). This reiteration, or performance, is not to be understood as voluntary. Butler writes that "performativity must be understood not as a singular or deliberate 'act', but, rather, as the reiterative and citational practice by which discourse produces the effects that it names" (2). Nor is this repetition to be understood deterministically, however. For the fundamental inadequacy of the citation to the norm it repeats — an inadequacy that, in Butler's Derridean logic, both inheres in the norm itself and drives the process of its citational supplementation — also assures that the norm itself will never be entirely fixed or fully instituted: "It is also by virtue of this reiteration that gaps and fissures are opened up as the constitutive instabilities in such constructions, as that which escapes or exceeds the norm, as that which cannot be wholly defined or fixed by the repetitive labor of that norm" (10). Butler thus sees hope for political transformation not in any dramatic contravention of the process by which sexual identities are generated but rather in the disjunctions inherent in the structure of the process itself: "If there is *agency*, it is to be found, paradoxically, in the possibilities opened up in and by the constrained appropriation of the regulatory law, by the materialization of that law, the compulsory appropriation and identification with those normative demands" (12).

Butler invokes Derrida in the hope of establishing a model for the construction of sexual identity that is neither voluntaristic nor deterministic. She sees the theory of performativity, thus reconceived, as nondeterministic because it makes the impossibility of the norm a condition for its continual propagation. How can constructionist theory be called deterministic when it assumes that the process of constructing sexual subjects its necessarily incomplete and inadequate? The fact that this failure inheres in the logic of performativity itself also spares her from having to account for that failure as the result of some form of voluntary, intentional resistance. As we saw in our reading of Derrida, however, the logic of supplementarity is no less deterministic for the inadequacy that drives it. The same is true for Butler's adaptation of Derrida in her theory of performativity. While any particular performance of sexual norms may be judged a failure — indeed, while they may *all* be judged as necessarily deficient — such failure itself is determined, in Bulter's logic, by the structure of performativity itself, which also dictates the norm's reiteration. *By incorporating failure into her model of identity formation, Butler merely widens the scope of that model's determining force: the same principle by which identity is enforced now accounts for its subversion as well.* Instead of personifying gender norms as she does in *Gender Trouble,* Butler therefore personifies the principle of performativity as the prime mover behind both the reiteration of norms and their "constitutive instabilities." As it happens, this personification has something in common with Foucault's personification of power in the first volume of *The History of Sexuality: it's always forcing sex on people.* Thus we encounter "the forcible production of 'sex'" (*BTM*, 12); "'sex' . . . as a kind of commandment or injunction" (14); "performativity" as "the forcible and reiterative practices of regulatory sexual regimes" (15); the embodiment of gender norms as "a compulsory practice, a forcible production" (231); and femininity as "the forcible citation of a norm" (232). The repeat offender here is the principle of repetition itself, performativity, which ordains that sex be imposed. Indeed, since the imposition never achieves the ideal it is meant to enforce, it ordains that sex be imposed perpetually. In short, Butler describes performativity as a serial rapist.

Of course, rape generally involves a victim as well as a rapist, and Butler's persistent rhetoric of violation serves to *imply* subjects whom we can envision as the perpetrators and targets of these violations even while she consistently denies that there is any subject that is not the product of performativity in the first place. For our construal of this process as political rather than natural once again demands that there be not only an oppressor — performativity — but also an oppressed distinct enough from the oppressor to be recognized as a victim: the subject. Thus, through her rhetoric Butler strives mightily to furnish us with the subject her theory both needs and denies. But her repeated use of adjectives like *forcible, compulsory,* and *constrained* to describe sex's imposition serves another purpose as well: it absolves the implied subject thus imposed upon of voluntary participation in the process. The subject that enforces or adheres to sexual norms is merely following orders. And this absolution, which effectively *differentiates* the subject from power by making its subjection comprehensive, therefore makes constraint the foundation for possible resistance. As an example of this paradoxical logic at work, Butler offers the recent embrace of the formerly derogatory word "queer" as a term of identification by those whom the word was and is used to ostracize:

> The term "queer" emerges as an interpellation that raises the question of the status of force and opposition, of stability and variability, *within* performativity. The term . . . has operated as one linguistic practice whose purpose has been the shaming of the subject it names, or rather, the producing of a subject *through* that shaming interpellation. "Queer" derives its force precisely through the repeated invocation by which it has become linked to accusation, pathologization, insult. This is an invocation by which a social bond among homophobic communities is formed through time. (*BTM*, 226)

Given all this, how are we to understand the process by which the term has been made "to signify a new and affirmative set of meanings"? (223). According to Butler, the shift demonstrates how the enforced repetition of sexual norms can produce the means of its own transformation: "To recast queer agency in this chain of historicity is thus to avow a set of constraints on the past and the future that mark at once the *limits* of agency and its most *enabling conditions*" (228). The potential for subversion comes not through an escape from the process of normalization but rather from within it as an effect of the fundamental deficiency that drives that process: "The resignification of norms is thus a function of their *inefficacy*, and so the question of subversion, of *working the weakness in the norm*, becomes a matter of inhabiting the practices of its rearticulation" (237). In other words, changing the norm is an indistinguishable part of participating in it—a participation which is, in any case, not a matter of choice but compulsory. The "queer" phenomenon not only exemplifies this process of change but thematizes it as the estrangement of the norm that is intrinsic to its inculcation. Its lesson is that while our perpetual "embodying of norms . . . is a compulsory practice," this fundamental subversion of personal agency provides its own opportunities for critique—ones that are all the more effective because they acknowledge in the very means of their realization the deficiency of the individual will that the norm supposedly operates to mythologize. Thus, Butler writes, "The incalculable effects of action are as much a part of their subversive promise as those we plan in advance" (241). The process by which performativity makes itself visible as such is the process by which the materialization of the norms it imposes might potentially be reversed. The acknowledgment that individual agency is an illusion may not be an entirely happy one, but it is nevertheless essential to the transformation of the normalizing process that makes agency what it is:

> It is one of the ambivalent implications of the decentering of the subject to have one's writing be the site of a necessary and inevitable expropriation. But this yielding of ownership over what one writes has an important set of political corollaries, for the taking up, reforming, deforming of one's words does open up the difficult future terrain of community, one in which the hope of ever fully recognizing oneself in the terms by which one signifies is sure to be disappointed. This not owning of one's words is there from the start, however, since speaking is always in some ways the speaking of a stranger through and as oneself, the melancholic reiteration of a language one never chose, that one does not find as an instrument to be used, but that one is, as it were, used by, expropriated in, as the unstable and continuing condition of the "one" and the "we," the ambivalent condition of the power that binds. (241–42)

The forcible performance of sexual identity here takes on the quality of spiritual possession, in which the actions of the possessed are always those of the occupying spirit. For Butler possession is a condition of discursive existence: "Speaking is always in some ways the speaking of a stranger through and as oneself." The state that was peculiar to the poet for writers like Shelley, Emerson, and Whitman is now a paradigm for subjectivity as such. Yet, strangely enough, although Butler figures possession as subjection, she also sees it as a potential source of resistance to subjection. By subverting the subject, possession opens up the possibility of a "future terrain of community." Subjects who do not exercise power but are instead "used" by it are subjects uncontaminated by power. They are therefore in a position to pursue a communal transcendence of it. To be "queer" for Butler is not to exchange being "used" by power for using power but rather to imagine that subjection to power promises exemption from it.

V

Butler's work is the most sweeping of recent attempts to radicalize Foucault's account of sexuality as a social construct. While this approach is currently hegemonic in literary studies of sexuality, it is not without rivals. Perhaps the most significant of these is the one advocated by Leo Bersani, who proposes to explore not how political relations construct sexuality but rather "the extremely obscure process by which sexual pleasure *generates* politics" ("RG," 208). This project has produced brilliant critical insights concerning not only contemporary sexual politics, both gay and straight, but also contemporary theoretical approaches to these issues. In fact, my own readings of Foucault and Butler are deeply indebted to Bersani. For example, consider the following comment from his 1987 essay "Is the Rectum a Grave?" on theorists of sexuality as diverse as Foucault and Catherine MacKinnon: "While it is undeniably right to speak . . . of the ideologically organizing force of sexuality, it is quite another thing to suggest . . . that sexual inequalities are predominantly, perhaps exclusively, displaced social inequalities . . . as if the sexual—involving as it does the source and locus of every individual's original experience of power (and of powerlessness) in the world: the human body—could somehow be conceived of apart from all relations of power, were, so to speak, belatedly contaminated by power from elsewhere" (220–21).

This simple but acute point lays much of the groundwork for my readings of power in Foucault and Butler. In his book *Homos* Bersani extends his critique to queer theory, arguing that it exemplifies a process by which "gay men and lesbians have nearly disappeared into their sophisticated awareness of how they have been *constructed as* gay men and lesbians" (*H*, 4). This focus on how homosexuality is socially constructed produces "*desexualizing* discourses," Bersani claims: "You would never know, from most of the works I discuss, that gay men, for all their diversity, share a strong sexual interest in other human beings anatomically identifiable as male" (5–6). While this type of work is obviously antihomophobic in intent, Bersani suggests that "it accomplishes in its own way the principal aim of homophobia: the elimination of gays" (5).

In "Is the Rectum a Grave?" Bersani traces this genocidal aim to what he sees as its basic animating principle. "There is a big secret about sex," he writes in the first sentence of the essay: "most people don't like it" (197). The reason they don't like it, he asserts, is because it threatens the self, at least momentarily, with disintegration. One of Bersani's main terms for this experience of disintegration is *jouissance*, which he describes as an "erotogenicity" that inheres not only in the body "but also in any activities and mental states or affective processes . . . that produce a certain degree of intensity in the organism and in so doing temporarily disturb psychic organization" (*H,* 101). Bersani speculates that "the origin of the excitement inherent in this erasure may . . . be in the biologically dysfunctional processes of maturation in human beings": "Overwhelmed by stimuli in excess of the ego structures capable of resisting or binding them, the infant may survive that imbalance only by finding it exciting. So the masochistic thrill of being invaded by a world we have not yet learned to master might be an inherited disposition, the result of an evolutionary conquest. This, in any case, is what Freud appears to be moving toward as a definition of the sexual: an aptitude for the defeat of power by pleasure, the human subject's potential for a jouissance in which the subject is momentarily undone" (100).

According to Bersani, we all feel the need for that pleasure, but we don't necessarily *like* feeling that need. He imagines that if a poll were taken in which individuals were asked if they liked sex, "people would probably answer the question as if they were being asked, 'Do you often feel the need to have sex?' and . . . these are two wholly different questions" ("RG," 197–98). The sexual compulsion may be hard to deny, but this doesn't mean people like it. The very fact that this *jouissance,* which Bersani also calls "self-shattering," momentarily undoes the subject also guarantees that it will be perceived as a *threat* by the subject. Bersani believes that male heterosexual–dominated society projects this threat onto female sexual pleasure and male homosexual pleasure because both entail an invasion of the body reminiscent of that primal invasion experienced by the infant. In the popular imagination, "women and gay men spread their legs with an unquenchable appetite for destruction. This is an image of extraordinary power" (211). At the same time, normative sexual pleasure is incorrectly defined as an exercise of mastery:

> It is possible to think of the sexual as, precisely, moving between a hyperbolic sense of self and a loss of all consciousness of self. But sex as self-hyperbole is perhaps a repression of sex as self-abolition. It inaccurately replicates self-shattering as self-swelling, as psychic tumescence. If, as these words suggest, men are especially apt to "choose" this version of sexual pleasure, because their sexual equipment appears to invite by analogy, or at least to facilitate, the phallicizing of the ego, neither sex has exclusive rights to the practice of sex as self-hyperbole. (218)

The threatening truth about sexuality is thus either repressed altogether or projected onto a particular sex (women) or sexual minority (gay men). This repression enables the creation of what Bersani elsewhere calls "authoritative selfhood," that is, the establishment of "identity *as* authority."[18]

Yet the repressed returns, Bersani claims, precisely in the spectacle of that sexual minority of gay men. The stigmatization of male homosexuality marks it as a potentially powerful vehicle for challenging the phallic ego. And challenging the ego is, in turn, a way to challenge the power that stigmatizes homosexuals in the first place. For if power is fundamentally relational, as Foucault states, and the existence of human relations depends upon the existence of individual selves to inhabit those relations, then the abolition of the individual self is also the abolition of power relations. This is why Bersani bemoans "the denial of the *value* of powerlessness in both men and women" (217). "The self which the sexual shatters provides the basis on which sexuality is associated with power," he writes. "As soon as persons are posited, the war begins" (218). On the other hand, "male homosexuality advertises the risk of the sexual itself as the risk of self-dismissal, of *losing sight* of the self, and in so doing it proposes and dangerously represents *jouissance* as a mode of ascesis" (222) and, therefore, resistance to power.

In the final chapter of *Homos* Bersani illustrates male homosexuality's potential in this regard through readings of Gide, Proust, and Genet. From the perspective of this study, his interpretation of Gide's *Immoralist* merits particular attention. It is the story of Michel, a wealthy intellectual, who travels with his wife to North Africa in order to recover from tuberculosis and discovers in the beauty of the native boys a reason to live. When his wife later contracts the same illness while they are in Europe, he rushes her back to Africa, where she dies, in part because of the haste of their journey. It is only when he is back in Africa that Michel realizes his real motive for returning: not to save his wife but to see the boys.

As Bersani explains, Michel's homoerotic passion "is a sexual preference without sex" (*H*, 118). Instead it takes the form of what Bersani calls a "radical slumming" (127). During travels in Sicily and North Africa, Michel seeks out "the dregs of society," whom he finds "delectable company." He develops a "horror of luxury, of comfort," begins to give away his property, and sleeps outdoors with Arabs.[19] As Bersani puts it, "his pederasty provides a sensual motive for an attack on all forms of property — on the self that belongs to him and also on all his possessions" (125). His sexless passion is thus an expression of what Bersani considers the deepest truth about sex: "It rejects personhood" (129). Being "self-less," Michel therefore rejects social relations, which depend upon the existence of selves (125). Gide's "fastidious sexuality is even more threatening to dominant ideologies" than "a man being penetrated by a man," writes Bersani, because "it eliminates from 'sex' *the necessity of any relation whatsoever*" (119–20). This rejection of the self and its relations makes Michel "a threat to the state" since a self is "the precondition for registration and service as a citizen" (127, 125). In answer to the question "Should a homosexual be a good citizen?" Bersani sees Gide saying *no*. Yet in this erotic asociality Bersani sees the promise of a new "community . . . in which it would no longer seem natural to define all relations as property relations" (128). For, as he writes with regard to Genet, "between oppression now and freedom later there may have to be a radical break with the social itself" (176)—a break to which the self-shattering of sex is the key.

I have summarized Bersani's discussion of Gide in some detail both because it exemplifies his theory of that "extremely obscure process by which sexual pleasure *generates* politics" and because, in certain respects at least, Bersani's Gide so closely resembles my Whitman. In particular, I have in mind Michel's radical slumming, so reminiscent of Whitman's avid immersion in the semiliterate worlds of streetcar drivers, firemen and, later, Civil War soldiers. Gide's "dregs of society" bear a more than chance resemblance, one suspects, to the "gay gang of blackguards" with whom Whitman frolics in "The Sleepers" (l. 41); his squalid Arab camps to Whitman's no less grim Army camps. More specifically, I have in mind the ascesis, or self-surrender, that this immersion involves in both cases—a surrender Whitman ascribes to possession and one that demands of him, as we have seen, even his body, "the vitality of [his] physical self." Of course, unlike Gide, Whitman portrays his sexuality by no means fastidiously. Yet there is in the overtly sexual passages themselves an element of self-sacrifice that anticipates the war writings so powerfully as to appear, in retrospect, to necessitate them. "A certain horrible pottage of human parts," D. H. Lawrence says *not* of Whitman's war poems but of his *sex* poems. "Just a horror." [20]

This resemblance makes all the more striking the difference between Bersani's conclusions and mine (or perhaps between Gide's and Whitman's).

Bersani's entire aesthetics—"ethics" might be a better term—turns on the assumed link between individuality and authority. Somehow dispense with the individual, he believes, and authority will not have a foothold. In this respect he is identical to the other theorists I have examined in this chapter. And in a certain Foucauldian sense he is, of course, correct. As we have seen, without the "person who acts" there can be no power relation. But this doesn't mean that the abolition of this person would constitute any sort of freedom. According to Foucault, when the person who acts is reduced to passivity, power is replaced by pure "determination," not freedom. Instead, it is sex itself that is liberated from power in Bersani's scheme. By undoing the self, it escapes forms of social regulation predicated on the self's existence. Yet by envisioning sex as antithetical to power, Bersani inadvertently places himself among those theorists he so convincingly criticizes for imagining that "the sexual . . . could somehow be conceived apart from all relations of power, were, so to speak, belatedly contaminated by power from elsewhere." Indeed, his entire sexual ethics is directed toward this end. Envisioning sexuality as a form of subjectivity in its own right, he envisions the erasure of subjective agency as the means of sex's emancipation in much the same way that Foucault and Butler imagine the decentering of the sexual subject as securing its autonomy.

As we have seen, by assigning the agency previously attributed to the subject to forces external to it, poststructuralism actually exempts the subject from involvement in those forces. For once such a force is imagined to exist and act independently of the subjects it affects instead of resulting from their concatenating actions, it also becomes possible to imagine that the force is actually extrinsic to subjects and therefore is imposed upon them. This line of flawed reasoning allows current theorists to portray subjects—including themselves and their readers—as invariably opposed to the forces that are nonetheless said to constitute subjects—as though these forces were entirely lacking in voluntary support. If the essentialism/constructionism distinction is misleading, then, it is because it is a distinction without a difference: the constructionist theory of the subject (or the performative theory, as it has been renamed by Butler) is simply a sophisticated defense of essentialist ontology.

While the theories of sexuality I have examined here are contradictory,

Foucault's relational theory of power may provide the makings of a viable alternative—especially as it is expressed in "The Subject and Power." There Foucault proposes that the subject be viewed as inhabiting a changing field of social and discursive possibilities that limits but does not determine its choices. Subjects are not products of this field; instead, *it* is the product of the interplay among their actions. While the existence of subjects is thus a logical precondition for the existence of the social arena, this does not mean they are independent of it. For subjects' freedom of action is always limited in practice by the relations in which they necessarily exist. As Foucault defines it here, power is one of the several types of relational actions that constitute the social field: it is "a mode of action upon the actions of others" ("SP," 220). Needless to say, if power relations are a consequence of the actions of subjects, then subjects cannot be products of power. Whether or not sexuality is a fiction, it is not something that power has implanted in people's unwilling minds and bodies, as Foucault often suggests in *The History of Sexuality*. At most one might be able to say of people's relationship to sexuality, as Foucault does of the Victorian bourgeoisie, that "they . . . tried it on themselves" (*HS*, 122)—and each other.

My understanding of Whitman as an author reflects this view of power as relational. As we have seen, revisionist critics often portray Whitman's poetry as an effort to reach a position exterior to his culture from which to reimagine it. His sexuality is read as an attempt to dissolve the category of the heterosexual individual upon which his culture is said to depend; his politics is said to challenge the representational foundations of the liberal state, if not of institutions as such. My reading suggests that Whitman's innovations arise from his participation in the project of asserting literature's authority against competing claims from rival forces within his culture, such as the nascent sexual sciences and the deteriorating national government. Does this mean that Whitman is less radical than he has previously been thought to be? I don't think so. All dissent involves competing claims of authority. A writer's politics is a function of the content of those claims, not their relation to authority in general. But it does mean that the literary grounds of Whitman's radicalism have been largely misunderstood—when they have not been neglected altogether. And it may mean that literary critics in general need to understand sex and politics more contextually than poststructuralist theory permits.

Abbreviations

BTM   Judith Butler. *Bodies That Matter: On the Discursive Limits of "Sex".* New York: Routledge, 1993.

C   Walt Whitman. *The Correspondence.* Ed. Edwin Haviland Miller. 6 vols. New York: New York University Press, 1961–77.

EL   Ralph Waldo Emerson. *Essays and Lectures.* Ed. Joel Porte. New York: Library of America, 1983.

EPF   Walt Whitman. *The Early Poems and Fiction.* Ed. Thomas Brasher. New York: New York University Press, 1963.

GF   Walt Whitman. *The Gathering of Forces.* Ed. Cleveland Rogers and John Black. 2 vols. New York: Putnam's, 1920.

GT   Judith Butler. *Gender Trouble: Feminism and the Subversion of Identity.* New York: Routledge, 1990.

H   Leo Bersani. *Homos.* Cambridge, Mass.: Harvard University Press, 1995.

HS   Michel Foucault. *The History of Sexuality, Volume 1.* Trans. Richard Hurley. New York: Random House, 1978.

LG   Walt Whitman. *Leaves of Grass.* Ed. Sculley Bradley and Harold W. Blodgett. New York: Norton, 1973.

LG 1855   Walt Whitman. *Leaves of Grass: The First (1855) Edition.* Ed. Malcolm Cowley. New York: Penguin, 1976.

LYM   Sylvester Graham. *A Lecture to Young Men.* 1834. Rpt., New York: Arno Press, 1974.

NUPM   Walt Whitman. *Notebooks and Unpublished Prose Manuscripts.* Ed. Edward F. Grier. 6 vols. New York: New York University Press, 1984.

OG   Jacques Derrida, *Of Grammatology.* Trans. Gayatri Chakravorty Spivak. Baltimore, Md.: Johns Hopkins University Press, 1976.

PW   Walt Whitman. *Prose Works, 1892.* Ed. Floyd Stovall. 2 vols. New York: New York University Press, 1963.

"RG"   Leo Bersani. "Is the Rectum a Grave?" *October* 43 (Winter 1987): 197–222.

"SP"   Michel Foucault. "The Subject and Power." In Hubert L. Dreyfus and Paul Rabinow, *Michel Foucault: Beyond Structuralism and Hermeneutics,* 208–26. 2nd ed. Chicago: University of Chicago Press, 1983.

SPP   *Shelley's Poetry and Prose.* Ed. Donald H. Reiman and Sharon B. Powers. New York: Norton, 1977.

V   Walt Whitman. *Leaves of Grass: A Textual Variorum of the Printed Poems.* Ed. Sculley Bradley et al. 3 vols. New York: New York University Press, 1980.

W   Henry David Thoreau. *Walden and Resistance to Civil Government.* Ed. William Rossi. 2nd ed. New York: Norton, 1992.

WWC   Horace Traubel. *With Walt Whitman at Camden.* 5 vols. Vols. 1–3 (New York: Rowman and Littlefield, 1961). Vol. 4, ed. Sculley Bradley (Philadelphia: University of Pennsylvania Press, 1953). Vol. 5, ed. Gertrude Traubel (Carbondale: Southern Illinois University Press, 1964).

Notes

Introduction

1. Plato, *The Collected Dialogues*, ed. Edith Hamilton and Huntington Cairns (Princeton: Princeton University Press, 1961), 492 (245a). On ancient Greek ideas about poetic inspiration and Plato's attitude toward them, see D. A. Russell, *Criticism in Antiquity* (Berkeley: University of California Press, 1981), 69–83.

2. On the connection between spiritual possession and democratic authority, see Nancy Ruttenburg, *Democratic Personality: Popular Voice and the Trial of American Authorship* (Stanford: Stanford University Press, 1998).

3. For psychological approaches, see David Cavitch, *My Soul and I: The Inner Life of Walt Whitman* (Boston: Beacon Press, 1985); and Edwin Haviland Miller, *Walt Whitman's Poetry: A Psychological Journey* (Boston: Houghton Mifflin, 1968). On Whitman's egotism, see Quentin Anderson, *The Imperial Self: An Essay in American Literary and Cultural History* (New York: Knopf, 1971); and R. W. B. Lewis, *The American Adam; Innocence, Tragedy, and Tradition in the Nineteenth Century* (Chicago: University of Chicago Press, 1955). On Whitman and the egotistical sublime, see Harold Bloom, *Poetry and Repression: Revisionism from Blake to Stevens* (New Haven: Yale University Press, 1976).

4. Allan Grossman, "The Poetics of Union in Whitman and Lincoln: An Inquiry into the Relationship of Art and Policy," in *The American Renaissance Reconsidered: Selected Papers from the English Institute, 1982–83*, ed. Walter Benn Michaels and Donald E. Pease (Baltimore: The Johns Hopkins University Press, 1985), 189.

5. Michael Moon, *Disseminating Whitman: Revision and Corporeality in "Leaves of Grass"* (Cambridge, Mass.: Harvard University Press, 1991), 14, 133, 59.

6. Michael Warner, "Whitman Drunk," in *Breaking Bounds: Whitman and Amer-*

ican Cultural Studies, ed. Betsy Erkkila and Jay Grossman (New York: Oxford University Press, 1996), 42.

7. Philip Fisher, "Democratic Social Space: Whitman, Melville, and the Promise of American Transparency," *Representations* 24 (Fall 1988): 60–101.

8. Wai Chee Dimock, *Residues of Justice: Literature, Law, and Philosophy* (Berkeley: University of California Press, 1996), 124. Some readers may object that the critique of individualism as characterized by critics like Warner and Moon is quite different from the "subtraction of differences" described by Fisher and Dimock. Indeed, for Moon and Warner individualism subtracts differences by serving as a norm for masculine identity, and Whitman's subversion of individualism thus liberates difference from normalization. But this does not change the fact that all four critics see Whitman as undermining the category of the individual. Furthermore, Moon and Warner's contention that individualism is discriminatory maintains the goal of subtracting differences in treatment (discrimination) while urging us to respect differences among groups. In this sense at least, their advocacy of difference is quite consistent with the promulgation of what Dimock calls "formal universals." Indeed, it may be seen as a normative injunction in its own right.

9. Whereas earlier Whitman scholarship discounted the relevance of English and European literary history for understanding his poetry on the grounds of American exceptionalism, more recent work has done the same in the name of a more political criticism. (The old exceptionalism, however, continues, as exemplified by Kenneth M. Price's *Whitman and Tradition: The Poet and His Century* [New Haven: Yale University Press, 1990], which, title notwithstanding, views Whitman's relation to British literature as one of simple opposition: "His poetic innovations are not the devices of a splendid isolation so much as they are a series of ingenious counters to English practice" [34]. Price accordingly devotes more space to the influence of Bryant than to that of Wordsworth.) A case in point is Moon's criticism of an apparently innocuous note to section 5 of "Song of Myself" in the Norton Critical Edition of *Leaves of Grass,* in which the editors connect the conjunction of body and soul in that section to the debate between body and soul in medieval literature. Moon charges the editors with "reduc[ing] the text's collage of intensely interactive persons, bodies, and parts of bodies to a literary-handbook notion of allegory, a simple variation on 'a fixed convention of medieval literature'" (*Disseminating Whitman,* 48). It seems as though the very attempt to situate or "fix" the passage in literary history offends Moon at least as much as the specific comparison being made. In other words, it seems as though he views literary-historical contextualization as merely an attempt to domesticate transgressive literature. But it's not clear why that should necessarily be so, nor why *social*-historical contextualization of the type Moon provides in his introduction should escape such a charge. The cumulative

result of this long-standing aversion to literary history in Whitman scholarship is a major gap in our understanding of the poet.

10. Christopher Marlowe, "Elegia I," ll. 5–34, *All Ovids Elegies,* in *The Complete Works of Christopher Marlowe,* ed. Roma Gill (Oxford: Clarendon Press, 1987), 1:13–14.

11. M. H. Abrams, *The Correspondent Breeze: Essays on English Romanticism* (New York: Norton, 1984), 28, 42. Of course, the shift was only partial; invocations to the gods or God continued during the Romantic period. Perhaps it could even be argued that the supernatural begins to fall under generic restrictions in this period, in the gothic narratives of Coleridge, Keats, and others, at the same time that sexuality begins to be freed of them.

12. *William Wordsworth,* ed. Stephen Gill (New York: Oxford University Press, 1984), 600.

13. Note, too, in this connection, Whitman's thoroughly Wordsworthian criticism of Keats' poetry for being "imbued with the sentiment, at second hand, of the gods and goddesses of twenty-five hundred years ago" (*NUPM* 5:1770). In fact, personification remains an important tool for Whitman in his treatment of sexuality, as we shall see in chapter 2. But Whitman's personifications are rarely of the conventional type that Wordsworth has in mind. Furthermore, they are far from clear-cut. Unlike the conventional personifications of eighteenth-century verse that Wordsworth has in mind, the "prurient provokers" of "Song of Myself" (section 28) could be actual people. As we shall see, this possibility is a crucial component of the poem's meaning. Finally, Whitman's use of personification in portraying sexuality fits Wordsworth's description of the one exception he grants himself in his "Preface to *Lyrical Ballads*": "They are, indeed, a figure of speech occasionally prompted by passion, and I have made use of them as such" (600). Why passion should provoke the use of personification is a topic I discuss in chapter 2.

14. Samuel Taylor Coleridge, "The Eolian Harp," *Poetical Works,* ed. Ernest Hartley Coleridge (New York: Oxford University Press, 1969), 100–102.

15. I have in mind here Michael Moon's claim that Whitman "created a liminal space of utopian potential in relation to" male homosexuality (*Disseminating Whitman,* 11).

16. See Betsy Erkkila, *Whitman the Political Poet* (New York: Oxford University Press, 1989), 145. For Erkkila's more recent modification of this position, see her essay "Whitman and the Homosexual Republic," in *Walt Whitman: The Centennial Essays,* ed. Ed Folsom (Iowa City: University of Iowa Press, 1994), 153–71.

17. Robert K. Martin, "Whitman and the Politics of Identity," in *Walt Whitman: The Centennial Essays,* ed. Ed Folsom (Iowa City: University of Iowa Press, 1994), 179–80.

18. See Kerry Larson, *Whitman's Drama of Consensus* (Chicago: University of Chicago Press, 1988), 150.

19. Thomas Yingling, "Homosexuality and Utopian Discourse in American Poetry," in Erkkila and Grossman, *Breaking Bounds,* 136.

20. Warner, "Whitman Drunk," 42.

21. Peter Bellis, "Against Representation: The 1855 Edition of *Leaves of Grass,*" *Centennial Review* 43 (Winter 1999): 73.

22. See Larson, *Whitman's Drama of Consensus,* 166.

23. Michel Foucault, *Discipline and Punish: The Birth of the Prison,* trans. Alan Sheridan (New York: Vintage, 1979), 30.

24. *The Complete Works of Ralph Waldo Emerson* (Boston: Houghton Mifflin, 1883), 12:86.

25. *The Poems of John Keats,* ed. Jack Stillinger (Cambridge, Mass.: The Belknap Press of Harvard University Press, 1978), l. 72 (371).

26. Hence this self is particularly on display in Romantic invocations and the genre to which they are most integral in the period, namely, the ode. See, in addition to Keats' "Ode to a Nightingale," Coleridge's "Dejection," Shelley's "Ode to the West Wind," and Whitman's "As I Ebb'd With the Ocean of Life."

27. After all, the Romantic idea of nature revitalized the theory of inspiration by assigning to poetry a living yet all-encompassing external source. Of course, it might be argued that the nature of the Romantics cannot support such an attribution either; hence Ruskin's analysis of the pathetic fallacy. But such an attribution is not, I think, inconsistent with the Romantic theory of inspiration, which indeed demands such transcendent categories of identity, whatever problems of credibility it may have posed in its own right.

28. See Foucault's related comments on the theory of ideology in *Power/Knowledge: Selected Interviews and Other Writings, 1972–77,* ed. Colin Gordon (New York: Pantheon, 1980), 118.

29. Robert Leigh Davis, *Whitman and the Romance of Medicine* (Berkeley: University of California Press, 1997). For a biographical approach to this material, see also Roy Morris, Jr., *The Better Angel: Walt Whitman in the Civil War* (New York: Oxford University Press, 2000).

Chapter 1: Sexual Hygiene: The Natural Gates and Alleys of the Body

1. Whitman moved from Brooklyn to Washington in late 1862 and regularly visited the army hospitals in and around the city from then through the end of the war and beyond. "Lew" is Lewis Brown, a friend of Sawyer as well as Whitman. For accounts of Whitman's life during the war, see Gay Wilson Allen, *The Soli-*

tary Singer: A Critical Biography of Walt Whitman (1955; rpt., Chicago: University of Chicago Press, 1985), 260–377; and Justin Kaplan, *Walt Whitman: A Life* (New York: Simon & Schuster, 1980), 270–328.

2. The failed pursuit of Sawyer forms one of the more poignant tales of unreciprocated love in Whitman's biography. See the previously cited letter of April 26, 1863, and Kaplan, *Walt Whitman: A Life*, 285–87.

3. Walt Whitman, *LG*, 324–25. Unless otherwise noted, subsequent citations of Whitman's poetry are from this edition.

4. Twice as many Civil War soldiers died of disease, or "fevers," as died of wounds — over four hundred thousand men. Among the chief culprits were typhoid, dysentery, malaria, tuberculosis, and pneumonia. Half of the six-volume *Medical and Surgical History of the War of Rebellion* (Washington, D.C.: GPO, 1879) is devoted to fevers.

The phrase "hectic red" derives from the opening section of Shelley's "Ode to the West Wind":

O wild West Wind, thou breath of Autumn's being,
Thou, from whose unseen presence the leaves dead
Are driven, like ghosts from an enchanter fleeing,

Yellow, and black, and pale, and hectic red,
Pestilence-stricken multitudes . . .
    (*SPP*, 221)

5. Henry James, "Mr. Walt Whitman," *The Nation*, November 16, 1865; rpt., *The American Essays of Henry James*, ed. Leon Edel (Princeton: Princeton University Press, 1989), 137, 136, 137.

6. M. H. Abrams, *The Mirror and the Lamp: Romantic Theory and the Critical Tradition* (New York: Oxford University Press, 1953), 189.

7. Whitman's use of martial language here in his love poetry clearly derives from the Petrarchan tradition. The relevance of that tradition to an understanding of the connection between sexuality and poetic agency in his poetry will be explicated in the next chapter.

8. The poem is printed in a section entitled "Poems Excluded from *Leaves of Grass*" in *LG* (613). For its publication history, see the editors' note (612).

9. It is worth noting that Whitman's dramatizations of sexual desire and activity are often attended by barrages of vocative O's. The 1855 version of "The Sleepers," for example, features an erotic dream sequence that begins: "O hot-cheeked and blushing! O foolish hectic! / O for pity's sake, no one must see me now! . . . my clothes were stolen while I was abed" (*LG* 1855, ll. 60–61). The evocation of sexual delirium in this passage relies in large part on the repeated O.

10. On Whitman's familiarity with the antebellum sexual hygiene movement, see Harold Aspiz, *Walt Whitman and the Body Beautiful* (Urbana: University of Illinois Press, 1980); Kaplan, *Walt Whitman: A Life*, 146–64; Michael Moon, *Disseminating Whitman*, 21–22; and David S. Reynolds, *Walt Whitman's America: A Cultural Biography* (New York: Knopf, 1995), 194–234.

11. On the shift in attitude toward sexuality in the 1830s, see Stephen Nissenbaum, *Sex, Diet and Debility in Jacksonian America: Sylvester Graham and Health Reform* (Westport, Conn.: Greenwood Press, 1980), 25–38.

12. On the growth of the sexual hygiene movement's medical and popular prestige, see Steven Seidman, *Romantic Longings: Love in America, 1830–1980* (New York: Routledge, 1991), 32–36; and Carroll Smith-Rosenberg, *Disorderly Conduct: Visions of Gender in Victorian America* (New York: Oxford University Press, 1985), 301–2, n. 23.

13. On Dixon, see Aspiz, *Whitman and the Body Beautiful*, 59–60; Moon, *Disseminating Whitman*, 22–23; and Martin Kaufman, "Edward H. Dixon and Medical Education in New York," *New York History* 51 (1970): 394–409. On Trall, see Aspiz, *Whitman and the Body Beautiful*, 44–46. On hydropathy, or the water cure, see Ronald G. Walters, *American Reformers, 1815–1860* (New York: Hill and Wang, 1978), 153–55; and Nissenbaum, *Sex, Diet and Debility*, 149–54. On the Fowlers, see Aspiz, *Whitman and the Body Beautiful*, 109–41; Madeleine Stern, *Heads and Headlines: The Phrenological Fowlers* (Norman: University of Oklahoma Press, 1971); and John Davies, *Phrenology, Fad and Science: A Nineteenth-Century Crusade* (New Haven: Yale University Press, 1955), 46–64. On their distribution of the 1855 edition of *Leaves of Grass*, see Kaplan, *Walt Whitman: A Life*, 198–99. It should be added that Whitman also admired a number of radical reformers—such as Robert Dale Owen and Frances Wright—whose views on sexuality were anathema to the sexual hygiene advocates. Whitman's father subscribed to Owen and Wright's *Free Inquirer* during Walt's youth. On their impact on Whitman, see Gay Wilson Allen, *The Solitary Singer: A Critical Biography of Walt Whitman*, rev. ed. (1967; rpt., Chicago: University of Chicago Press, 1985), 8, 29–30, 138–39.

14. On Whitman's reviews of health reform literature, see Aspiz, *Whitman and the Body Beautiful*, 60–61, 114–15; Thomas L. Brasher, *Whitman as Editor of the Brooklyn Daily Eagle* (Detroit: Wayne State University Press, 1970), 179–87; and Moon, *Disseminating Whitman*, 22. On his sale of such literature in his Brooklyn shop in the early '50s, see Aspiz, *Whitman and the Body Beautiful*, 115; and Kaplan, *Walt Whitman: A Life*, 161. On his contributions to the Fowler & Wells publication *Life Illustrated*, see Aspiz, *Whitman and the Body Beautiful*, 115. (These articles are collected in Walt Whitman, *New York Dissected*, ed. Emory Holloway and Ralph Adimari [New York: Rufus Rockwell Wilson, 1936)]. On his references to Lorenzo Fowler's phrenological examination in his reviews of *Leaves of Grass*, see Aspiz,

Whitman and the Body Beautiful, 126–27. Fowler's phrenological description of Whitman is printed in *Faint Clews and Indirections: Manuscripts of Walt Whitman and his Family,* ed. Clarence Gohdes and Rollo G. Silver (Durham: Duke University Press, 1949), 233–36. On Whitman's plans for a lecture series, see Aspiz, *Whitman and the Body Beautiful,* 50.

15. Thomas Laqueur, *Making Sex: Body and Gender from the Greeks to Freud* (Cambridge, Mass.: Harvard University Press, 1990), 228–29. Compare Ed Cohen's argument that Victorian anti-masturbation authors portrayed the onanist as "the embodiment of anti-social impulses" (*Talk on the Wilde Side* [New York: Routledge, 1993], 61); G. J. Barker-Benfield's view that "masturbation . . . expressed the desire for total sexual autonomy" (*The Horrors of the Half-Known Life: Male Attitudes Toward Women and Sexuality in Nineteenth-Century America* [New York: Harper and Row, 1976], 22–24); and Steven Seidman's assertion that as "a solitary act aimed at sensual gratification, masturbation violated the norms of proper sex" (*Romantic Longings,* 23).

16. The phrase "masturbation phobia" is Barker-Benfield's; see *Horrors,* 163–74.

17. Carroll Smith-Rosenberg, "Sex as Symbol in Victorian Purity: An Ethnohistorical Analysis of Jacksonian America," *American Journal of Sociology,* 84 suppl. (1978): S226–27. See also Vern L. Bullough and Martha Voght, "Homosexuality and Its Confusion with the 'Secret Sin' in Pre-Freudian America," in Vern L. Bullough, *Sex, Society, and History* (New York: Science History Publications, 1976), 112–24. It must be noted that Smith-Rosenberg's claim about the connection between masturbation and homosexuality is not intended as an explanation of the anti-masturbation phenomenon as a whole. The "code word" thesis is only one of several explanations she advances in her important essay.

18. Moon, *Disseminating Whitman,* 11.

19. Stephen Nissenbaum calls Graham's *Lecture* "the first important expression of a new fear of human sexuality that would become one of the trademarks of the later nineteenth century" (*Sex, Diet and Debility,* 4).

20. William A. Alcott, for example, clearly differentiates between them: While "solitary vice is more unnatural than social, that form of social vice called sodomy is equally unnatural; and if possible, still more revolting." Nevertheless, Alcott views the social vice of sodomy as less common, and therefore less threatening, than masturbation: "I would fain hope, this abomination is as yet but little known, or practised in this country, beyond our dungeons and prisons" (*The Physiology of Marriage* [Boston, 1866; rpt., New York: Arno Press, 1974], 68). Reformers could discuss homosexuality without mentioning masturbation at all. When Orson S. Fowler wrote about a murder supposedly motivated by homosexual love, he labeled it only as a case of perverted "amativeness"—the phrenological term for heterosexual love —and made no reference to onanism (*Creative and Sexual Science, or Manhood,*

Womanhood, and their Mutual Interrelations . . . [New York: Physical Culture Publishing, n.d. (1870)], 224–25).

21. Of course, certain writers did think that one way was *more* pernicious than the other. But they nevertheless thought *both* ways were pernicious, which means they did not think its solitary or group practice was what *made* masturbation pernicious. After commenting that masturbation was "so common . . . with boys, that it is more frequently performed in company than solitary," James C. Jackson goes on to argue that "strange as it may at first seem to the reader, this is one of the redeemingly active influences; for it is far better that all vice should be social than that it should be solitary" (*The Sexual Organism, and Its Healthful Management* [1861; rpt., New York: Arno Press, 1974], 60). At first glance this passage would seem to lend weight to Laqueur's claim that it was the asocial nature of masturbation that troubled reformers. (It certainly suggests that homosexuality was not Jackson's prime concern.) But the social character of male masturbation here is itself the consequence of the commonness of the "vice." According to Jackson, the fact that masturbation *is* so common partly explains the prevalence of disease in the general population. "Company" was at best a mitigating circumstance in individual cases; it was the symbol of an epidemic in the case of the social whole. The fact that Jackson considered masturbation an epidemic despite the mitigating circumstance that it was usually performed "in company" demonstrates that he did not condemn it because he thought it was asocial.

22. Cohen, *Talk on the Wilde Side*, 47.

23. Moon, *Disseminating Whitman*, 21.

24. Alcott, *Physiology*, 70.

25. See Nissenbaum, *Sex, Diet and Debility*, 117–18.

26. Ibid., 109; Smith-Rosenberg, "Sex as Symbol," S223; Graham, *LYM*, 25.

27. Smith-Rosenberg, "Sex as Symbol," S231, S218, S231; Cohen, *Talk on the Wilde Side*, 62; Moon, *Disseminating Whitman*, 25.

28. Smith-Rosenberg quotes the latter passage to support her previously cited argument that sexual hygiene authors "saw young men as a potentially despotic power." My point, of course, is that the passage demonstrates the opposite. However, by taking issue with Smith-Rosenberg and Laqueur I do not mean to question their general contention that sexual hygiene was a response to economic and social change in the period—a view also shared by Nissenbaum and Barker-Benfield. Specifically, I find Smith-Rosenberg's argument that hygiene writers were reacting against capitalism's erosion of the economic independence of farmers, merchants, and artisans entirely convincing. I am less convinced, however, by her apparent belief that these authors were more anxious about the Jacksonian youth's social autonomy than they were about his economic dependency.

29. R. N. Barr, "Spermatorrhoea," *The Ohio Medical and Surgical Journal* 7, no. 3 (1855): 174–75.

30. Fowler, *Creative and Sexual Science*, 52 (Fowler's emphasis).

31. [Samuel Gridley Howe], *On the Causes of Idiocy; Being the Supplement to a Report by Dr. S. G. Howe and the other Commissioners Appointed by the Governor of Massachusetts to Inquire into the Conditions of the Idiots of the Commonwealth, Dated February 26, 1848* (Edinburgh and London, 1848); quoted in William H. Parker, M.D., *The Science of Life; or Self-Preservation. A Medical Treatise on Nervous and Physical Disability, Spermatorrhoea, Impotence, and Sterility, with Practical Observations on the Treatment of Diseases of the Generative Organs* (Boston: Peabody, 1881), 138.

32. *Onania, or the heinous sin of self-pollution, and all its frightful consequences in both sexes considered* (1724), quoted in [Samuel A.] Tissot, M.D., *Treatise on the Diseases Produced by Onanism* (New York, 1832), 47 (my emphasis).

33. Roberts Bartholow, *Spermatorrhoea: Its Causes, Symptoms, Results and Treatment*, 4th rev. ed (New York: William Wood, 1879), 11–12 (my emphasis).

34. John Cowan, M.D., *The Science of a New Life* (1869; rpt., New York: Source Book Press, 1970), 99. On "amativeness," see Lorenzo Fowler, *The Principles of Phrenology and Physiology Applied to Man's Social Relations* (New York: Fowler, 1842), 10–18, and O. S. Fowler, *Amativeness*, rev. ed. (New York: Fowler and Wells, 1889), both reprinted in *Sex and Science: Phrenological Reflections on Sex and Marriage in Nineteenth-Century America* (New York: Arno Press, 1974).

35. Jackson, *The Sexual Organism*, 72.

36. On the evangelical origins of the sexual hygiene movement, see Walters, *American Reformers*, 21–38, 145–46.

37. [Andrew Jackson Davis], *Appetites and Passions: Their Origin, and How to Cast Them Out. A Lecture, by Andrew Jackson Davis, at Dodsworth Hall, N.Y., Sunday Morning, Jan. 25, 1863* (New York, n.d.), 4–5. On Davis, see Walters, *American Reformers*, 166–69. Analogies between desire and demonic possession are common among sexual hygiene writers as well. For examples, see Edward Dixon, *A Treatise on Diseases of the Sexual Organs: Adapted to Popular and Professional Reading, and the Exposition of Quackery, Professional and Otherwise* (New York, 1845), 235, 252; Howe, *Causes of Idiocy*, quoted in Parker, *Science of Life*, 141; and Graham, *A Lecture to Young Men*, 42.

38. Charles Rosenberg, *No Other Gods: On Science and American Social Thought* (Baltimore: Johns Hopkins University Press, 1976), 29. Thus, when medical historian H. Tristram Englehardt, Jr., writes that in the eighteenth and nineteenth centuries masturbation was held to be a "disease entity," he means not a *biological* entity but a "causal mechanism" by which a "heterogeneous set of signs and symptoms

was unified" ("The Disease of Masturbation: Values and the Concept of Disease," in *Sickness and Health in America: Readings in the History of Medicine and Public Health*, ed. Judith Walzer Leavitt and Ronald Numbers [Madison: University of Wisconsin Press, 1978], 15–16).

39. Nissenbaum, *Sex, Diet and Debility*, 4. See also Nissenbaum (140–73) on Graham's role in the formation of the sexual hygiene movement and his impact on later reformers.

40. Ibid., 132.

41. By the "functions of organic life" Graham means the involuntary functions of the digestive, pulmonary, and circulatory systems — "the various organs [that] preside over all the processes of vital chemistry" — as opposed to the functions of "animal life," which involve "the organs of sensation, perception, intellection, volition" and "the muscles of voluntary motion" (*LYM*, 15).

42. Cowan, *The Science of a New Life*, 98. After heredity (98), diet was "next in the list" of Cowan's "causes that conspire to a growth of licentiousness." On nineteenth-century views of heredity, see Rosenberg, *No Other Gods*, 25–53.

43. Rosenberg, *No Other Gods*, 27.

44. The idea that one could abstain from sensuality during conception may seem paradoxical to readers today, but there can be little doubt that many nineteenth-century sexual reformers envisioned something of this kind. As Nissenbaum points out, Graham extolled marriage largely because he thought "marital sex . . . was simply not as exciting as nonmarital sex" (*Sex, Diet and Debility*, 119). Sociologist Steven Seidman states the paradox bluntly, if perhaps unwittingly: "Victorian advice writers endorsed the importance of sex in marriage provided that it was moderate in frequency *and did not incite sensual desires*" (*Romantic Longings*, 26; my emphasis). However, some reformers retained an older view that linked the conception of healthy offspring to the amount of bodily energy, or heat, expended during intercourse. See, for example, Fowler, *Creative and Sexual Science*, 129. On the history of medical theories of conception, see Laqueur, *Making Sex*.

45. Jackson, *Sexual Organism*, 12.

46. Ibid., 10.

47. Dixon, *Treatise on Diseases of the Sexual Organs*, xi, quoting *Hamlet*, act 1, scene 5, lines 64–70. Dixon omits line 68 and misquotes line 69. For text and variants, see *Hamlet, Prince of Denmark*, ed. Philip Edwards (Cambridge: Cambridge University Press, 1985), 108. The "pure fountain of maternal love" is presumably the breast — a source from which offspring might literally "imbibe" a sexual taint, physicians and reformers believed, should the mother's diet, behavior, or feelings during lactation be less than temperate. See Rosenberg, *No Other Gods*, 28–29; Smith-Rosenberg, "Sex as Symbol."

48. M. Lallemand, *A Practical Treatise on the Causes, Symptoms, and Treatment of Spermatorrhoea,* ed. and trans. Henry J. McDougall, 3rd Amer. ed. (Philadelphia: Blanchard and Lea, 1858), 146.

49. Letter published in Homer Bostwick, *A Treatise on the Nature and Treatment of Seminal Diseases, Impotency, and Other Kindred Affections; with Practical Directions for the Management and Removal of the Cause Producing Them; Together with Hints to Young Men* (New York, 1848), 126; quoted in John S. Haller and Robin M. Haller, *The Physician and Sexuality in Victorian America* (New York: Norton, 1974), 222.

50. Jackson, *The Sexual Organism,* 77. This quotation merely voices the pervasive view of masturbation as involuntary that is implicit in descriptions of it as a disease and of its practitioner as its "victim."

51. According to Graham's formula, "the more it is yielded to, the more it is increased" (*LYM,* 30).

52. George R. Calhoun, *Report of the Consulting Surgeon on Spermatorrhoea, or Seminal Weakness, Impotence, the Vice of Onanism, Masturbation, or Self-abuse, and Other Diseases of the Sexual Organs* (Philadelphia: Howard Association, 1858), 3.

53. Thus Calhoun writes that "Onanism, or Self-Abuse, is, beyond all question, the most frequent and universal cause of Spermatorrhoea, Sexual Weakness, and Impotence of the genital organs," and that the "indulgence of the sexual passion, to *excess,* in the natural intercourse of the sexes, is also a fruitful cause" (*Spermatorrhoea,* 4, 7).

54. Lallemand, *Spermatorrhoea,* 160.

55. Marris Wilson, M.D., *On Diseases of the Vesiculæ Seminales: and Their Associated Organs. With Special Reference to the Morbid Secretions of the Prostatic and Urethral Mucous Membrane,* appended to Lallemand, *Spermatorrhoea,* 349.

56. Woodward, *Hints for the Young,* 22–23 (quoting from a letter addressed to him).

57. Ibid., 7.

58. Bartholow, *Spermatorrhoea,* 22.

59. Smith-Rosenberg, "Sex as Symbol," S230.

60. John Humphrey Noyes, *Male Continence* (Oneida: Office of the Oneida Circular, 1872), 7.

61. Ibid., 8–10. On Noyes and Graham, see Nissenbaum, *Sex, Diet and Debility,* 166.

62. Albert Hayes, *Science of Life* (Boston: Peabody Medical Institute, 1868), 146.

63. Lallemand writes of several such cases. Of one he reports that "he made a strong resolution to correct himself, but the habit had become so strong, that he often had recourse to it, unconsciously, during sleep" (*Spermatorrhoea,* 136).

Another case study concisely presents the conflict between a deteriorating will and an expanding automatism: "The habit at length overcame the will, and even took its place, provoking the same acts during sleep" (138).

64. Bartholow, *Spermatorrhoea*, 22.

65. Parker, *Science of Life*, 154. Cf. *LYM*, 20 (cited earlier), and Tissot, *Treatise on . . . Onanism*, 37.

66. Hayes, *Science of Life*, 153.

67. Woodward, *Hints to the Young*, 11; Alcott, *Physiology of Marriage*, 81; Tissot, *Treatise on . . . Onanism*, 18–19, 24. Tissot also identifies the masturbator's head with that of the penis when he cites the case of a patient whose "pupil was extraordinarily dilated" and whose eyes "abundantly" exuded a "whitish matter" (12). The equation of the sensualist's or onanist's body with an erect penis would appear to be a more spectacular version of the involuntary priapism, or "painful and long-continued erections of the penis" noted by various authors in the victim of excesses (Calhoun, *Spermatorrhoea*, 15).

68. Jackson, *Sexual Organism*, 145.

69. Dixon, *Treatise on Diseases*, 218.

70. Fowler, *Creative and Sexual Science*, 809 (on masturbation).

71. Calhoun, *Spermatorrhoea*, 13.

72. [Samuel Woodward], "Insanity, Produced by Masturbation" *Boston Medical and Surgical Journal* 12 (1835): 109. One historian has plausibly linked the notion of masturbatory insanity to the rise of the insane asylum in the eighteenth century, where doctors, actually observing masturbation among their patients, might have mistakenly assumed it was the cause of their insanity. See E. H. Hare, "Masturbatory Insanity: The History of An Idea," *Journal of Mental Science* 108 (1962): 12. Woodward was himself director of the Massachusetts Lunatic Asylum at Worcester when he published the essay cited earlier. See Nissenbaum, *Sex, Diet and Debility*, 121, n. 3.

73. Thomas Low Nichols, *Esoteric Anthropology*, rev. ed. (London: Nichols, n.d.), 286.

74. Woodward, *Hints to the Young*, 28.

75. Isaac Ray, *A Treatise on the Medical Jurisprudence of Insanity*, ed. Winfred Overholser (Cambridge, Mass.: Harvard University Press, 1962), 190, 143–44, 190, 145.

76. William Acton, *The Functions and Disorders of the Reproductive Organs in Childhood, Youth, Adult Age, and Advanced Life Considered in Their Physiological, Social, and Moral Relations* (London, 1871), 67, 65; Dixon, *Treatise on Diseases*, 244; Hayes, *Science of Life*, 152; Calhoun, *Spermatorrhoea*, 13; Fowler, *Creative and Sexual Science*, 346.

77. John Wiltbank, *Introductory Lecture for the Session, 1853–54* (Philadelphia: Edward Grattan, 1854), 7, quoted in Smith-Rosenberg, *Disorderly Conduct*, 183.

78. Thomas Laycock, *A Treatise on the Nervous Diseases of Women; Comprising an Inquiry into the Nature, Causes, and Treatment of Spinal and Hysterical Disorders* (London, 1840). Quoted in Mary Poovey, "'Scenes of an Indelicate Character': The Medical 'Treatment' of Victorian Women," *Representations* (special issue: *Sexuality and the Social Body in the Nineteenth Century*), 14 (Spring 1986): 146.

79. Stephen Tracy, *The Mother and Her Offspring* (New York, 1860), xv; quoted in Charles Rosenberg and Carroll Smith-Rosenberg, "The Female Animal: Medical and Biological Views of Women," in Rosenberg, *No Other Gods*, 55.

80. Marshall Hall, *Commentaries on Some of the More Important of the Diseases of Females* (London, 1827), 2; quoted in Rosenberg and Smith-Rosenberg, "Female Animal," 55. Cf. Haller and Haller: "The whole vasomotor system of the female was far more excitable than that of the male, marking her with a tendency to greater tension, irritability, and emotionalism. Laughing, crying, blushing, and quickened heart beat were all marks of her peculiar mental state. She was more prone to hysteria, hypnotism, trances, superstitions, as well as pity, sympathy and charity" (*Physician and Sexuality*, 73–74).

81. Rosenberg, *No Other Gods*, 76.

82. Acton, *Functions and Disorders*, 115; Dr. Robert Brundenell Carter, quoted in Poovey, "Scenes of an Indelicate Character," 163, n. 55; Fowler, *Creative and Sexual Science*, 123; Acton, *Functions*, 116, 117–19.

83. Bartholow, *Spermatorrhoea*, 44, 21–22.

84. Wilson, in Lallemand, *Spermatorrhoea*, 365, quoting from Hufeland, "Art of Prolonging Life"; Hayes, *Science of Life*, 179.

85. R. J. Culverwell, *Self-Preservation, Manhood, Causes of its Premature Decline . . .* (New York, 1830), 82, quoted in Rosenberg, *No Other Gods*, 82; Hayes, *Science of Life*, 176.

86. Cowan, *Science of a New Life*, 118. This argument was a staple of the literature. Compare the following: "With the progress of the habit the penis becomes relaxed, the erections feeble: the corpora cavernosa either atrophy, or their vessels lose their tonicity, whereby an apparent diminution in bulk takes place; the corpus spongiosum and the glans also shrink, so that the prepuce appears unnaturally elongated. The testes may increase in size, become tender and 'irritable,' or they may undergo a certain degree of atrophy; the latter is the more usual result" (Bartholow, *Spermatorrhoea*, 30–31). "The diminution of the size of the penis is one of the first and most obvious effects of this bad habit. The virile organ becomes shrunk to less than half its former outline" (Hayes, *Science of Life*, 180).

87. John B. Newman, *The Philosophy of Generation* (New York, 1849), 63, quoted

in Rosenberg, *No Other Gods,* 82. For a similar account of the absorption of the onanist's testicles into the abdomen, see Wilson, in Lallemand, *Spermatorrhoea,* 351.

88. Ambroise Paré, *On Monsters and Marvels,* trans. Janis L. Pallister (Chicago: University of Chicago Press, 1982), 31–32; quoted in Laqueur, *Making Sex,* 127.

89. Laqueur, *Making Sex,* 127; Gaspard Bauhin, *Theatrum anatomicum* (Basel, 1605), 181, quoted in Laqueur, 127.

90. Eve Kosofsky Sedgwick suggests another way of linking early-nineteenth-century views on masturbation with notions of homosexuality that emerged later in the century. "Among the sexual dimensions overridden within the past century by the world-historical homo/hetero cleavage is the one that discriminates, in the first place, the autoerotic and the alloerotic," Sedgwick writes. She speculates that this earlier system of categorization may well have given us in the masturbator "the proto-form of modern sexual identity itself." In her account, the solipsistic character of masturbation, as it was conceived in the period leading up to the creation of modern sexual identities, provided a model of *sexuality as identity* that facilitated the conceptualization of sexual identities as we now know them: "That it was this particular, apparently unitary and in some ways self-contained, autoerotic sexual identity that crystallized as the prototype *of* 'sexual identity' made that isolating embodiment of 'the sexual' easier" ("Jane Austen and the Masturbating Girl," in *Questions of Evidence: Proof, Practice, and Persuasion Across the Disciplines,* ed. James Chandler, Arnold I. Davidson, and Harry Harootunian [Chicago: University of Chicago Press, 1994], 112, 113, 123–24). Sedgwick's historical argument is predicated on her belief that masturbation was defined as a solipsistic deviation from the fundamentally social purpose of sexual activity — "the channeling of healthy desire back into itself," in Laqueur's words. It should now be evident, however, that male masturbation was *not* conceived as a "self-contained" activity in nineteenth-century America; on the contrary, it was viewed as both a symptom and an instance of the male self's *violation* by an agency external to it. Further, it is precisely this vision of male masturbation as an invasion of the body that links masturbation "phobia" to modern homophobia.

Chapter 2: Sexuality and Poetic Agency

1. See, for example, Harold Bloom, "The Real Me," *New York Review of Books,* April 26, 1984, 3–7.

2. Calvin Beach, review in the New York *Saturday Press,* May 19, 1860, quoted in Gay Wilson Allen, *The Solitary Singer: A Critical Biography* (Chicago: University

of Chicago Press, 1985), 261; D. H. Lawrence, *Studies in Classic American Literature* (1923; rpt., New York: Penguin Books, 1977), 172, 176; M. Jimmie Killingsworth, *Whitman's Poetry of the Body* (Chapel Hill: University of North Carolina Press, 1989), 117–18.

3. Betsy Erkkila, *Whitman the Political Poet* (New York: Oxford University Press, 1989), 106. Cf. David S. Reynolds, *Walt Whitman's America* (New York: Knopf, 1995), 200; Harold Aspiz, "Walt Whitman: The Spermatic Imagination," *American Literature* 56, no. 3 (October 1984): 379–95.

4. Some Whitman critics have singled out Orson Fowler as particularly akin to Whitman in his celebration of sexuality and have contrasted both writers to a supposedly more puritanical hygienic norm. "Like Whitman," writes M. Jimmie Killingsworth, "Orson Fowler . . . celebrated sexual energy and fulfillment" (*Whitman's Poetry of the Body*, 55). David S. Reynolds states that "with Fowler as with Whitman, all organs and acts connected with sex were holy" (*Walt Whitman's America*, 210). Both critics also attribute Whitman's separation from Fowlers and Wells to Orson Fowler's own departure from the firm. But this reading of Fowler is misleading. As Stephen Nissenbaum has demonstrated, in Whitman's time radical and conservative authors on sexuality shared the same view of sexual physiology; indeed, many so-called free-lovers were also followers of Graham. Fowler himself, who was a major publisher and distributor of sexual hygiene literature, drew eagerly on Graham. His book *Amativeness* typically warned of the medical dangers not only of masturbation but also of promiscuity and marital excess. (See Stephen Nissenbaum, *Sex, Diet and Debility in Jacksonian America: Sylvester Graham and Health Reform* [Westport, Conn.: Greenwood Press, 1980], 140–54.) In short, Fowler was part of the hygienic mainstream, not a dissenter from it. His reverence for the reproductive instinct motivated him to seek ways to regulate and protect it, not to liberate it from regulation. If Whitman's views on sexuality differed from those of the moral reformers, it was not because of Fowler's influence.

5. "Spontaneous Me" first appeared in the second edition of *Leaves of Grass* (1856). The related passages from "Song of Myself" and "The Sleepers" (discussed later) appeared in the first edition of 1855.

6. See Robert K. Martin, *The Homosexual Tradition in American Poetry* (Austin: University of Texas Press, 1979), 27.

7. Ibid., 17.

8. This link has been recognized in different ways by previous critics, most notably Martin (*Homosexual Tradition*, 19–21) and Michael Moon (*Disseminating Whitman: Revision and Corporeality in "Leaves of Grass"* [Cambridge, Mass.: Harvard University Press, 1991], 38–47).

9. In this connection, note Moon's reading of various metaphors for writing in this passage (*Disseminating Whitman*, 46–47) as well as one detail Moon omits: the presence of the word "pen" in "pendant" (l. 215).

10. I therefore disagree with Martin when he claims that the line describes "a fantasy of mass fellatio" and asserts that "the woman disappears completely from the poem" in the final stanza, presumably because she has been replaced by the poet, for whom she previously provided cover (*Homosexual Tradition*, 20–21). Such a reading cannot fully account for Whitman's use of the word "pendant," which can describe a woman's breasts. Nor do I agree entirely with Moon's more nuanced revision of Martin's reading, according to which the twenty-ninth bather, in the course of the passage, becomes "neither determinately male or female" by merging with but not into the speaker (*Disseminating Whitman*, 43). Both readings overstate the subordination of the woman's sexual presence to that of the speaker as a result of misconstruing the scene described in the final stanza. While it is certainly true, as both critics argue, that the woman serves as a vehicle for Whitman's own sexual desires, and while it is also true, as Moon contends, that Whitman's use of the female figure for this purpose does not prevent him from allowing her a good deal of erotic force in her own right—*as a woman*—it is also a fact that she remains not only present but graphically—which is to say *anatomically—female* throughout the passage. Indeed, she is never more so than in the final stanza. In other words, this isn't so much poetic transvestism or androgyny as it is poetic transsexuality. (I recognize, however, that the sexual act performed in the passage is more debatable than is the sex of the performer. That is to say, one could accept that the twenty-ninth bather remains very much a female presence throughout the passage and still view the sexual act she performs as oral, not genital, sex. While I *don't* view it this way, I also don't think this view would greatly affect my reading.)

11. Consider the following passage by Noyes:

The effects of nervous exaltation may be good as well as evil. Herein the spiritual view is perhaps a little different from the medical. A degree of excitement which would injure a sick man may be harmless and even invigorating to the healthy. . . . We must not seek examples of nervous phenomena exclusively among the weaklings of debauchery, as writers on sexual pathology generally do. Human nature certainly does not reach its normal condition till it is the temple of the Holy Spirit, filled with all the fullness of God. A nervous system in that condition can bear a weight, not only of suffering but of glory, which would destroy ordinary health. Paul's philosophy teaches that even the Lord's Supper, received unworthily, may work damnation, thus causing physical weakness and death. (See I Cor. XI: 29, 30.) The ultimate way to escape nervous injury will be found, not in the direction of abstinence from excitement, but in the toning of the nervous system to the divine standard of health by fellowship with resurrection-life. (*Male Continence* [Oneida: Office of the Oneida Circular, 1872], 20–21)

12. Albert Hayes, *Science of Life* (Boston: Peabody Medical Institute, 1888), 151; Roberts Bartholow, *Spermatorrhoea: Its Causes, Symptoms, Results and Treatment*, 4th rev. ed. (New York: William Wood, 1879), 49.

13. William Acton, *The Functions and Disorders of the Reproductive Organs* (London, 1871), 75 (quoting Ritchie, *An Inquiry into a Frequent Cause of Insanity in Young Men*), 69 (quoting Rousseau, *Confessions*), 75 (quoting Ritchie), 65. For the Rousseau passage, see Jean-Jacques Rousseau, *Oeuvres Complètes*, ed. Bernard Gagnebin and Marcel Raymond (Paris: Bibliothèque de la Pléiade, 1959), 1:115. The connection between language and sexual desire in Rousseau's *Confessions* has, of course, been central to deconstructive discussions of language — about which Acton seems oddly prescient despite his condemnation of those aspects of Rousseau that deconstruction arguably celebrates. See *OG*, 141–64; Paul de Man, *Allegories of Reading: Figural Language in Rousseau, Nietzsche, Rilke, and Proust* (New Haven: Yale University Press, 1979), 278–301. Acton's analysis differs from Derrida's in connecting masturbation to Rousseau's inept *speech*. According to Derrida's reading of the *Confessions*, it is writing, as a supplement to Rousseau's ineptitude in spoken intercourse, that most resembles masturbation — itself a supplement for sexual intercourse. (As Derrida explains, Rousseau applies the word "supplement" to both writing and masturbation.) It is also worth noting that Acton's interest in Rousseau's tendency to "stammer words without ideas [balbutier . . . des paroles sans idées]" anticipates, in its own peculiar fashion, the centrality of "the moment of dispossession in favor of the arbitrary power play of the signifier," in Paul de Man's account of Rousseauian — and, indeed, all — *textuality* (*Allegories of Reading*, 296).

14. M. Lallemand, *A Practical Treatise on the Causes, Symptoms, and Treatment of Spermatorrhoea*, ed. and trans. Henry J. McDougall, 3rd Amer. ed. (Philadelphia: Blanchard and Lea, 1858), 189.

15. What follows in this section is a brief exploration of the poetic resources on which Whitman may have drawn, directly or indirectly, in fashioning his view of the relations among male sexual desire, male homosexuality, and poetic agency. It is not intended to be an exhaustive survey; such a literary history would require several volumes. Nor is it meant to delineate a heretofore unrecognized homosexual tradition in European poetry. My subject is the resources available for a male homosexual poetics in a poetic tradition that is not only *apparently* but, for the most part, *actually* heterosexual. Finally, my choice of examples has been driven as much by

their exemplarity — by which I mean their embodiment of widely influential poetic ideas, figures, and principles pertinent to Whitman — as it has been by historical evidence, such as it is, of Whitman's actual reading. Nevertheless, Whitman's familiarity with several of the examples I cite is all but certain and his knowledge of the others is, in my view at least, highly probable. (For evidence on this last point, see the remaining notes in this section.)

16. I emphasize the word *possible* to make clear that I am *not* claiming traditional personifications of love are *necessarily* homoerotic in intention or effect. Rather, my point is that the poetic tradition's treatment of Cupid constitutes a potential resource for poets seeking to delineate a male homosexual poetics despite his central role in the poetic depiction of heterosexual desire.

17. Christopher Marlowe, "Elegia I," ll. 5–34, *All Ovids Elegies,* in *The Complete Works of Christopher Marlowe,* ed. Roma Gill (Oxford: Clarendon Press, 1987), 1:13–14. I have modernized Marlowe's spelling and punctuation.

18. For evidence that Whitman read Marlowe's translation of Ovid, compare these lines from Marlowe's translation of the first elegy

> With muse upreared I meant to sing of arms,
> Choosing a subject fit for fierce alarms.
>
> .   .   .   .
>
> When in this work's first verse I trode aloft,
> Love slacked my muse, and made my numbers soft.

to the following epigram Whitman wrote to introduce *Drum-Taps* in 1871:

> Aroused and angry,
> I'd thought to beat the alarum, and urge relentless war;
> But soon my fingers fail'd me, my face droop'd, and I resign'd myself,
> To sit by the wounded and soothe them, or silently watch the dead.
>   (*V,* 3:630)

Whitman later incorporated these lines into "The Wound-Dresser." I have been unable to discover whether Whitman read Marlowe's version of Ovid before 1871. For evidence that he did read some Marlowe very early, see his epigraph from Marlowe in his 1842 newspaper obituary for the poet McDonald Clarke, reprinted in *Walt Whitman of the New York "Aurora": Editor at Twenty-Two,* ed. Joseph Jay Rubin and Charles H. Brown (Westport, Conn.: Greenwood Press, 1972), 105.

19. That is, Cupid's intervention traditionally coincides with the poet's first encounter with his or her beloved instead of preceding it: "In all this the poetic cart, so to say, is put before the amatory horse. Propertius and Tibullus had been moved to write poetry by love. Ovid is peremptorily drafted by Cupid into the ranks of the

elegists; on protesting that he has nothing (i.e. nobody) to write about, he is told that Cupid can soon see to that" (E. J. Kenney, "Introduction" to Ovid, *The Love Poems*, trans. A. D. Melville [New York: Oxford University Press, 1990], xiv). This comment puts into perspective the complaints cited at the beginning of this chapter about the generic quality of the female lovers in Whitman's poetry. The subordination of the particular beloved to love itself, whether personified or not, has a long poetic history. Indeed, from classical love elegy to Renaissance sonnet, the beloved has almost always been an idealized "nobody." My source for Ovid's Latin is *Amores*, ed. E. J. Kenney (Oxford: Oxford University Press, 1961).

20. This is perhaps even more obvious in the Latin, where what is "slacked" (weakened) is the speaker's *nervos*—a word here meaning muscles but with strong phallic overtones. Compare *Amores* 3:7, a poem entirely devoted to the subject of sexual impotence: "quid vetat et *nervos* magicas torpere per artes?"; in Marlowe, "Why might not then my *sinews* be enchanted?" I am indebted to Ann Cumming here and elsewhere for her expertise in Latin literature.

21. Compare Ovid's less suggestive Latin: "Arma gravi violentaque bella parabam / edere"; literally, "I was preparing to tell of arms and violent wars in solemn meter" (dactyllic hexameter, the proper epic meter, instead of elegaic couplets, the traditional meter of Roman love elegy and that of the *Amores*).

22. Petrarch was, of course, steeped in Ovid. See Robert Durling's introduction to *Petrarch's Lyric Poems: The "Rime Sparse" and Other Lyrics*, trans. and ed. Robert M. Durling (Cambridge, Mass.: Harvard University Press, 1976), 26–33. For a different approach to the connection between Whitman and the Petrarchan tradition, see Roland Greene, *Post-Petrarchism: Origins and Innovations of the Western Lyric Sequence* (Princeton: Princeton University Press, 1991), 133–52. As Greene points out (138), Whitman refers to Petrarch in some notes on his reading; whether he actually read Petrarch or merely read about him is unclear. (For Whitman's notes, see *NUPM*, 5:1864.) The evidence of his poetry, however, suggests a fairly detailed knowledge of Petrarchan conventions, if not of their originator. In fact, it is hard to believe that as avid a reader of Shakespeare as Whitman could fail to absorb those conventions, if only in mock-Petrarchan form.

23. This paragraph summarizes the argument of Nancy J. Vickers in her influential essay "Diana Described: Scattered Woman and Scattered Rhyme," in *Writing and Sexual Difference*, ed. Elizabeth Abel (Chicago: University of Chicago Press, 1982), 95–109.

24. Sir Philip Sidney, *Astrophil and Stella*, sonnet 20; in *Sir Philip Sidney*, ed. Katherine Duncan-Jones (Oxford: Oxford University Press, 1989), 160–61.

25. Of course, in theory the psychoanalytic reading of Petrarchism is capable of accommodating this personification of Love as male; after all, castration anxiety

centrally involves the father as well as the mother. As we shall see, the biggest problem with this approach to Petrarchism is not the way it genders the psychic threat posed by sexual desire (Vickers demonstrates that female characters can pose the same risks Cupid does) but rather its assumption that the unity of the self is paramount to Petrarchan poetics.

26. Vickers' claim that "if the speaker's 'self' (his text, his 'corpus') is to be unified, it would seem to require the repetition of [his beloved's] dismembered image" ("Diana Described," 102) thus identifies the poet's self and his poetry overhastily. The modern origin of this view of the Petrarchan lyric as an exercise in preserving oneself by fetishistically worshiping another appears to be John Freccero's landmark essay "The Fig Tree and the Laurel: Petrarch's Poetics" (*diacritics* 5, no.1 [1975]: 34–40). "The fundamental strategy of the *Canzoniere*," Freccero writes, is "the *thematics* of idolatry transformed into the *poetics* of presence" (40).

27. *Astrophil and Stella*, sonnet 90 (201). Compare, among others, sonnet 28, where love is again identified as the source of poetic agency: "I, in pure simplicity, / Breathe out the flames which burn within my heart, / Love only reading unto me this art" (ll. 12–14).

28. *Petrarch's Lyric Poems*, 73, ll. 1–15. The translation is my own, as are those of the subsequent passages I quote from Petrarch. For Petrarch's Italian, see *Petrarch's Lyric Poems*, 169.

29. It is worth noting that the poem (no. 73) whose opening stanza I quoted is precisely the kind Vickers has in mind when she writes about Petrarch's self-defensive fragmentation of Laura's body: it is the last in a series of three *canzoni* entirely devoted to the praise of Laura's eyes.

30. "Anzi mi struggo al suon de le parole" (l. 14); literally, "Instead I melt in the sound of the words."

31. According to Durling, "Since Petrarch did not have the apostrophe as part of his punctuation, but simply ran elided words together, there was for him hardly any orthographic distinction between *Laura* and *l'aura* (breeze) . . ." (introduction to *Petrarch's Lyric Poems*, 27).

32. See M. H. Abrams, "The Correspondent Breeze: A Romantic Metaphor," in his *The Correspondent Breeze: Essays on English Romanticism* (New York: Norton, 1984), 33–39.

33. Sonnet 133, my translation. For the Italian, see Durling, *Petrarch's Lyric Poems*, 271.

34. Sonnet 194, ll. 1–4, my translation. Ibid., 341.

35. For a survey of homoerotic connotations in seventeenth-century devotional poetry, see Rick Rambuss, "Pleasure and Devotion: The Body of Jesus and Seven-

teenth-Century Religious Lyric," in *Queering the Renaissance,* ed. Jonathan Gold-berg (Durham: Duke University Press, 1994), 253–79.

36. John Donne, *Holy Sonnets,* 10; in *John Donne,* ed. John Carey (Oxford: Oxford University Press, 1990).

37. Donne's is not the only nor the most direct reinvention of Petrarchan con-ventions for devotional purposes in the period. The sixteenth-century mystic Saint Teresa of Avila records a rather Petrarchan vision of a small seraph piercing her heart repeatedly with an arrow. This vision occasioned Richard's Crashaw's verse fantasy of being similarly pierced by *her* in his poem "The Flaming Heart" (*English Seventeenth-Century Verse,* vol. 1, ed. Louis L. Martz [New York: Norton, 1963], 278–81). For an attempt to read Crashaw's poem as homoerotic, see Rambuss, "Pleasure and Devotion," 269–71.

38. Of course, these are not mutually exclusive possibilities (Ovid and Petrarch employ both ideas), nor are they always easy to distinguish. My point is simply that, unlike the poetry of Petrarch or Sidney, that of the Romantics is not exclusively nor even largely amatory in focus (though they do, of course, write love poetry). As a result, the idea of love as a direct source of inspiration plays a relatively minor role in their work. But this only makes all the more striking the figurative uses to which they *do* put sexuality, even in the absence of an overtly amatory theme. Whereas the amatory tradition from at least Ovid to the Renaissance sonneteers and elegists tends to posit a *genetic* connection between desire and poetic creation, the Romantics posit a relation of *similarity.*

39. On Whitman's knowledge of Shelley, see Floyd Stovall, *The Foreground of "Leaves of Grass"* (Charlottesville: University of Virginia Press, 1974), 243–48. As Stovall notes (244), Whitman's copy of Shelley's *Works* is now housed in the library at Bryn Mawr College; Shelley's prose writings on poetics are heavily marked. On Whitman's debt to Romantic concepts of inspiration, see Kaplan, *Walt Whitman: A Life* (New York: Simon & Schuster, 1980), 189. Byron may be an exception to the consensus I am outlining here by way of Shelley. His satirical opening to the third canto of *Don Juan* — "Hail Muse! *et caetera*" — suggests that he may view the notion of inspiration merely as a convention to be travestied (*Don Juan,* ed. Leslie Marchand [Boston: Houghton Mifflin, 1958], act 3, scene i, line 1). But this atti-tude may only apply to more conventional personifications of inspiration; as Abrams has noted, elsewhere Byron seems to participate in the Romantic view of nature — specifically the wind — as a catalyst of poetic creation ("Correspondent Breeze," 31).

40. Shelley probably found the seeds of this view of the poet in Wordsworth's 1800 "Preface to *Lyrical Ballads*": "Poems to which any value can be attached, were never produced . . . but by a man . . . of more than usual organic sensibility." "What

is a poet? . . . He is a man . . . endued with more lively sensibility, more enthusiasm and tenderness . . . and a more comprehensive soul, than are supposed to be common among mankind" (*Selected Poems and Prefaces,* ed. with an introd. by Jack Stillinger [Boston: Houghton Mifflin, 1965], 448, 453). The same idea turns up repeatedly in Emerson, perhaps most notably in his early lecture "The Poet and the Times," which Whitman attended in New York in 1842: "Him the circumstance of life dazzles and overpowers whilst it passes, because he is so delicate a meter of every influence" (*The Early Lectures of Ralph Waldo Emerson,* 3 vols., ed. Robert E. Spiller and Wallace E. Williams [Cambridge, Mass.: Harvard University Press, 1972], 3:358).

41. Steven Marcus notes another, perhaps related, connection between Romantic portrayals of the poet and medical ones of the masturbator. Citing Acton's description of the antisocial tendencies of the victim of masturbatory insanity, Marcus writes that "it might be difficult to find a more apt or prettier description of the romantic artist: the Ancient Mariner, the poet of 'Alastor,' Endymion, any one of Byron's early heroes fit this bill of particulars. This hardly indicates that these characters masturbated themselves into insanity; it does serve to show, however, how in a single culture one set of descriptive terms is forced into the service of representing a variety of states, in this case, extreme states of mental alienation" (*The Other Victorians: A Study of Sexuality and Pornography in Mid-Nineteenth Century England,* 2nd ed. [New York: Basic Books, 1974], 21). Marcus is correct in urging caution since similar descriptions may have different explanations. Nevertheless, the language Shelley uses to describe the poet's sensitivity — in particular, his use of the term "organization" — is drawn from the vocabulary of the biological sciences of his period. Drawing on the same vocabulary, for example, Graham uses the terms "organization" and "constitution" interchangeably. In other words, Shelley is invoking an emerging scientific discourse on nervous sensitivity to describe the nature of poetic inspiration. (Little wonder, considering that Shelley's vegetarian polemic *A Vindication of Natural Diet* [1813] anticipates Graham's major preoccupations by over twenty years, according to Nissenbaum [*Sex, Diet and Debility,* 46–49].) When Shelley wrote the *Defense* (1821), this scientific discourse on the nervous system already included sexuality in its domain: Tissot's *Treatise on the Diseases Caused by Onanism* (1758) is largely devoted to the effect of sex on the nervous system. Within a few years of the publication of the *Defense,* it would also include the poet, whose delicate organization is diagnosed by Lallemand (1836) as a nervous disorder with potentially dangerous sexual consequences. Later in the nineteenth century, in the work of Krafft-Ebing, this discourse provided the foundation for the medical definition of male homosexuality (see D. A. Miller, *The Novel and the Police* [Berkeley: University of California Press, 1988], 154, n. 6); at the same time, with the unin-

tentional assistance of Romantic poetics, it paved the way for the distinctly modern association of poetry with male homosexuality and effeminacy.

42. I have elided an important phrase: "This power arises from within" (504). In doing so, I am deliberately dodging the issue of whether the *Defense* conceives of inspiration as descending upon the poet from without or arising from within. Abrams cites this passage as evidence of an emerging, naturalistic view of inspiration, according to which "an inspired poem or painting is sudden, effortless, and complete, not because it is a gift from without, but because it grows of itself, in a region of the mind which is inaccessible either to awareness or control" (*The Mirror and the Lamp*, 192). As Abrams also notes, however, the *Defense* is inconsistent on this point, elsewhere echoing the ancient theory of divine visitations. Nor, I think, are the two accounts entirely incompatible, as they appear in Shelley, considering that his main analogy for the naturalistic, or organic, theory of poetic invention — embryonic growth — assumes some form of fertilization from without (*SPP*, 504).

43. The exception to the hygienic aversion to all forms of rapture is Noyes, whose views on sexuality, while parallel to Graham's in some respects — for example, on the issue of male orgasm — were antagonistic to the principles of orthodox moral reform on most issues. While Shelley's Romantic morality is the reverse of Graham's, both nevertheless trace the moral corruption of their time to the same socioeconomic forces: industrialization and the rise of the market economy. (See also Wordsworth's "Preface to *Lyrical Ballads*" in *Selected Poems and Prefaces*, 448.) The difference is that while Graham sees the market as undermining individual independence — a process he translates into bodily debilitation — Shelley sees it as elevating the selfish principle at the expense of sympathy and community. Put another way, Graham fears the workingman's loss of autonomy, whereas Shelley fears the rise of an economy fueled solely by competition. These social concerns are not in themselves contradictory, but the solutions to them envisioned by Graham and Shelley are.

44. It also appears to be at the heart of the mid-century transformation of French poetry principally enacted by Whitman's contemporary, Charles Baudelaire. For a brilliant reading of the artist as prostitute in Baudelaire (one that anticipates my own reading of Whitman), see Leo Bersani, *The Culture of Redemption* (Cambridge, Mass.: Harvard University Press, 1990), 63–86. To my knowledge, Bersani is the only critic of nineteenth-century poetry — or, indeed, any poetry — who addresses the relations between sexuality and poetic agency in ways comparable to those I am proposing here. That he should do so in a discussion of Baudelaire, Whitman's French counterpart in the historical shift from Romantic to Modern, is particularly striking. (I read Bersani's book after having already formulated a version

of this argument in my dissertation.) Whereas Whitman, in my account, sees the penetration-inspiration analogy as enabling him to present male homosexuality as a mark of poetic vocation, Baudelaire, in Bersani's account, sees the prostitution-inspiration analogy as suggesting that the artist is by nature androgynous: "The Baudelairian artist — as well as the Baudelairian lover[—]are androgynous not because they share so-called masculine and feminine features, but rather because the very notion of combining features is superseded by a sense of the comparative irrelevance of how movement toward self-erasure is directed. . . . In aspiring to a state of completeness, creatures . . . reach toward the ultimate difference-from-themselves that is self-effacement" (70).

45. See M. H. Abrams, "Structure and Style in the Greater Romantic Lyric," in *The Correspondent Breeze*, 76–108. On Whitman's early knowledge of Coleridge's work, see Stovall, *The Foreground of "Leaves of Grass"*, 110–12. Whitman reviewed the *Biographia Literaria* as a newspaper editor. On the basis of this review, Stovall plausibly speculates that Whitman knew Coleridge's poetry more intimately than he did his prose.

46. Samuel Taylor Coleridge, "The Eolian Harp," ll. 1–43, in *Poetical Works*, 100–102. The poem is addressed to Coleridge's bride, Sarah Fricker Coleridge, and was written during their honeymoon.

47. On the topos of the wind harp, see Abrams, *The Correspondent Breeze*, 25–43. Shelley uses it in the second paragraph of his *Defense* (480); Wordsworth in Book 1 of *The Prelude;* and Coleridge (again) in "Dejection: An Ode." For American examples see Ralph Waldo Emerson's "May-Day" and "Maiden Speech of the Æolian Harp" in *Collected Poems and Translations*, ed. Harold Bloom and Paul Kane (New York: Library of America, 1994), 131–48, 228–29; and Henry David Thoreau's "Rumors from an Aeolian Harp" in *Collected Poems of Henry Thoreau*, ed. Carl Bode (Chicago: Packard, 1943), 53.

48. According to Mary Jacobus, "Representation only begins at the point where Eolianism — the fiction of unmediated expression — is eschewed. . . . [T]hinking can only begin where the monuments and arbitrary signs of language take over from sound (pure voice or breath) and speech (pure presence). In any event, it is clear that writing, the permanent record of thought, involves both the muting of voice — a kind of deafness — and the death of presence" ("Apostrophe and Lyric Voice in *The Prelude*," in *Lyric Poetry: Beyond New Criticism*, ed. Patricia Parker and Tilottama Rajan [Ithaca: Cornell University Press, 1985], 177–78).

49. On invocation, see Jonathan Culler, "Apostrophe," in his *The Pursuit of Signs: Semiotics, Literature, Deconstruction* (Ithaca: Cornell University Press, 1981), 135–54. Here he argues that "the poet makes himself a poetic presence through an image of voice, and nothing figures voice better than the pure *O* of undifferenti-

ated voicing" (142), adding that "the apostrophic postulation of addressees refers one to the transforming and animating activity of the poetic voice. The 'you' is a projection of that voice" (148). As forms of personification, apostrophe and invocation have been major preoccupations for deconstructive Romanticists. The locus classicus is the work of Paul de Man. See the following essays: "Hypogram and Inscription" in *The Resistance to Theory*, ed. Wlad Godzich (Minneapolis: University of Minneapolis Press, 1986), 27–53; "Autobiography as De-Facement" (67–82) and "Wordsworth and the Victorians" (83–92), both in his *The Rhetoric of Romanticism* (New York: Columbia University Press, 1984).

50. Thus, Anne Mellor cites the poem as an example of "the male poet's attempt to usurp female procreative power" (*Romanticism and Gender* [New York: Routledge, 1993], 20).

51. See note 48.

52. Shelley, "Ode to the West Wind," ll. 53–54, in *SPP*, 223. Other obvious examples include Keats' "Ode to a Nightingale" and Whitman's "As I Ebb'd with the Ocean of Life."

53. In fact, recent work on rape in Romanticism generally seems to focus on the figure of the poet as a kind of rapist. See, for example, Nancy A. Jones, "The Rape of the Rural Muse: Wordsworth's 'The Solitary Reaper' as a Version of Pastourelle" (263–77), and Froma I. Zeitlin, "On Ravishing Urns: Keats in His Tradition" (278–302), both in *Rape and Representation*, ed. Lynn A. Higgins and Brenda R. Silver (New York: Columbia University Press, 1991).

54. "Instinct and Inspiration," in *The Complete Works of Ralph Waldo Emerson*, vol. 12, *Natural History of the Intellect and Other Papers*, ed. Edward W. Emerson (Boston: Houghton Mifflin, 1904), 86, 77.

55. Wordsworth, "Preface to *Lyrical Ballads*," in *Selected Poems and Prefaces*, 448–49. Compare Shelley's *Defense*, cited earlier, and Emerson: "The whole art of man has been an art of excitation" ("Instinct and Inspiration," 69). Wordsworth's distaste for the literature of "gross and violent stimulation"—"frantic [i.e., Gothic] novels, sickly and stupid German Tragedies, and deluges of idle and extravagant stories in verse" ("Preface," 449)—anticipates Graham's invective against stimulating foods. Further, both authors blame the same broad social changes for the problem. For example, Wordsworth complains of "the increasing accumulation of men in cities, where the uniformity of their occupations produces a craving for extraordinary incident." Nevertheless, there is an essential difference here. Wordsworth eschews "gross and violent stimulants" in favor of more gentle ones because he believes this approach will ultimately *increase* the capacity for excitement in his reader, whereas the popular alternatives merely produce "savage torpor." Graham and his followers, on the other hand, shun *all* forms of excitement, gentle and vio-

lent, on the grounds that nervous stimulation of any kind inexorably leads to debility. For them, therefore, there could be no significant difference between the popular literature Wordsworth attacks and his own: both threaten to debilitate the reader.

56. Moon interprets this passage as describing the soul reaching to hold the speaker's beard and feet from *on top of him:* "What is clearly figured here is the . . . reaching by the top figure to hold the head ('beard') and feet of the recumbent one" (*Disseminating Whitman*, 48). Perhaps this reading results from his assumption that the scene is a purely sexual one. Thus, he never even discusses the fact that the speaker's sexual partner happens to be his *soul* and belittles previous efforts to take account of this fact. In any case, it seems clear enough that the speaker's soul reaches to hold his beard and feet from *within* him, that is, that it *fills* his body.

57. The scholarship relating to Emerson's influence on Whitman — and the impact of "The Poet" in particular — is considerable. On the textual evidence, see Stovall, *The Foreground of "Leaves of Grass,"* 282–305.

58. Stovall notes this echo of Emerson's essay, along with a host of others, in the last chapter of his study (301). However, he underestimates the importance of the parallel for understanding the passage in Whitman.

59. In Poem 315 ("He fumbles at your Soul") Emily Dickinson rewrites the same passage in Emerson's essay in a way that also combines poetic and erotic possession:

> He fumbles at your Soul
> As Players at the Keys
> Before they drop full Music on —
> He stuns you by degrees —
> Prepares your brittle Nature
> For the *Ethereal Blow*
> By fainter Hammers — further heard —
> Then nearer — Then so slow
> Your breath has time to straighten —
> Your Brain — to bubble Cool —
> Deals — One — imperial — Thunderbolt —
> That scalps your naked Soul —
>
> When Winds take Forests in their Paws —
> The Universe — is still —

(*The Complete Poems of Emily Dickinson*, ed. Thomas H. Johnson [Boston: Little, Brown, 1955], 148; my emphasis.) Compare Dickinson's "Ethereal Blow" to Emerson's "ethereal tides." Dickinson's conceit here turns on her pun on blow: the blow that "He" strikes upon the keys of the speaker's soul is also a breath of inspiration that "He" *blows* into her.

60. "The Poet and the Times," *The Early Lectures of Ralph Waldo Emerson*, 3 vols., ed. Robert E. Spiller and Wallace E. Williams (Cambridge, Mass.: Harvard University Press, 1972), 3:361; my emphasis.

61. Whitman's brief but enthusiastic notice, which gives the title of Emerson's lecture as "Poetry and the Times," can be found in *Walt Whitman of the New York "Aurora"*, 105.

62. On the circumstances of the book's composition, see the editor's note in *EPF*, 124–26.

63. On the temperance movement, see Nissenbaum, *Sex, Diet and Debility*, 69–85, and Ian Tyrrell, *Sobering Up: From Temperance to Prohibition in Antebellum America, 1800–1860* (Westport, Conn.: Greenwood Press, 1979). According to Nissenbaum, Graham began his speaking career as a temperance lecturer, as did other sexual hygiene advocates. Many of the hygiene authors discussed in chapter 1 also wrote temperance tracts; and the hygiene tracts themselves, of course, generally eschewed all consumption of alcohol.

64. For a reading of *Franklin Evans* in which the content of Evans' dream vision plays a prominent role, see Michael Warner, "Whitman Drunk," in *Breaking Bounds: Whitman and American Cultural Studies*, ed. Betsy Erkkila and Jay Grossman (New York: Oxford University Press, 1996), 30–43.

65. Coleridge, *Poetical Works*, 195–96.

66. Of course, one may want to read passages where Evans, under the influence, compares himself to "a ship upon the ocean without her mainmast" (*EPF*, 213), or where he explains how drinking "darkened . . . all his powers of penetration" (206) in light of Whitman's later conversion of the hygiene movement's feminized onanist into the male homosexual bard. These readings are crude, but no more so than Whitman's novel. For a fine interpretation of another Whitman temperance narrative, "The Child and the Profligate," in relation to his later treatment of sexuality, see Moon, *Disseminating Whitman*, 26–36.

67. Whitman's remarks to Traubel continue as follows: "In three days of constant work I finished the book. Finished the book? I finished myself. It was damned rot — rot of the worst sort — not insincere perhaps, but rot nevertheless."

68. See John Addington Symonds, "A Problem in Greek Ethics," in John Addington Symonds and Havelock Ellis, *Sexual Inversion* (1897; rpt., New York: Arno Press, 1975). According to David Halperin, Symonds originally composed this essay in 1873 (*One Hundred Years of Homosexuality and Other Essays on Greek Love* [New

York: Routledge, 1990], 154, n. 12). For Symonds' treatment of the issue with respect to Whitman, see his *Walt Whitman: A Study* (London: Routledge, n.d.), 85–100.

69. According to Lorenzo Fowler, "adhesiveness" is the phrenological term for friendship and other social "attachments not founded upon the generative instinct." It describes "the disposition of adhering to, remaining with and embracing the object of affection without regard to sex" (*The Principles of Phrenology and Physiology*, in *Sex and Science*, 29). Whitman uses the term to describe specifically male-male affection. For an example of the pledge against masturbation, see the "life-boat resolution" in Orson Fowler's *Amativeness* (in *Sex and Science*, 50).

70. All emphasis and capitalization in the passages quoted from this notebook, here and elsewhere, are Whitman's own. For a detailed account of the different color inks, the underlinings and double-underlinings, and other forms of emphasis that Whitman employs in this notebook — most of them impossible to reproduce in print — see the textual notes in *NUPM*, 2:886–90. Part of the manuscript is reproduced in black and white in *NUPM*, vol. 3, following page 1100.

71. See *NUPM*, 2:889, n. 65.

72. *Whitman's Manuscripts, "Leaves of Grass" (1860): A Parallel Text*, edited with an introduction by Fredson Bowers (Chicago: University of Chicago Press, 1955), 114. I have quoted the manuscript version of the poem simply for aesthetic reasons. In lineating the manuscript version, where line breaks are hard to determine, I have followed the published text and the pattern of capitalization in the manuscript. (Capital letters usually indicate of a new line in Whitman's text.) The words in brackets are canceled in the manuscript but restored in the published version. Whitman's "Calamus" cluster was introduced, with "Children of Adam" (whose composition it preceded), in the 1860 edition of *Leaves of Grass*. Its purpose, as Whitman states in the poem that introduces the cluster, is "to celebrate the need of comrades" ("In Paths Untrodden," l. 19).

73. Ecclesiastical in origin, this formula is taken up by British criminal law in Sir Edward Coke's *Third Part of the Institutes of the Laws of England* (1797). For more on the subject, see Ed Cohen, *Talk on the Wilde Side* (New York: Routledge, 1993), 103–25.

74. For traditional interpretations of this passage as an experience of mystical unity, see Malcolm Cowley's introduction to *LG* 1855, where he cites the passage as an example of "a rapt feeling of union or identity with God (or the Soul . . .)" (xii); and James E. Miller, Jr., who argues that the passage exhibits an "intimate fusion of the physical and the spiritual" in which "body and soul become one" (*A Critical Guide to "Leaves of Grass"* [Chicago: University of Chicago Press, 1957], 10). This reading has persisted in more recent criticism. For example, Martin writes that the passage displays "a new knowledge of the unity and interrelatedness of all

life" (*The Homosexual Tradition*, 18); Paul Zweig concludes that it constitutes an "illuminated moment when Whitman's 'twoness' dissolves in an act of love" (*Walt Whitman: The Making of the Poet* [New York: Basic Books, 1984], 252); and Betsy Erkkila that it "revis[es] the traditional debate between body and soul by integrating them" (*Whitman the Political Poet*, 97). My own reading is closer to that of Allen Grossman, who argues that the passage represents a "sexual union reconstructed as a moment of primal communication" in which the "Whitmanian voice" becomes "uncanny—a servant to persons, but not itself personal" ("The Poetics of Union in Whitman and Lincoln: An Inquiry toward the Relationship of Art and Policy," in *The American Renaissance Reconsidered*, ed. Walter Benn Michaels and Donald Pease [Baltimore: Johns Hopkins University Press, 1985], 195).

75. The book, eventually published in 1875 as *Memoranda During the War*, is in fact largely devoted to the hospitals. Material from *Memoranda During the War* was later incorporated into *Specimen Days & Collect* (1882). See *PW*, 1:viii.

76. See also Whitman's letters dated March 6, 1863, to his brother Thomas Jefferson Whitman (*C*, 1:76–77), and October 11, 1863, to Abby H. Price (161–64), as well as the letter dated April 15, 1863, to his mother (89), which is cited in the next chapter.

77. Here I am in agreement with Eve Kosofsky Sedgwick, who writes that "Whitman's unrelenting emphasis . . . on *incarnating* a phallic erethism . . . had a double effect. Put schematically, rather than having a phallus, he enacted one. Seeming at first to invite a naively celebratory, male-exalting afflatus of phallic worship, the deeper glamour of this pose lay in the drama . . . of being like a woman, since to have to enact rather than possess a phallus is (in this system) a feminine condition" (*Between Men: English Literature and Male Homosocial Desire* [New York: Columbia University Press, 1985], 204). Although schematic, these remarks substantially anticipate my own reading of the relation between Whitman's phallic and "feminine" modes.

78. Clara Barrus, *Whitman and Burroughs, Comrades* (1931; rpt., Port Washington, N.Y.: Kennikat Press, 1968), 339. The phrase comes from Burroughs' journal entry of January 28, 1903. Burroughs was one of Whitman's closest friends during and after the war. Compare this statement with the following remarks by Burroughs: "With all his rank masculinity, there was a curious feminine undertone in him which revealed itself in the quality of his voice, the delicate texture of his skin, the gentleness of his touch and ways, the attraction he had for children and the common people. A lady in the West, writing to me about him, spoke of his 'great mother-nature'" (*Walt Whitman: A Study* [1896; rpt., New York: AMS Press, 1969], 49). For a roughly contemporaneous study that interprets Whitman's supposed femininity as evidence of sexual perversion, see W. C. Rivers, "Whitman's

Femininity," in his *Walt Whitman's Anomaly* (London: George Allen, 1913), 20–33. For a rejoinder to Rivers from an important early partisan of both Whitman and "sex-inversion," see Edward Carpenter, *Some Friends of Walt Whitman: A Study in Sex-Psychology,* The British Society for the Study of Sex Psychology, 13 (London: Athenæum Press, 1924), 13–16.

79. Compare Emily Dickinson, poem 258 ("There's a certain slant of light"): "Heavenly hurt, it gives us— / We can find no scar, / But internal difference / Where the Meanings, are—" (*The Complete Poems of Emily Dickinson,* 118, ll. 5–8). Consider also Oliver Wendell Holmes' comparison of inspiration to "vascular and nervous excitement" in "Exotics" and to "a bullet in the forehead" in *The Autocrat at the Breakfast Table* (1857), both quoted in G. Ferris Cronkhite, "Some Varieties of Inspiration," in *Aspects of American Poetry: Essays Presented to Howard Mumford Jones,* ed. Richard M. Ludwig (Columbus: Ohio State University Press, 1962), 3–60. Cronkhite's essay remains a helpful survey of American views on inspiration from Emerson to Hart Crane—with the unfortunate exception of Dickinson.

80. Erkkila, *Whitman the Political Poet,* 145. For Erkkila's more recent modification of this position, see her essay "Whitman and the Homosexual Republic," in *Walt Whitman: The Centennial Essays,* ed. Ed Folsom (Iowa City: University of Iowa Press, 1994), 153–71. Erkkila's sublimation argument goes back at least to Gay Wilson Allen: "Whitman's erotic impulses made him feel alienated. . . . [H]e fantasized solutions to his personal problems; hence his cult of 'Calamus' (or 'manly love'), which he sublimated into universal brotherhood, and his role as 'the poet of democracy'" (*The New Walt Whitman Handbook* [1975; rpt., New York: New York University Press, 1986], 58).

81. Martin, "Whitman and the Politics of Identity," *Walt Whitman: The Centennial Essays,* 179–80.

82. Emerson, "Poetry and Imagination," *The Complete Works of Ralph Waldo Emerson,* vol. 8, *Letters and Social Aims,* 72.

83. Harold Aspiz, "Walt Whitman: The Spermatic Economy," *American Literature* 56, no. 3 (1984), 384.

84. I have in mind, in particular, Aspiz's reading of "Song of Myself," section 28:

Sexual experts, it will be recalled, generally held that the loss of semen would result in debility and mental derangement unless sufficient semen has been conserved to maintain physical and mental well-being. When one has learned to retain semen during sexual union, according to Dr. Stockman, "in the course of an hour the physical tension subsides, the spiritual exhilaration increases, and not uncommonly visions of transcendent life are seen and consciousness of new powers experienced." Apparently, the "prurient provokers" who threaten to rob the "udder" of the Whitman persona's heart of its "withheld drip" have failed; he has retained enough semen . . . to "super-think." Perhaps the persona was only fantasizing the sensations of sexual ecstasy while conserving the flower of his blood in order to conjure up these "full-sized" and "golden" visions. ("The Spermatic Imagination," 387)

85. The main theoretical rallying point for this project (though by no means the only one) has been the work of Judith Butler. See, for example, "Critically Queer," in her *BTM*, 223–42. I discuss this project, and Butler's place in it, more fully in chapter 4.

86. Moon, *Disseminating Whitman*, 145, 110, 150, 156. Moon makes these two arguments about two different editions (1856 and 1860) of *Leaves of Grass*. For a summary of Moon's argument and a critique somewhat different in emphasis from the one I pursue here, see my "Whitman and His Doubles: Division and Union in *Leaves of Grass* and Its Critics," *American Literary History* 6, no. 1 (1994): 119–39.

87. Moon's effort at ideological exculpation is relatively supple. Another option for critics sharing his overall agenda is simply to *deny* that the poetry exhibits any sexual violence or subordination. This route has been taken recently by two readers of "Song of Myself." In his book *Whitman's Poetry of the Body* M. Jimmie Killingsworth argues that the passivity of the speaker in section 5 when his soul plunges its tongue into his heart "might suggest that the poet wished to purge aggression from his sexual ideal" (40). It seems not to occur to Killingsworth that the speaker's apparent eagerness to have something plunged through his breastbone into his heart suggests otherwise. There is a reason, however, that Whitman refers in another poem to his "savage soul's volition" ("Not Heaving from my Ribb'd Breast Only," l. 5). Christopher Newfield undertakes a similar sanitization of section 28, in which the speaker is apparently raped by a "red marauder": "Whitman does *not* link intersubjectivity to servility. . . . To take only one well-known example, the seduction sequence of stanza 28 of 'Song of Myself' concludes in the next stanza in an erotic 'reception' that lacks compensatory aggression. . . . The sodomized narrator is not subordinated by the act, as he shows by experiencing enough equality with the penetrator to assume his vulnerability and ask about his mood" ("Democracy and Male Homoeroticism," *Yale Journal of Criticism* 6, no. 2 [1993]: 44). Newfield refers here to the rhetorical question "Did it make you ache so, leaving me?" (l. 643). Evidently he thinks this is Whitman's way of asking "How was it for you?" But this is hardly enough to erase the significance of the rape-and-pillage conceit that dominates the major portion of the passage (which Newfield wisely neglects to quote).

88. On this general point Moon and I are in complete agreement. For references to contrary views, see note 3 in this chapter.

Chapter 3: Masses and Muses

1. Michael Moon, *Disseminating Whitman* (Cambridge, Mass.: Harvard University Press, 1991), 14, 11; my emphasis. Compare this to David S. Reynolds' more openly traditional view of the work of art as something that assimilates the culture of its time only to transcend it. See his *Beneath the American Renaissance: The Subversive Imagination in the Age of Emerson and Melville* (Cambridge, Mass.: Harvard University Press, 1989), 563–67.

2. Betsy Erkkila, *Whitman the Political Poet* (New York: Oxford University Press, 1989), 10, 188.

3. M. Jimmie Killingsworth, "Tropes of Selfhood: Whitman's 'Expressive Individualism,'" *The Continuing Presence of Walt Whitman: The Life After the Life,* ed. Robert K. Martin (Iowa City: University of Iowa Press, 1992), 51.

4. "*Leaves of Grass:* A Volume of Poems Just Published," Brooklyn *Daily Times,* September 29, 1855; rpt., *LG,* 777.

5. I have chosen the original version not only out of preference but also because it includes the opening lines quoted later. The passage here quoted differs substantially in only one line from the final version. In 1867 Whitman removed the potentially incendiary reference to the Eucharist (l. 174) and replaced it with what is, for him, a relatively neutral one: "When I can touch the body of books by night or by day, and when they touch my body back again." How Whitman thought masons could procreate in their overalls must remain a mystery. For his revisions of the passage, see *V,* 1:98.

6. Whitman probably inherited his skepticism about the Eucharist from his Quaker mother and her family. (Quakers reject the rite altogether.) Nevertheless, the contrast between it and the reproductive powers of its bakers appears to have been shocking enough for Whitman — who doubtless intended to shock initially — to suppress the line in later editions of *Leaves of Grass.* It is worth noting that Emerson left the Unitarian ministry in 1832 because he found the rite a "painful impediment" to devotion: "To eat bread is one thing; to love the precepts of Christ and resolve to obey them is quite another" ("The Lord's Supper," *EL,* 1137).

7. Abraham Lincoln, "The Repeal of the Missouri Compromise and the Propriety of its Restoration: Speech at Peoria, Illinois, in reply to Senator Douglas, October 16, 1854," *Abraham Lincoln: His Speeches and Writings,* ed. Roy P. Basler (New York: Da Capo Press, 1990), 313. Lincoln was still a Whig at the time he gave this speech. The views he expresses, however, are entirely consistent with the platform of the Republican party, which he joined before the presidential election of 1856.

8. William M. French, ed., *Life, Speeches, State Papers, and Public Services of Gov. Oliver P. Morton* (Cincinnati, 1866), 88–89; *Annual Message of Alexander W.*

Randall, Governor of the State of Wisconsin, and Accompanying Documents (Madison, 1860), 24. Both are quoted in Eric Foner, *Free Soil, Free Labor, Free Men: The Ideology of the Republican Party Before the Civil War* (New York: Oxford University Press, 1970), 57. On the Kansas-Nebraska Act, see James M. McPherson, *Battle Cry of Freedom: The Civil War Era* (New York: Oxford University Press, 1988), 121–29.

9. See Gay Wilson Allen, *The Solitary Singer: A Critical Biography of Walt Whitman* (Chicago: University of Chicago Press, 1985), 89–91 (on Whitman's support of the Wilmot Proviso and his dismissal from the Brooklyn Daily *Eagle*) and 102–3 (on his editorship of the *Freeman*).

10. Lincoln, "Agriculture: Annual Address before the Wisconsin State Agricultural Society, at Milwaukee, Wisconsin, September 30, 1859," *Speeches and Writings,* 502.

11. Horace Greeley, *Hints Toward Reforms* (New York: Harper and Bros., 1850), 354.

12. Lincoln, *Speeches and Writings,* 307, 313.

13. Jean-Jacques Rousseau, *The Social Contract,* chapter 15: "On Deputies or Representatives," *Rousseau's Political Writings,* ed. Alan Ritter and Julia C. Bondanella, trans. Bondanella (New York: Norton, 1988), 143–44.

14. *Narrative of the Life of Frederick Douglass, an American Slave, Written by Himself,* edited with an introduction by Houston A. Baker, Jr. (New York: Penguin, 1982), 56–57. In *Uncle Tom's Cabin* (1852) Stowe makes the same link between slaves and politicians through the character of "black Sam": "Black Sam, as he was commonly called, from his being about three shades blacker than any other son of ebony on the place, was revolving the matter [of Tom's sale] profoundly in all its phases and bearings, with a comprehensiveness of vision and a strict lookout to his own personal well-being, that would have done credit to any white patriot in Washington" (*Uncle Tom's Cabin or, Life among the Lowly,* edited with an introduction by Ann Douglas [New York: Penguin, 1981], 95–97; see also 135–40).

15. Stowe, *Uncle Tom's Cabin,* 43.

16. Douglass makes the same point, albeit in a more ominous tone, in his fictionalized account of the successful slave rebellion aboard the *Creole* in 1841, which was led by a man named Madison Washington: "In the short time he had been on board," the first mate says of Washington after the mutiny, "he had secured the confidence of every officer. . . . His manners and bearing were such, that no one could suspect him of a murderous purpose. The only feeling with which we regarded him was, that he was a powerful, good-disposed negro" ("The Heroic Slave" [1853] in *The Oxford Frederick Douglass Reader,* ed. William L. Andrews [New York: Oxford University Press, 1996], 160). But it is Melville, in *Benito Cereno* (1856), who makes this point most ominously.

17. *The Federalist Papers,* edited with an introduction by Garry Wills (New York: Bantam, 1982), 46–48.

18. Thus, Madison responded to criticisms of the Constitution's stipulation that only nine of the thirteen states need ratify it by implying that ratification by all thirteen state legislatures, as mandated by the Articles of Confederation, would be less democratic than his scheme for ratification by extragovernmental state conventions, since the latter would allow the people themselves to decide: "In one particular it is admitted that the [Constitutional] Convention have departed from the tenor of their commission. Instead of reporting a plan requiring the confirmation *of the Legislatures of all the States,* they have reported a plan which is to be confirmed by the *people,* and may be carried into effect by *nine States only"* (*Federalist* No. 40, 199; Madison's emphasis). On the significance of this passage for the Federalist view of representation, see Bruce Ackerman, *We the People,* vol. 1, *Foundations* (Cambridge, Mass.: Harvard University Press, 1991), 178.

19. See McPherson, *Battle Cry,* 47–145.

20. By contrast, in *Walden* Thoreau castigates the very same class of people for their *servility,* which he sees as born of economic dependency. Further, he lists voting as one example of the artisanal class's slavish behavior:

> It is very evident what mean and sneaking lives many of you live, for my sight has been whetted by experience; always on the limits, trying to get into business and trying to get out of debt, a very ancient slough, called by the Latins *æs alienum,* another's brass, for some of their coins were made of brass; still living, and dying, and buried by this other's brass; always promising to pay, promising to pay, to-morrow, and dying to-day, insolvent; seeking to curry favor, to get custom, by how many modes, only not state-prison offences; lying, flattering, voting, contracting yourselves into a nutshell of civility, or dilating into an atmosphere of thin and vaporous generosity, that you may persuade your neighbor to let you make his shoes, or his hat, or his coat, or his carriage, or import his groceries for him. . . . I sometimes wonder that we can be so frivolous, I may almost say, as to attend to the gross but somewhat foreign form of servitude called Negro Slavery, there are so many keen and subtle masters that enslave both north and south. (*W,* 4).

21. Again, compare Emerson:

> It is easy to see that every man represents a new and perfect style of oratory, and each, if he speak long enough, and the matter is important enough to show his genius, will actually come to the verge of good deliverance; — comes so near that the professional poet or orator begins to feel himself quite superfluous: —

What need of the deputy, when here the principal can state his own case? But neither of the speakers quite hits it, and none does, of thousands and thousands; and in a nation, the one or two who do best, are separated by a whole length from all the rest. And this in the expression of right and wrong respecting their own affairs. An obscure old instinct revives in the beholder, that this man who does what the beholder had panted in vain to do, or said what he was bursting to speak, is himself, himself with some advantages, — and he begins to love him as himself. ("The Poet and the Times," *The Early Lectures of Ralph Waldo Emerson,* ed. Robert E. Spiller and Wallace E. Williams [Cambridge, Mass.: Harvard University Press, 1972], 3:355)

22. *Early Lectures of Ralph Waldo Emerson,* 3:356–57.

23. Emerson's view of poets as a new nobility bears comparison to the eighteenth-century idea of a natural aristocracy — an idea Madison probably has in mind in the *Federalist* No. 10 when he writes of "a chosen body of citizens, whose wisdom may best discern the true interest of their country, and whose patriotism and love of justice will be least likely to sacrifice it to temporary and partial considerations."

24. Emerson, *Letters and Social Aims,* 274–75, paraphrasing Socrates in Plato's *Phaedrus,* 245a: "If any man come to the gates poetry without the madness of the Muses, persuaded that skill alone will make him a good poet, then shall he and his works of sanity with him be brought to nought by the poetry of madness, and behold, their place is nowhere to be found" (trans. R. Hackforth, in Plato, *The Collected Dialogues,* ed. Edith Hamilton and Huntington Cairns [Princeton: Princeton University Press, 1961], 492).

25. Erkkila, for example, writes that this passage "undoes traditional hierarchies by presenting each person as part of a seemingly indiscriminate mass" (*Whitman the Political Poet,* 88). Kerry Larson sees it as evidence of an "additive appetite [that] names whatever it sees" (*Whitman's Drama of Consensus* [Chicago: University of Chicago Press, 1988], 126). M. Wynn Thomas describes it as imputing "to American society the unity in diversity Whitman believed characterized the natural order" (*The Lunar Light of Whitman's Poetry* [Cambridge, Mass.: Harvard University Press, 1987], 84).

26. I therefore disagree with Philip Fisher's important reading of Whitman as an exponent of a purely "cellular" form of national identity, according to which the identity of the group would merely be a function of the formal equivalence of its component parts — individual, familial, local, regional, and so on. In my reading, such formal equivalences only tell half the story. The other half has to do, in part, with making those equivalences *recognizable* to the people involved as a foundation for the identity of a People. For Whitman this is the work of poetic representation,

whose very function as a means of unification, and *not* of individuation, differentiates it and its practitioners from the components thus united. See Philip Fisher, "Democratic Social Space: Whitman, Melville, and the Promise of American Transparency," *Representations* 24 (Fall 1988): 60–101.

27. Most recent interpretations of Whitman's politics agree that *Leaves of Grass* was largely conceived to fill the role of a literature of national unity during a time of deepening sectional crisis. This much seems beyond debate. Where my account differs is in arguing that Whitman's view of poetry as a form of *representation* — akin to the kind called for by Madison but ultimately more authentic — is the key to his vision of it as a power for national unity. Others studies, by contrast, have argued either that Whitman's poetics is essentially *anti*representational (Erkkila, *Whitman the Political Poet;* Thomas, *The Lunar Light of Whitman's Poetry*) or — what amounts to the same thing — that it seeks to replace a flawed system of political union with a "consensual framework" that can achieve national unanimity (Larson, *Whitman's Drama of Consensus,* xiv). Both these arguments portray Whitman opposing representation in favor of some more radical means of national unification. For the essay that ignited recent interest in Whitman's Unionism, see Allen Grossman, "The Poetics of Union in Whitman and Lincoln: An Inquiry Toward the Relationship of Art and Policy," in *The American Renaissance Reconsidered,* ed. Walter Benn Michaels and Donald Pease (Baltimore: Johns Hopkins University Press, 1985).

28. For a contrary view of Whitman's poetic treatment of Lincoln — one that draws on psychoanalysis — see Vivian R. Pollack, "Whitman Unperturbed: The Civil War and After," *Walt Whitman: The Centennial Essays,* ed. Ed Folsom (Iowa City: University of Iowa Press, 1994), 30–47.

29. In Lincoln's "First Inaugural Address, March 4, 1861," one reads:

No State, upon its own mere motion, can lawfully get out of the Union . . . *resolves* and *ordinances* to that effect are legally void, and . . . acts of violence, within any State or States, against the authority of the United States, are insurrectionary or revolutionary, according to circumstances.

I therefore consider that in view of the Constitution and the laws, the Union is unbroken; and to the extent of my ability I shall take care, as the Constitution itself expressly enjoins upon me, that the laws of the Union be faithfully executed in all the States. . . . I trust this will not be regarded as a menace, but only as the declared purpose of the Union that it will constitutionally defend and maintain itself. (*Speeches and Writings,* 582–83)

30. By contrast, when he wrote "The Eighteenth Presidency!" in 1856, Whitman appears not to have had a party. Nominally a tract in support of John C. Frémont,

the Republican candidate for president, it mentions him almost as an afterthought in a short paragraph headed "To Fremont, of New York" and makes no direct endorsement of his candidacy, instead choosing to offer him some rather stern advice: "Whenever the day comes for him to appear, the man who shall be the Redeemer President of These States . . . is not to be exclusive, but inclusive" (*NUPM*, 6:2133). As many scholars have noted, Whitman's portrait of the ideal president, earlier in his manifesto, as a plain workingman descending on the capital from the West resembles Lincoln—about whom Whitman knew little in 1856—more than it does Frémont.

31. See Allen, *Solitary Singer*, 282–331.

32. Quoted in B. L. Rayner, *The Life of Thomas Jefferson* (Boston: Lilly, Wait, Colman and Holdin, 1834), 356.

33. The sketch names the battle as "White Oaks Church," which is interpreted by the editor of the notebooks to be that of White Oak Swamp (see the headnote to "Scene in the Woods," *NUPM*, 2:651). On the Seven Days' Battles, see McPherson, *Battle Cry of Freedom*, 464–71.

34. *The Works of Virgil*, trans. Davidson (London: Henry Bohn, 1867), 196–97. I am grateful to Jeffrey Knapp for pointing out the relevance of the Roman custom to my reading of Whitman's poem, and to Ann Cumming for guiding me to this example of it. Other echoes of the *Aeneid* in "A March" include the "crowd of bloody forms," which is reminiscent of Virgil's description of dead souls in the underworld in Book 6. Whitman owned a two-volume edition of the Davidson translation, published in New York in 1857; it is now in the Oscar Lion Collection at the New York Public Library. The first flyleaf bears the following inscription in Whitman's hand, followed by his initials: "Had this volume with me in N.Y.—Washington—and in Canada—1862 to 1889—(the edge-stains are from breaking a bottle of Virginia wine in a trunk with it on a journey during the war there)" (*Walt Whitman and the Civil War*, ed. Charles I. Glicksberg [1933; rpt., New York: A.S. Barnes, 1963], 83).

35. Thus, even the most astute of recent studies on Whitman's politics mistakes "the departure of such coveted abstractions as Democracy, Personality, Love, or Union" in the poems we are considering for evidence of "*Drum-Taps'* confused flight from advocacy" (Larson, *Whitman's Drama of Consensus*, 222). Unlike Larson's book, which attempts to read Whitman's politics as "an evolving drama integral to the poem's design" (xvi), other recent studies of Whitman's politics have mostly stuck to the "coveted abstractions."

36. For a more detailed reading of the relationship between these two poems— and what that relationship says about the one between writing and the body in Whitman's work as a whole—see my "Whitman's 'Strange Hand': Body as Text in *Drum-Taps*," *ELH* 58 (Winter 1991): 935–55.

37. William Wordsworth, *The Prelude: 1799, 1805, 1850,* ed. Jonathan Words-worth, M. H. Abrams, and Stephen Gill (New York: Norton, 1979), 1:1. My text is the 1850 version. Whitman read, clipped, and annotated a review of *The Prelude* in 1851, along with three other articles on Wordsworth (see Stovall, *Foreground of "Leaves of Grass,"* 238–41). While Whitman generally denied the influence of English poets, it seems probable that he read *The Prelude.*

38. I am grateful to Michael Fried for alerting me to the effect of this phrase.

39. This image also occurs in Whitman's prose memoirs of the war. For example, it turns up in "A Night Battle, Over a Week Since"—one of the best war pieces in *Specimen Days*—where he laments "the red life-blood oozing out from head or trunks or limbs upon that green and dew-cool grass" (*PW,* 1:46). In "Unnamed Remains the Bravest Soldier," the essay that immediately follows, he describes the typical battlefield death as follows: "Likely the typic one of them (standing, no doubt for hundreds, thousands,) crawls aside to some bush-clump, or ferny tuft, on re-ceiving his death-shot—there sheltering a little while, soaking roots, grass and soil with red blood." (*PW,* 1:49).

40. Whitman's hospital notebooks were often composed of wove paper whose mesh texture, designed to approximate that of cloth, could have reminded him of the dressings used in the hospitals. One fragment of a draft of "The Wound-Dresser" survives in a notebook with this kind of paper. For a description of the paper, see *NUPM,* 2:603; for the draft lines, see 610.

41. On the conflicting aspects of the literary imperative to *see* in the great prose descendant of *Drum-Taps,* Crane's *Red Badge of Courage,* see Michael Fried, *Real-ism, Writing, Disfiguration: On Thomas Eakins and Stephen Crane* (Chicago: Uni-versity of Chicago Press, 1987), 93–161. On the politics of this imperative in Crane's works, see Walter Benn Michaels, "Colored Lines" (forthcoming, *The Cambridge Literary History of America*).

42. As Edmund S. Morgan and Bruce Ackerman have both pointed out, invoking the presence of the People has always been an essential part of the rhetoric of politi-cal representation. See Ackerman, *We the People,* vol. 1, *Foundations,* 184; Morgan, *Inventing the People: The Rise of Popular Sovereignty in England and America* (New York: Norton, 1988). Both books have strongly influenced my views on political representation and its relation to literary representation in the United States. For an important discussion of this relationship in revolutionary France, one that has also influenced my own argument, see Susan Maslan, "Resisting Representation: Theater and Democracy in Revolutionary France," *Representations* 52 (Fall 1995): 27–52.

43. Timothy Sweet has argued that "in *Drum-Taps* Whitman attempts to make sense out of the violence of war . . . by . . . detach[ing] wounds and deaths from the

body (often, without explicitly acknowledging them) and attach[ing] them to the discourse of the state. The topoi deny that violence is meaningless; this denial requires that the individual body disappear into ideology" (*Traces of War: Poetry, Photography, and the Crisis of the Union* [Baltimore: Johns Hopkins University Press, 1990], 15). It should be evident by now that I disagree strongly with this view, as any sensitive reader of "The Wound-Dresser" and similar poems in *Drum-Taps* inevitably must. It is hard to imagine how Whitman could have done more than he does to make the injuries of the war present to the reader. If the almost unbearable profusion of injuries in "The Wound-Dresser" is not enough for Sweet, what would be? One suspects that Sweet's real animus is not against Whitman so much as it is against the inevitable difference between language and its referents. What Sweet disapproves of is not *how* Whitman represents the wounded, but the fact that he *represents* them instead of somehow *presenting* them. But even this doesn't do justice to Sweet's argument, for even if Whitman *were* somehow able to make the wounded present, they would certainly not say, as Sweet does, that the violence of the war was "meaningless." In this account, the imputation of meaning to violence is always misrepresentation; but, of course, if the violence *were* meaningless — that is, if it were perceived by its participants as meaningless — then there would have been no *reason* for its instigation. The truth is that meaning is not something that is *added to* acts of war after the fact; meaning is internal to the acts themselves and to the people who engage in them. The imputation of meaning to war's violence — Sweet's most basic charge against Whitman — cannot in itself be a misrepresentation of war. This is not to say, however, that Whitman doesn't turn the injuries he represents in his poems to his own uses; again, it is hard to imagine a writer doing otherwise. It is a mistake, however, to assume that doing so necessarily involves denying the reality of injury or the pain of its victims. In fact, it is by forcefully evoking these realities that Whitman succeeds in presenting himself as an embodiment of the injured.

44. I am not the first reader to notice this fact. See Kaplan, *Walt Whitman: A Life*, 265, and Larson, *Whitman's Drama*, 221.

45. Whitman either read, or had read to him, at least the first book of Rousseau's *Social Contract*. (See his detailed notes on it in *NUPM*, 5:1845–46.) He was therefore familiar with Rousseau's definition of the general will (Book 1, Chapter 6), though not necessarily with his denunciation of political representation (Book 3, Chapter 15).

46. See Fried, *Realism, Writing, Disfiguration*, for a masterful discussion of this issue. I should add that the possibility that the reader's awareness of the writer's language *as language* will be heightened by efforts to annul it increases greatly when that effort is thematized openly, as it sometimes is in Whitman. The opening of the

1855 version of "A Song for Occupations" is one example, and Whitman's realization of this possibility may be what led him to drop those lines from the poem.

47. I owe this observation to Michael Fried.

Chapter 4: Lines of Penetration

1. This paragraph is a composite of most of the critical works I have mentioned in previous chapters, including those of Betsy Erkkila, M. Jimmie Killingsworth, Robert K. Martin, Michael Moon, and M. Wynn Thomas. It does not necessarily represent the total view of any single critic.

2. Rousseau, *On Social Contract,* in *Rousseau's Political Writings,* ed. Alan Ritter and Julia C. Bondanella, trans. Bondanella (New York: Norton, 1988), 92–93. In Derrida's gloss, "Total alienation is the total reappropriation of self-presence" (*OG,* 295).

3. *Rousseau's Political Writings,* 92.

4. The interpolation is from the original French text. See Jacques Derrida, *De la grammatologie* (Paris: Les Éditions de Minuit, 1967), 227 (my emphasis).

5. I am grateful to Susan Maslan for discussions of Derrida's reading of *On Social Contract.*

6. M. H. Abrams, *The Mirror and the Lamp: Romantic Theory and the Critical Tradition* (New York: Oxford University Press, 1953), 190.

7. Steven Knapp, *Literary Interest: The Limits of Anti-Formalism* (Cambridge, Mass.: Harvard University Press, 1993), 48.

8. On the differences and similarities, see Foucault's critique of Derridean *écriture* in his essay "What Is an Author?," in *Language, Counter-Memory, Practice: Selected Essays and Interviews,* ed. Donald F. Bouchard (Ithaca: Cornell University Press, 1977), 119–20. Foucault's critique anticipates my own, yet his alternative to Derrida's personification of writing—discourse—is merely another personification.

9. Michel Foucault, "Truth and Power," in *Power/Knowledge: Selected Interviews and Other Writings, 1972–77,* ed. Colin Gordon (New York: Pantheon, 1980), 117.

10. For a fuller exegesis of Foucault's definition of power as well as a critique of other theoretical assessments of it, both positive and negative, see my essay "Foucault and Pragmatism," *Raritan* 7, no. 3 (1988): 94–114.

11. "Intellectuals and Power: A Conversation between Michel Foucault and Gilles Deleuze" (1972), in *Language, Counter-Memory, Practice,* 207–8. Compare Foucault's remarks on the "specific intellectual" in "Truth and Power," *Power/ Knowledge,* 127–33.

12. Here I differ with most critics of Foucault, who tend to see his construction-

ism as an outgrowth of his theory of power. What I am suggesting is that his theory of power, properly understood, belies his constructionism.

13. Interpolations in the original French are from Michel Foucault, *Histoire de la sexualité 1: La volonté de savoir* (Paris: Gallimard, 1976), 20. Subsequent references will be cited parenthetically in the text following the page number of the English translation and separated from it by a slash.

14. By "elsewhere" I mean not only in other works, such as "The Subject and Power," which is late, but also elsewhere in *The History of Sexuality, Volume One.* Thus, Foucault's definition of power in the section entitled "Method" (92–102) seems to me entirely consistent with the definition of power relations he outlines in "The Subject and Power." My point, in other words, is not that Foucault's view of power changed (though that may be true) but rather that—at least in the first volume of *The History of Sexuality*—he held two contrary views simultaneously: the relational view, in which power is an inevitable attribute of the interaction between people, who are thereby assumed to be independent agents *irreducible to power,* and the constructionist view, with which my critique is exclusively concerned.

15. A fuller exploration of the influences on Butler's work would include Irigaray, Kristeva, Lacan, and Wittig. However, I don't believe that widening the discussion to include them would require any fundamental alteration of the critique I offer here.

16. In other words, the problem of personification is a logical and not simply a semantic or grammatical one, as Butler sometimes implies. Her commitment to the idea of identity as an imposition requires her to invent a constituent subject to impose it.

17. More precisely, she invokes Derrida's use of the term "iterability" in his essay on J. L. Austin entitled "Signature, Event, Context" (in Derrida, *Limited Inc* [Evanston: Northwestern University Press, 1988], 1–23). But the notion of iterability is a variation on the Derridean terminology I have already introduced.

18. Leo Bersani, *The Culture of Redemption* (Cambridge, Mass.: Harvard University Press, 1990), 3.

19. André Gide, *The Immoralist,* trans. Richard Howard (New York: Vintage, 1970), 155–56; quoted in Bersani, *Homos,* 126–27.

20. D. H. Lawrence, *Studies in Classic American Literature* (1923; rpt., New York: Penguin, 1977), 171, 176.

Index

abolitionism, 96, 98

Abrams, M. H., 5, 20, 149, 195n. 42

Ackerman, Bruce, 210n. 42

Acton, William A., 41–43, 59–60

adhesiveness, 81, 200n. 69

agency: Butler on, 160–64; Derrida on, 147–48; Foucault on, 150–52, 154–56; poetic, 19–22, 57–92, 107–8; political, 100–107; poststructuralism on, 144; sexual, 32–41, 46–59. *See also* will

Alcott, Louisa May, 85

Alcott, William, 14, 25, 39

Allen, Gay Wilson, 202n. 80

amativeness, 30, 179n. 20

amatory poetry, 4, 6, 61–66, 72, 76, 89, 91

apostrophe, 11, 21, 50, 52, 125, 177n. 9, 196–97n. 49

Articles of Confederation, 114

Aspiz, Harold, 202–3nn. 83, 84

authority, poetic, 1, 3–4; and homosexuality, 7–8, 89–92, 124–28, 135–36, 142–43; and popular authority, 8–12, 107–18, 125–26, 135–36, 143; sexuality as source of, 8. *See also* inspiration

authority, popular, 1, 93–141, 144; and

homosexuality, 9–12, 124–26, 135–36, 141, 143; Madison on, 102–3, 206n. 18; and poetic authority, 8–12, 107–18, 125–26, 135–36, 143. *See also* representation, political

automatism: poetic, 59, 61–69, 80–81, 88; political, 100–101; sexual, 34–42, 59, 68–69; verbal, 59–60, 147–50, 155–56, 163–64

Barker-Benfield, G. J., 179n. 15

Baudelaire, Charles, 195–96n. 44

Bellis, Peter, 9

Bersani, Leo, 12, 15–16, 144, 165–69, 195–96n. 44; on authority, 166–69; on constructionism, 165; and Foucault, 165, 167, 169; on Gide, 167–68; on pleasure, 165–66; on self, 166–68

breeze. *See* inspiration: wind as source of

Burroughs, John, 201n. 78

Butler, Judith, 12, 14, 16, 144, 157–64, 213n. 16; on agency, 160–64; and Derrida, 160–61; and Foucault, 158–60, 162; on performativity, 161–62; on political representation, 158; and Romantics, 164; use of personification

Butler, Judith (*continued*)
by, 160, 162, 213n. 16; use of rape as
metaphor by, 162
Byron, George Gordon, Lord, 193n. 39

Cohen, Ed, 24, 27, 179n. 15
Coleridge, Samuel Taylor, 5, 77, 91, 148,
154, 175n. 11; "Eolian Harp, The," 7,
69–72, 74–75; "Kubla Khan," 79
Confederacy, 114, 138
Congress, Continental, 114
Congress, U.S., 10, 103–4; wartime,
114–15, 117
Constitution, U.S., 98
Cowan, John, 30, 32, 44
Cowley, Malcolm, 200n. 74
Culler, Jonathan, 196–97n. 49
Cupid, 4, 6–7, 61–67, 77, 190n. 19

Davis, Robert Leigh, 16
de Man, Paul, 189n. 13
Derrida, Jacques, 13, 16, 144–50, 152–53,
155, 157, 160–61, 189n. 13; on political
representation, 146–47; on textual
system, 147–50, 152–53, 155; use of
personification by, 148
desire, sexual: as coercive, 28–31, 34, 46,
48–53, 61–65, 73–74; as disease, 26, 30–
31; female, 42–43; feminization of men
by, 41–45, 49–50, 55–59; and inspiration, 4–8, 15, 20–22, 58–59, 67, 69–92,
142–43; as invasive, 6–7, 15, 20–22, 28–
34, 43, 45–46, 52, 61–63, 66–67, 74, 91,
142; object of, 28, 47, 49, 50, 52, 62;
personification of, 6–7, 29–31, 46–55,
61–65, 73; poetic *vs.* hygienic descriptions of, 8, 68–69, 73–74; as possession,
8, 29–30, 46–74; and the will, 21, 34, 39,
82–84, 142. *See also* homosexuality,
male; sexual hygiene movement
devotional poetry, 4–6, 66–67, 89, 91
Dickinson, Emily, 198–99n. 59, 202n. 79

Dimock, Wai Chee, 3, 174n. 8
Dixon, Edward, 22, 33
Donne, John, 5, 66–67, 72
Douglass, Frederick, 15, 99, 205n. 16
Durling, Robert M., 192n. 31

Emerson, Ralph Waldo, 143, 148, 153, 164,
207n. 23; "Inspiration," 107; "Instinct
and Inspiration," 13; "Lord's Supper,
The," 204n. 6; "Poet, The," 10–13, 71, 76,
107–10; "Poet and the Times, The," 77,
107, 206–7n. 21; "Poetry and Imagination," 89
Erkkila, Betsy, 48, 89, 94, 175n. 16,
200–201n. 74, 207n. 25
Eucharist, 95, 204nn. 5, 6

feminization: of male masturbator, 41–45;
of male poet, 6–7, 49–50, 55, 58–59,
86–87
Fisher, Philip, 2, 174n. 8, 207–8n. 26
Foucault, Michel, 12, 14–16, 144, 150–60,
162, 164–65, 170, 212n. 8, 212–13n. 12,
213n. 14; Butler on, 158–59; on confession, 155–56; on constituent subject,
150–51; constructionism of, 153–57,
212–13n. 12; on freedom, 151–52; on
political representation, 154–55; on
power, 151–56, 170, 213n. 14; and sexual
hygiene movement, 154–55; use of
personification by, 154–55, 162
Fowler, Orson S., 13, 22, 41–42, 59, 91,
179n. 20, 187n. 4
Freccero, John, 192n. 26
Free Soil ideology, 96–97, 105–6, 113
Freud, Sigmund, 6–7, 166
Fried, Michael, 211–12n. 46

genre, 4–5, 62, 69, 72
Gide, André, 167–68
Graham, Sylvester, 14, 23–32, 37–39, 41,
44, 60, 68–69, 91, 182nn. 41, 44

Greeley, Horace, 97
Grossman, Allen, 2, 200–201n. 74

Holmes, Oliver Wendell, 202n. 79
homophobia, 15, 45, 166
homosexuality, male: in Donne's poetry, 5,
    66–67; as egalitarian, 90–91; as incar-
    nation of desire's structure, 15, 55, 74,
    89; and inspiration, 6–8, 11, 15, 20–22,
    74–92, 140–43; and masturbation, 23–
    24, 45, 52; and poetic authority, 7, 74, 81,
    124–28, 135–36, 143; and political
    resistance, 7, 93–94; and popular
    authority, 9–12, 124–26, 135–36, 141–
    43; as self-betrayal, 82–84, 166. *See also
    under* Whitman, Walt, writings of
hospitals, Union Army, 18–19, 84–88, 91,
    115–18, 121
House of Representatives, U.S., 98

identity, sexual, 22, 89, 144, 157–64
inspiration, 1–8, 10, 19–22, 58–92, 107–8,
    115; and alcohol, 78–80; in Coleridge's
    poetry, 7, 69–72, 74–75, 79; and cries
    of sexual pleasure, 6, 59, 72, 74; in
    Emerson, 76–77, 89, 107–8; feminization
    of male poet by, 6–7, 58–59, 71–72; as
    homoerotic, 6–8, 11, 15, 20–22, 74–92,
    140–43; hospitals as source of, 19–21,
    84–88, 116–18, 122–24, 134–36;
    ingestion as metaphor for, 85, 118; as
    invasive, 6–7, 20–22, 68, 71–72; James
    on, 19–20; and orgasm, 6, 21, 58, 72, 88,
    108, 117; in Ovid's *Amores*, 61–62; in
    Petrarch's *Rime Sparse*, 64–66; Plato on,
    1, 107; and poetic authority, 1, 3–4, 91–
    92; and popular authority, 11–12, 107–8;
    116–18; Romantic naturalization of, 5–8,
    12, 15; and sexual intercourse, 4–8, 58–
    59, 67, 69–77, 84, 108, 195–96n. 44; in
    Shelley's poetry and prose, 1, 4, 13, 67–
    69, 71–72; in Sidney's *Astrophil and*

Stella, 63–64; theories of, 1, 5–6, 13, 15,
    19–20, 67–69, 148–49; wind as source of,
    5, 10, 65–66, 70–72, 74; in Wordsworth's
    poetry and prose, 5, 124. *See also under*
    Whitman, Walt, writings of
intention, authorial, 3–4, 147–50, 164
interests, political, 101–5, 108, 143
invention, poetic. *See* inspiration
invocation, 11, 18, 21, 56, 65, 67, 70–75,
    111, 125

Jackson, James, 30, 32, 34–35, 180n. 21
Jacobus, Mary, 196n. 48
James, Henry, 19–20, 108, 141
Jefferson, Thomas, 105, 117, 136

Kansas-Nebraska Act, 96
Keats, John, 13, 175n. 13
Kenney, E. J., 190n. 19
Killingsworth, M. Jimmie, 187nn. 2, 4,
    203n. 87, 204n. 3
Knapp, Steven, 150

Lallemand, François, 35, 60–61, 69,
    183n. 63
Laqueur, Thomas, 23, 44, 180n. 21
Larson, Kerry, 176nn. 18, 22, 207n. 25,
    209n. 35
Lawrence, D. H., 47, 168
Lincoln, Abraham, 96–98, 114–15,
    208–9n. 29
literary history, 3, 7–8, 12, 77, 143, 170
Love. *See* Cupid
love poetry. *See* amatory poetry

Madison, James, 102–4, 108–9, 114, 140,
    143, 206n. 18
Marcus, Steven, 194n. 41
Marlowe, Christopher, 6, 62, 190n. 18
Martin, Robert K., 54, 89, 175n. 17, 188n.
    10, 200–201n. 74

masturbation: as antisocial, 23–24; and convulsions, 38–40; erosion of self-control by, 35–41; and homosexuality, 23–24, 45, 180n. 21; and male autonomy, 27; and object of desire, 28; and penis, 43–45; *vs.* reproduction, 24; sexual hygiene movement on, 23–45; and voice, 41, 59–61; in Whitman's poetry, 46

Mellor, Anne, 197n. 50

Mexican War, 96, 100

Miller, James E., Jr., 200n. 74

Moon, Michael, 2, 24, 27, 90–91, 93, 174n. 9, 175n. 15, 188n. 10, 198n. 56, 203n. 86

Morgan, Edmund S., 210n. 42

nervous system, 41–43, 193n. 41

Newfield, Christopher, 203n. 87

Nissenbaum, Stephen, 31, 179n. 19, 180n. 26

Noyes, John Humphrey, 37–38, 188n. 11

orgasm, 6; as convulsion, 35–38, 57; as excessive, 25, 37; and inspiration, 6, 21, 58, 72, 88, 108, 117; sexual hygiene movement on, 25, 35–39, 57; and will, 36–37

Ovid, 4, 15, 61–63, 66, 72, 74, 76, 190nn. 18, 19

Paré, Ambroise, 44

parties, political: Douglass on, 99; Whitman on, 104–6, 108

people, the: as effect of poetry, 108–14, 139–44; Whitman's embodiment of, 132–37

personification, 6, 70, 175n. 13; poststructuralist uses of, 14, 148, 154–55, 160, 162; of sexual impulse, 6–7, 29–31, 46–55, 61–66, 73

Petrarch, Francesco, 15, 64–66, 70, 72, 73, 76, 191n. 22

Petrarchism, 62–67, 86, 177n. 7

Pierce, Franklin, 104

Plato, 1, 107, 207n. 24

possession, erotic, 8, 29–30, 46–74

possession, poetic. *See* inspiration

possession, spiritual, 30, 59, 66

poststructuralism. *See* subject, poststructuralist critique of

presidency, U.S., 98, 104–5, 109

Price, Kenneth, 174n. 9

principle, political, 101–5

procreation, 70–71, 86–87

rape: and inspiration, 5, 66–67, 71–77, 91; and male sexual desire, 13, 29–31, 45–50, 73; and subject formation, 154–55, 162

representation, political, 9, 15–16, 94, 98–108, 114–15, 117; in "Calamus," 9–12; *vs.* direct democracy, 102, 105; Douglass on, 99; Madison on, 102–3; in poststructuralism, 146–47, 153, 158; Rousseau on, 98–99; Thoreau on, 100–105; Whitman on, 98, 104–6

Reynolds, David S., 187n. 4

Rosenberg, Charles, 30–31

Rousseau, Jean-Jacques, 13, 41, 60, 98–99, 101, 145–50, 153, 189n. 13

sectional crisis, 103

Sedgwick, Eve Kosofsky, 186n. 90, 201n. 77

Seidman, Steven, 179n. 15, 182n. 44

self: in poetry, 1–4, 12–13, 18–21, 61–69, 71, 73–74, 78–80, 84, 88–89, 91, 107–8, 125–26, 142–43; in politics, 103, 108, 113; renunciation of, 19–22, 66–67, 83–84, 87–88, 102–5, 107–8, 114, 117, 126, 143, 147, 164, 166–69; as restrictive, 13–15, 166–70. *See also* subject, poststructuralist critique of

self-control: addiction and, 78–80; Emerson on, 107–8; eroded by masturbation, 35–41; *vs.* inspiration, 58, 71, 73–74, 107–8,

142–43; Whitman on, 80–84; in women, 42–43

sensibility, poetic: Emerson on, 107, 193–94n. 40; Shelley on, 67–68; Wordsworth on, 193n. 40

sexual hygiene movement, 7–8, 14–15, 22–45, 55, 57–59, 73–74, 81; on automatism, 28, 34–41, 73; on diet, 8, 26–27, 31–32; and exorcism, 30; on feminization of men, 41–45; on heredity, 8, 32–33; and homophobia, 45; on insanity, 40–41; on orgasm, 25, 35–39; on orifices, 39–40; on sexual coercion, 8, 33–34; on voice, 41, 59–61

sexuality: and authority, 8; cultural elevation of, 8; feminine, 28, 41–43; and inspiration, 4–8, 15, 20–22, 58–59, 67, 69–72, 142–43; jurisdiction over, 8; poststructuralist theories of, 12–15, 144–70. *See also* desire, sexual; homosexuality, male

Shakespeare, William, 33

Shelley, Percy Bysshe, 67–69, 71–74, 91, 140, 143, 193n. 39, 194n. 41, 195n. 43, 197n. 52; "Defense of Poetry, A," 1, 4, 13, 67–69, 71; "Ode to the West Wind," 71, 177n. 4; "With a Guitar. To Jane," 72

Sidney, Sir Phillip, 63–64, 66, 76

slavery, 15, 96–101, 106, 206n. 20; and apportionment, 98; and industrial labor, 97; and political representation, 98–101, 205n. 14

Smith-Rosenberg, Carroll, 23, 27, 36, 180n. 28

sodomy, 45, 83, 200n. 73

spermatorrhoea, 35–39, 61

Stowe, Harriet Beecher, 99, 205n. 14

subject, poststructuralist critique of, 12–15, 144–45, 148–51, 157, 169–70; and homosexuality, 12–15, 144–45, 157–70; and theory of inspiration, 12–14, 144–45, 149

sublimation, 9, 77, 139, 202n. 80

Sweet, Timothy, 210–11n. 43

Symonds, John Addington, 80–81

temperance movement, 2, 78–81

Thomas, M. Wynn, 207n. 25

Thoreau, Henry David, 15, 100–105, 136, 153, 206n. 20

Traubel, Horace, 80

Vickers, Nancy J., 191n. 23, 192nn. 26, 29

Virgil, 123–24, 209n. 34

virtue, civic, 101–3, 106, 108, 136

voice, poetic: 70–72; alterity of, 3–4, 107–8, 119; automatism of, 59, 61–69, 80–81, 88, 126; individuality of, 71; and popular authority, 106–10, 122–23; and self-betrayal, 82–84

Warner, Michael, 2, 9, 174n. 8

Whitman, Thomas Jefferson, 115–16

Whitman, Walt: and Lewis Brown, 18; on the Capitol, 10–12, 84–85, 117; on common people, 94–98, 105–6, 109, 143; and Peter Doyle, 81–84; on Eucharist, 95, 204nn. 5, 6; free soil ideology of, 96–97, 113; and Gide, 168; hospital work of, 15–17, 18–19, 84–88, 91, 115–19, 127–28; individualism of, 1–3; journalism of, 96–97; on Keats, 175n. 13; on *Leaves of Grass*, 87–88, 94, 141; letters of, 18–19, 84–86, 115–17; nationalism of, 9; notebooks of, 81–84, 118–19, 128, 131, 210n. 40; on nursing, 86–87; originality of, 88–89; poetic antecedents of, 61–72, 122–23; on political representation, 98, 104–6; on the presidency, 98, 104–5, 109; reading, 123, 190n. 18, 191n. 22, 193n. 39, 196n. 45, 208n. 34, 210n. 37, 211n. 45; sacrifice of body by, 88, 134–36, 168; and Thomas Sawyer, 18; on self-control, 80–84; and sexual hygiene, 22–23, 48,

Whitman, Walt (*continued*)
  52–53; as slave, 141; on slavery, 96–97;
  transferential narratives of, 120–40;
  Unionism of, 114–15; on virtue, 106; in
  Washington, D.C., 115; weight of, 86,
  116
Whitman, Walt, works by: "Bad Wounds,"
  116; "Calamus," 9–12, 83; "Children of
  Adam," 9, 47; "Come up from the Fields
  Father," 127; "'Convulsiveness,'" 117–18;
  "Crossing Brooklyn Ferry," 2; "Death of
  a Pennsylvania Soldier," 132–33; "Death
  of a Wisconsin Officer," 131; *Drum-Taps*,
  19–20, 117–41; "Earth, My Likeness,"
  83; 1855 Preface to *Leaves of Grass*, 6,
  57, 59, 106, 109, 140; "Eighteenth
  Presidency!, The," 15, 104–6, 108, 125,
  133, 208–9n. 30; "Epictetus Notebook,
  81–84; "Female Nurses for Soldiers," 86–
  87; *Franklin Evans*, 15, 77–80, 199n. 66;
  "From Pent-up Aching Rivers," 47–48,
  50, 52, 55, 57; "Happy Hour's Command,
  A," 127–28, 131; "In Paths Untrodden,"
  11–12; *Leaves of Grass*, 87–88, 94, 141;
  "*Leaves of Grass*: A Volume of Poems
  Just Published," 94; "Look Down Fair
  Moon," 138–40; "Lo, Victress on the
  Peaks," 131; "March in the Ranks, Hard-
  Prest, and the Road Unknown, A,"
  119–24, 127–29, 132, 138; "Night Battle,
  Over a Week Since, A," 210n. 39; "Not
  Heaving from my Ribb'd Breast Only,"
  203n. 87; "Not My Enemies Ever Invade
  Me," 20–21, 50; "O Tan-Faced Prairie-
  Boy," 124–25; "Reconciliation," 137–40;
  "Scene in the woods on the Peninsula,"
  118–19; "Sleepers, The," 7, 15, 49, 52,
  54–55, 58, 75, 168, 177n. 9; "Soldiers and
  Talks," 118–19; "So Long!" 57, 94; "Song
  for Occupations, A," 94–98, 104, 107,
  110–12, 114, 139; "Song of Myself," 15–
  16, 48, 50–59, 74–77, 80, 82, 84–86, 91,
  106, 111–14, 117, 130–31, 134–35, 174n.
  9, 175n. 13; "Song of the Answerer,"
  108–10, 140; "Song of the Banner at
  Daybreak," 121; *Specimen Days*, 86–88,
  116–19, 127–28, 131–33, 210n. 39;
  "Spirit Whose Work Is Done," 18–21,
  58–59, 84–85, 88, 116–19, 121, 127;
  "Spontaneous Me," 46, 48–50, 55, 57;
  "Starting from Paumonok," 81; "Vigil
  Strange I Kept on the Field One Night,"
  124, 126–29; "When I Heard at the
  Close of Day," 9–11, "Wound-Dresser,
  The," 87, 124, 128–36, 139, 190n. 18,
  210–11n. 43
Whitman, Walt, writings of: absence of
  possessive pronouns in, 50, 122, 132;
  ambiguity of sexual episodes in, 48–59;
  apostrophe in, 11, 21, 50, 52, 125, 177n.
  9; bleeding in, 120–22, 130–31, 210n. 39;
  body as representational in, 116–18,
  122–23, 128, 136; Calamus plant in, 11–
  12; comradeship in, 80–81; democratic
  fraternity in, 109; demonstrative
  adjectives in, 135–36; depersonalization
  of body in, 134–36; desire as feminizing
  in, 49–50, 55, 58–59, 86–87; embodiment of others by speaker in, 115–39;
  feminine desire in, 49, 55–59; fusion of
  sexual and poetic drives in, 4, 73–89, 91–
  92; grass in, 130–31; heterosexual desire
  in, 47–50, 55–59; homosexuality in, 2, 7,
  9–12, 18–22, 46–61, 73–94, 115–17,
  124–37, 141; inclusiveness of, 112;
  incorporation of readers into, 111, 129–
  30, 139–40; injury in, 54, 84, 88, 116–18,
  120–24, 131–33; inspiration in, 4, 10–12,
  18–22, 73–89, 91–92, 110, 115, 122–27,
  134–36, 148, 164; invocation in, 11, 18,
  21, 56, 75, 111, 125; kissing in, 18–19,
  126–27, 134–35, 138; leaves in, 127, 130;
  linguistic medium in, 57, 93–96, 104,
  110–11, 136–40, 211–12n. 46; mastur-

bation in, 46, 51–54; orgasm in, 21, 58–
59, 90, 117; penetration of body in, 6–9,
21, 45–52, 54–55, 75, 90; people as
muses in, 11, 18–21, 85–86, 88, 110–11,
118–36; personification in, 6, 46–55, 73;
physical presence in, 53, 94–97, 110,
124, 129–32, 134–36, 138–40; poet as
representative in, 106–14, 124–26, 134–
39; possession in, 20, 45–59, 88, 117,
122–24, 136, 141; redness in, 19, 86–87,
115–16; resumption in, 124, 128–29;
sexual coercion in, 46, 48–54, 74–75;
sexualization of inspiration in, 4–8, 12,
73–89, 91–92; silence in, 124–25, 138;
substitution of speaker for others in, 109,
111, 121–22, 124–25, 129, 133, 135–36;
swelling in, 85–87, 115; trembling in,
57–59; verse form in, 2, 113; vignettes,
137–40; withdrawal from society in, 12;
women in, 47–48, 55–59, 77–78, 86–87;
work in, 94–98, 105–6, 113; wounded in,
120–25, 131–34
will: and desire, 21, 32–41, 59, 61–68, 142–
43; general, 101, 136; of legislator, 15–
16, 101; of poet, 20, 59, 66–68, 107–8,
142–43; and representation, 98–99, 101;
of slave, 15, 99–100. *See also* agency
Wilmot Proviso, 96
wind. *See under* inspiration
Woodward, Samuel, 14, 38, 40
Wordsworth, William, 6, 10–11, 14, 73,
127, 175n. 13, 193n. 40, 197–98n. 55

Yingling, Thomas, 9

BAKER & TAYLOR